Extractive Industries and Changing State Dynamics in Africa

AF835128

This book uses extractive industry projects in Africa to explore how political authority and the nation-state are reconfigured at the intersection of national political contestations and global, transnational capital. Instead of focusing on technological zones and the new social assemblages at the actual sites of construction or mineral extraction, the authors use extractive industry projects as a topical lens to investigate contemporary processes of state-making at the state–corporation nexus.

Throughout the book, the authors seek to understand how public political actors and private actors of liberal capitalism negotiate and redefine notions and practices of sovereignty by setting legal, regulatory and fiscal standards. Rather than looking at resource governance from a normative perspective, the authors look at how these negotiations are shaped by and reshape the self-conception of various national and transnational actors, and how these jointly redefine the role of the state in managing these processes for the 'greater good'. *Extractive Industries and Changing State Dynamics in Africa* will be useful for researchers, upper-level students and policy-makers who are interested in new articulations of state-making and politics in Africa.

Jon Schubert is a Leverhulme Early Career Fellow at the Anthropology Department at Brunel University London, UK, and the author of *Working the System: A Political Ethnography of the New Angola*.

Ulf Engel is Professor of Politics in Africa at Leipzig University, Germany, Professor Extraordinary in the Department of Political Science at Stellenbosch University, South Africa, and a visiting professor at the Institute for Peace and Security Studies at Addis Ababa University, Ethiopia.

Elísio Macamo is Professor of African Studies, Director of the Centre for African Studies and Head of the Social Sciences Department at the University of Basel, Switzerland.

Routledge Studies in African Development

HIV and East Africa
Thirty years in the shadow of an epidemic
Janet Seeley

Development Discourse and Global History
From colonialism to the sustainable development goals
Aram Ziai

Higher Education and Capacity Building in Africa
The geography and power of knowledge under changing conditions
Hanne Kirstine Adriansen, Lene Møller Madsen and Stig Jensen

Gender and the Political Economy of Conflict in Africa
The persistence of violence
Meredeth Turshen

Social Innovation in Africa
A practical guide for scaling impact
Ndidi Okonkwo Nwuneli

Political Transition and Inclusive Development in Malawi
The democratic dividend
Edited by Dan Banik and Blessings Chinsinga

National Liberation Movements as Government in Africa
Edited by Redie Bereketeab

Hunger and Poverty in South Africa
The Hidden Faces of Food Insecurity
Jacqueline Hanoman

Extractive Industries and Changing State Dynamics in Africa
Beyond the Resource Curse
Edited by Jon Schubert, Ulf Engel and Elísio Macamo

Extractive Industries and Changing State Dynamics in Africa

Beyond the Resource Curse

Edited by
Jon Schubert, Ulf Engel and
Elísio Macamo

Routledge
Taylor & Francis Group
LONDON AND NEW YORK

First published 2018
by Routledge
2 Park Square, Milton Park, Abingdon, Oxon OX14 4RN

and by Routledge
52 Vanderbilt Avenue, New York, NY 10017

First issued in paperback 2020

Routledge is an imprint of the Taylor & Francis Group, an informa business

© 2018 selection and editorial matter, Jon Schubert, Ulf Engel and Elísio Macamo; individual chapters, the contributors

The right of Jon Schubert, Ulf Engel and Elísio Macamo to be identified as the authors of the editorial material, and of the authors for their individual chapters, has been asserted in accordance with sections 77 and 78 of the Copyright, Designs and Patents Act 1988.

All rights reserved. No part of this book may be reprinted or reproduced or utilised in any form or by any electronic, mechanical, or other means, now known or hereafter invented, including photocopying and recording, or in any information storage or retrieval system, without permission in writing from the publishers.

Trademark notice: Product or corporate names may be trademarks or registered trademarks, and are used only for identification and explanation without intent to infringe.

British Library Cataloguing in Publication Data
A catalogue record for this book is available from the British Library

Library of Congress Cataloging in Publication Data
Names: Schubert, Jon, 1982- editor. | Engel, Ulf, editor. | Macamo, Elísio Salvado, editor.
Title: Extractive industries and changing state dynamics in Africa : beyond the resource curse / edited by Jon Schubert, Ulf Engel, and Elísio Macamo.
Description: First Edition. | New York : Routledge, [2018] |
Series: Routledge studies in African development | Includes bibliographical references and index.
Identifiers: LCCN 2018006662 (print) | LCCN 2018010288 (ebook) | ISBN 9781351200639 (eBook) | ISBN 9780815391845 (hardback)
Subjects: LCSH: Mineral industries--Africa. | Local government--Africa. | Industrial policy--Africa.
Classification: LCC HD9506.A2 (ebook) | LCC HD9506.A2 E978 2018 (print) | DDC 338.2096--dc23
LC record available at https://lccn.loc.gov/2018006662

ISBN 13: 978-0-367-66609-5 (pbk)
ISBN 13: 978-0-8153-9184-5 (hbk)

Typeset in Goudy
by Taylor & Francis Books

Contents

Illustrations

Figures

Tables

About the contributors

Editors

Ulf Engel is Professor of Politics in Africa at Leipzig University. He is also Professor Extraordinary in the Department of Political Science at Stellenbosch University and a visiting professor at the Institute for Peace and Security Studies at Addis Ababa University. His research is on the African peace and security architecture as well as processes of violent respatialisation on that continent. His most recent publication, co-edited with Heidrun Zinecker, Frank Mattheis, Antje Dietze and Thomas Plötze, is *The New Politics of Regionalism: Perspectives from Africa, Latin America and Asia-Pacific* (Routledge 2016).

Elísio Macamo is Professor of African Studies at the University of Basel. He is also the Director of the Centre for African Studies and Head of the Social Sciences Department at the University of Basel. His research interests cover methodological issues in Area Studies as well as development, politics, knowledge and risk. His most recent publication is *The Taming of Fate* (CODESRIA 2016).

Jon Schubert is a Leverhulme Early Career Fellow at the Anthropology Department at Brunel University London, and the author of *Working the System: A Political Ethnography of the New Angola* (Cornell University Press 2017). Following research on authoritarianism and political legitimacy, bureaucracy, class formation and legacies of violence in Angola and Mozambique, he is currently researching 'the afterlives of oil-backed infrastructures in the port city of Lobito, Angola' (2018–2021). He holds a Ph.D. in African Studies from the University of Edinburgh (2014) and has previously taught and carried out research at the universities of Leipzig, Halle-Wittenberg and Geneva.

Contributors

Jana Hönke is Associate Professor and Rosalind Franklin Fellow in International Relations at the University of Groningen. She is the author of

Transnational Companies and Security Governance (2013) and co-editor of *Governing (In)Security in the Postcolonial World* (2012) and *The Global Making of Policing* (2016). Her articles have appeared in *Security Dialogue, African Affairs, International Political Sociology, Environment and Planning D: Society and Space* and *Governance*, among others. Her current work revolves around infrastructure globalities and includes ERC-funded research in Tanzania, Mozambique, China and Brazil and with international organisations.

Rita Kesselring is a senior lecturer at the Institute for Social Anthropology, University of Basel, Switzerland. She was a research fellow at the Human Rights Institute, University of Connecticut, the Department of Anthropology, University of Cape Town and the Dag Hammarskjöld Institute for Peace and Conflict Studies, University of the Copperbelt, Zambia. She is the author of *Bodies of Truth: Law, Memory and Emancipation in Post-apartheid South Africa* (Stanford University Press 2016) and leads the interdisciplinary project 'Valueworks: Effects of Financialisation along the Copper Value Chain'. Her current work is on governance, the body and the built environment in new mining towns in Zambia.

Sonwabile Mnwana is Associate Professor of Sociology at the University of Fort Hare, South Africa. He is also a research associate at the Society, Work and Development Institute (SWOP), University of the Witwatersrand, Johannesburg. He holds a Ph.D. in Social Sciences. Broadly, his research focuses on land, large-scale natural resource extraction and rural social change.

Paul Nugent is Professor of Comparative African History at the University of Edinburgh, divided between History and the Centre of African Studies. He is a past president of AEGIS, the European African Studies association, and currently the holder of an ERC Advanced Grant for the project 'African Governance and Space: Transport Corridors, Border Towns and Port Cities in Transition' (AFRIGOS).

Padil Salimo is a Ph.D. fellow at Roskilde University in Denmark and the University of Dar-es-Salaam in Tanzania. He is affiliated as a research associate at the Institute for Poverty, Land and Agrarian Studies (PLAAS), University of the Western Cape, Cape Town. His research is funded by the Danish Ministry of Foreign Affairs under the Hierarchies of Rights programme.

Monica Skaten has been conducting research into the Ghanaian petroleum industry since 2012. Her Ph.D. thesis focused on the political processes of the downstream industry in Ghana. She currently works as a research fellow at the Centre of African Area Studies in Kyoto, Japan.

Erika Tchatchouang is a Cameroonian researcher at the Catholic University of Central Africa and Director-Cameroon of the African Centre for

Research on Energy and Mining Policies (CARPEM), specialising in International Environmental Law, Human Rights and Humanitarian Action. She is working on a thesis on the protection of human rights in the development of extractive resources in Africa. She has over thirteen years of experience in the monitoring of development projects, the promotion of human rights, environmental protection and adult education through her organisation of and participation in training, seminars, international conferences and workshops.

Acknowledgements

This book grew out of a workshop on 'State-making at the nexus of extractive industries in Africa', convened by the editors at the Stellenbosch Institute of Advanced Studies (STIAS) in March 2016. The workshop was financed by and organised as part of the research project 'Changing Stateness in Africa', itself part of the Research Priority Programme SPP1448 of the German Research Foundation (DFG), 'Adaptation and Creativity in Africa'.

Many thanks to Henrik B. Geyer, Jo Venter and Nel-Marie Loock at STIAS for providing such an excellent environment for the workshop. In addition to thanking the DFG/SPP1448, STIAS and Lena Dallywater for helping lay the groundwork for this volume, the editors would like to thank the contributors for their committed work, as well as the invited discussants who enriched the workshop with their valuable comments: Sylvia Croese, Davide Chinigò, Janis van der Westhuizen, Gerrie Swart, Peter Fourie and Scarlett Cornelissen.

The editors are also very grateful to the series editor, Helena Hurd, and the managing editor, Leila Walker, at Routledge, for their hands-on support and enthusiasm throughout the publication process. Many thanks also to the production manager, Ed Gibbons, and the copyeditor, Philipp Parr, whose diligence helped the manuscript glide smoothly through the production stage. Andrea Behrends, Tobias Haller, Agathe Mora and Jason Sumich provided critical feedback and support during various stages of this project.

Introduction

Boom and bust: extractive industries and African states in the twenty-first century

Jon Schubert, Ulf Engel and Elísio Macamo

Following a 'lost decade' for 'the developing world' – a shorthand devised by magazine journalists and policy analysts to bemoan the lack of progress and development in Africa, a 'continent mired in poverty' – the dominant Afro-pessimism of the mid-1990s to mid-2000s eventually gave way to a more hopeful picture.[1] This was largely the result of a period of sustained high commodity prices and high global demand for natural resources between 2004 and 2014 (see Hendrix and Noland 2014, 3), which, coupled with technological advancements (ultra-deepwater/pre-salt drilling, surface/strip mining, heavy sands refining) and, not least, advice from institutions such as the World Bank (Lange 2011, 233–234), opened up new 'resource frontiers' across the African continent. The discovery of natural gas reserves below the seabed off the coasts of Mozambique and Tanzania, and of oil deposits under Lake Albert between Uganda and the DRC, as well as promises of a 'blue economy' (see Chapter 3, this volume), created a climate of 'bonanza', with major international corporations rushing to secure concessions and exploration rights. Politics followed suit, with the African Union (AU) adopting at its February 2009 summit the 'Africa Mining Vision 2020', which called for a 'holistic' approach to development through investment in extractives.[2] Investors were euphoric, while African governments were left flush with money from royalties and signing bonuses.

This commodity-driven boom of the mid-noughties, as well as the resulting increase in GDP growth rates across much of the continent, has – to a certain extent – changed the dominant popular narratives about Africa. Lamentations about a 'lost' continent mired in permanent crisis gave way to an optimistic 'Africa rising' narrative, including the preaching of an 'almost obsessive gospel about the role of the middle class in the continent's rapid and accelerated development' by international financial institutions (Melber 2015, 248) and the peddling of 'a crude binary construction of Africa that has shifted almost overnight from basket case to bonanza' (Taylor 2016, 10).

This rapid influx of money led scholars, but also policy designers and advisers from bi- and multilateral development partners of these African countries, to concern themselves with how best to mitigate potential negative consequences from the boom, and help the concerned countries avoid the proverbial 'resource curse' (see below), so as to ensure that mining and oil exploration contribute 'as much as possible to economic development and poverty alleviation' (Davis and Tilton 2005, 233). Articles like 'Saving Ghana from Its Oil' (Van Gyampo 2011), for example, argued that countries where a resource boom was expected should prepare themselves to remedy their perceived policy and administrative deficiencies, although other scholars analysed this very tendency of pre-emptive policy reform more critically (Donner 2009; Weszkalnys 2014; Phillips et al. 2016). Thus, high market demand, coupled with strong normative policy advice, increased the pressures on resource-producing countries to enact new legislation that would give them greater fiscal revenues, grant them automatic equity stakes for national oil and minerals companies, and allow them to set local content (employment, training, 'public' services) targets for international investors (Andreasson 2015, 313).

However, declining demand for coal and minerals in East Asia, and the opening up of the exploration of shale gas in North America, led to a precipitous drop in world market prices for natural resources from about mid-2014 onwards. This clearly revealed the fragility and structural limits of Africa's resource-dependent economic boom (see Taylor 2016). New investments were halted or postponed, and many resource-dependent African states saw a drastic reduction in their fiscal, royalty and export revenues. It also put many governments in a much weaker position vis-à-vis foreign investors. Faced with the need to attract investors despite lower expected returns, which made many planned projects much less economically viable, governments more readily bowed to investors' demands, granting them, for example, fiscal or labour law exemptions to reduce seed and operating costs and maximise corporate profits.

Clearly, the insertion of African polities into global economic forces has for a long time been based on crude extraction rather than transformative production, and there is an evident need to historicise such resource dependence and the cyclical downturns of commodity booms (Jacobs 2013, 29; Chapter 1, this volume). However, we hold that the boom-and-bust cycle of the past two decades was coupled with the rise of a specific and dominant normative international framework ('good governance') and the parallel 'unleashing' of transnational economic interests (usually, and ahistorically, conceptualised as 'globalisation'), which have strongly impacted the imaginaries and practices of the state in Africa. So, while the current economic crisis is real in many countries, it also creates a specific analytical moment: crisis and efficiency are potent political imaginaries that are generative of ideas and practices of 'stateness'. What are the imbrications of state, corporate and civil society actors around the planning and implementation of large-scale extractive industry projects? How do these interactions change the ideas, practices and capacities of states in Africa? How are the dynamics of these interactions changing in the current climate of crisis, after ten years of riding the wave of the boom? And how may we, by adopting this approach, say something new about state dynamics in Africa?

Accounting for state formation in Africa continues to be, as it would appear, a particularly vexing problem in the social sciences. On the one hand, it has often been understood as the process of setting up institutions corresponding to a normative idea of the modern (for which read Western, liberal democratic) state. This view has tended to assume that the difficulties encountered by African modern polities in building the state are technical in nature: that is, a failure of modernisation, to put it broadly. However, the imposition of a normative analytical account of statehood fails to do justice to the contingent nature of politics. If we follow this idea of contingency, then state-building processes are, on the other hand, forms of political action. This means that setbacks experienced by African countries in becoming 'modern' nation-states are not the result of technical failure, but rather outcomes of political interactions which are intrinsically contingent; there is not one single model of stateness. This often results in tautological explanations, based on some essentialist, culturalist reductionism: African states are failing because this is Africa, or so the view goes. We therefore follow a processual view of state dynamics (e.g. Migdal and Schlichte 2005; Hagmann and Péclard 2010) that is grounded on the assumption that social processes produce their own dynamics, and that the consequences of social processes are responses to the practices that constitute them. We may then conceptualise stateness – the ensemble of imaginaries and practices that constitute the field of 'the state' – as an open-ended process of formation that is always contested and incomplete, and constantly remade by processes of negotiation, accommodation, complicity and resistance between different state and non-state actors.

Changing stateness

What we propose, then, is to take such a processual approach to the state, and use the negotiations taking place around the exploitation of the continent's mineral resources as a privileged empirical way in to look at the changing dynamics and processes of stateness. We term this 'privileged' because, due to the capital-intensive and technologically complex nature of large-scale extractive projects, new ventures in Africa are usually undertaken by multinational corporations rather than domestic companies (Jones 2008, 10). The dominance of transnational, non-state actors in what is arguably a key source of revenue for many African states has in turn given rise to a series of (in our view debatable) assumptions about how the activities of transnational mining and oil corporations 'hollow out' or weaken the state. One of the challenges we see, therefore, is to do justice to the realities we attempt to describe without falling into extremes by reproducing simple stories of corporate overlords exploiting poor African countries (or the greed of African leaders to do so) and destroying local livelihoods, or, conversely, uncritically hailing the socio-economic benefits generated by large-scale extractive projects (see Golub 2014, 2). It is true that a great number of African countries are still largely dependent on the export of one or a few primary natural resources. This situation structurally affords the corporate actors engaged in natural resource extraction inordinate economic and political weight. Because of the great socio-economic impact of extractives, the planning, development and implementation of extractive industry projects then engages a diverse cast of players – government and administration, corporations and investors, unions and civil society organisations, local communities and international advocacy organisations, and donors and development actors – in multiple constellations, whose interactions we can chart to overcome an overly state-centred perspective on processes of state-building.

In addition, these processes of negotiation around resource extraction, though they are very much a question of national development, take place against the backdrop of competing, globally circulating ideas about the best way forward in natural resource extraction. These include cultural transfers of managerial ideals promoted to increase efficiency and reduce friction and wastage from the interference of the state, usually glossed as 'neoliberalism' (Ferguson 2010; von Schnitzler 2016). Here we can observe how, across Africa, governments of every political stripe actively promote a 'business-friendly climate' of economic liberalism and a reliable regulatory framework to attract foreign direct investment (FDI). This often comprises promises of reducing state interference in the smooth functioning of the markets and the commercial operations of companies, freely given by governments or demanded by investors, including tax breaks and exemptions from national regulatory regimes, such as employment, local content or environmental laws.[3]

Parallel to, and sometimes in tension with, these economics-based tenets of unfettered market forces stand developmental ideas about the positive role of extractive industries in promoting 'sustainable' and 'inclusive' economic growth for the respective countries, promoted variously and with different emphases by international financial institutions (IFIs), bi- and multilateral donors, the governments themselves (especially those with a developmental bent) and, to a certain extent, civil society actors. Under a programmatic discourse of emancipatory references, such investments and greater flexibilisation of the market are said to promote formal employment, a broadening of the skills base, cheaper (and cleaner) energy and higher fiscal revenues redistributed to target communities for local development.

Finally, there is also a globally circulating and locally adapted criticism of (or warnings against) the potential negative impact of extractive industries, chiefly on the environment, local communities and the economies and politics of the countries concerned (the infamous 'resource curse'), mobilised to various degrees under headers like 'transparency', 'equitable growth' and '(corporate) social responsibility' by the actors identified above alongside international advocacy organisations, such as Publish What You Pay (PWYP), Global Integrity the Extractive Industries Transparency Initiative (EITI; see below).

Charting how these different, overlapping and competing ideas are mobilised by different actors to influence the ways in which states manage the activities of and revenues from extractive industries helps reveal the processes of negotiation and accommodation that stand at the heart of processes of changing stateness, while at the same time avoiding a perspective on these processes that is confined to national boundaries.

Rather than, as has often been the case, studying how states can influence the governance of natural resource extraction, we advocate a non-deterministic, empirically grounded viewpoint that enables us to look at how the different ways of dealing with the challenges and opportunities posed by natural resource extraction change the ideas and practices of African states. Much of the scholarly literature on the governance of extractive industry investment seeks to ascertain the presence or absence of 'good governance' in the industry, according to generally accepted international norms, to explain the causes of this presence or absence, and normatively prescribe policy remedies. We suggest taking a somewhat different approach in examining how extractive industry investments and activities influence the changing roles, legitimacies, capacities and authorities of the state. In other words, we seek to make the tensions and negotiating processes around the activities of extractive industries analytically fruitful, and understand empirically what forms of stateness emerge from the interactions around these activities. This allows us to think through the processes of state formation in Africa in a novel and productive way. Indeed, one of the key problems of the political sociology of Africa is that socio-political phenomena are viewed as deviations from a norm – a fallacy that Mahmood Mamdani (1996, 12) describes as 'history by analogy'. Neo-patrimonialism, for example, describes the failure of the African state to be 'normal' (measured against the universalised benchmark of an ideal Western state), and thus implicitly or explicitly suggests there is no way in which politics could ever change in Africa.

The dynamics and controversies around extractive industries demonstrate, however, that things are very much in flux. The challenge, then, consists in accounting for both the power of ideas about 'good' ways of pursuing resource extraction and the structural and political forces that shape these negotiations. This will allow us to understand changing forms of stateness by being attuned to the multiple, unexpected and open outcomes of these processes.

Conceptual parameters

We develop our approach from a number of conceptual premises and engage with debates on both the state in Africa and extractive industries, as well as the links between the two. Although the 'state failure' literature in African Studies has been thoroughly criticised (see Wai 2012), ideal-typical (Westphalian, Weberian) notions of the state – as rational-legal, territorially coherent representative of public authority and holding a monopoly of force – still often dominate media and scholarly accounts of the state in Africa. And while the choice of words might have become somewhat less pathologising since its heyday, when African nations were variously characterised as 'weak' (Jackson and Rosberg 1982), 'failing' (Herbst 1996), 'collapsing' (Zartman 1995; Allen 1999), 'criminal' (Bayart et al. 1999) or 'shadow' states (Reno 2000), the predominant sentiment often remains strikingly similar, with experts on democratic process and the correct functioning of the state diagnosing and condemning the shortcomings of African states. Given such a perspective, the involvement of external non-state actors in service provision or state-building – such as mining companies or INGOs – is usually also seen as a consequence of 'limited statehood', 'where the state does not have the administrative capacity (either material or institutional) to exercise effective control over activities within its own borders' (Krasner and Risse 2014, 564). Such scholarship is then interested in the 'success' of such interventions in providing services and collective goods 'even under extremely adverse conditions of fragile or failed statehood' (ibid.; see also Cooper 2002 on the gatekeper state).

Similar normativity also often pervades analyses of African states as 'neo-patrimonial', through which scholars seek to make sense of a blurring between the public and the private (for a critical overview, see Erdmann and Engel 2007). Constructed as an inherent characteristic of the predatory state (Bayart et al. 1999) or as cornerstone of the 'traditional' African cultural logic (Chabal and Daloz 1999), neo-patrimonialism is seen as the root cause of underdevelopment and conflict and is placed in contrast with the modern, rational-legal functioning of the idealised and universalised Weberian state. Beyond the normative assumptions implicit in these approaches, such binary opposition tends to ignore the reciprocity implied in Weber's analysis of a legitimate type of authority and overlook processes of adaptation and *bricolage* for which drawing on social imaginaries of personal relations and legal-rational bureaucracy allows (Koechlin 2013, 93; see also Bierschenk and Olivier de Sardan 2014). Neo-patrimonialism has therefore become

> a catch-all conceptual staple in Africanist scholarship for accounting for and explaining nearly every perceived African socio-political malaise, difficulty or problem – corruption, institutional decay, communication breakdown, authoritarian rule, development failure, economic dysfunction, poor growth, civil and political unrest and especially armed conflicts (all of which are the markers of so-called state failure).
>
> (Wai 2012, 31)

We do not claim to reinvent the wheel entirely here; after all, a processual approach to the state has previously yielded insightful analytical perspectives (e.g. Migdal and Schlichte 2005; Hagmann and Péclard 2010). We simply assume that states' functions, as well as people's expectations of what states should do, are changing under uneven processes of globalisation, and that these changes may be observed and made analytically fruitful. However, to avoid the trappings of normativity and state-centredness, we prefer to talk in this volume about stateness as a process, rather than statehood as an ideal-type status/endpoint, somewhat analogous to the differentiation between state formation (open-ended) versus state-building (intentional, directed).

Our epistemology is, then, based on historical and recent empirical observations in which different forms of sovereignty are practised beyond the state and by a variety of non-state actors. Indeed, much of the literature on African states under the conditions of globalisation has 'overstated the case that global economic (and other) forces have crippled the state … [as] many international and transnational forces have propped it up more than they have sabotaged it' (Migdal and Schlichte 2005, 9). What we can see is that core functions of the state in Africa are redefined as the continent is respaced (Engel 2009; Engel and Nugent 2010): new actors beyond the state have arisen (from warlords to transnational companies, from new churches to external interventions); new 'spatialities of power' – micro-regions, border regimes, local powers, transnational networks – have become important from an everyday life perspective, or are given new attention. At the same time, external actors, such as the BRIC nations (Brazil, Russia, India and, most importantly, China), are changing the conditions under which African states are integrated into the global economy.

The nexus of extractive industries speaks to and crystallises all of these developments: a multiplicity of non-state actors (multinational companies, civil society associations and transnational advocacy organisations, international regulatory bodies) deploy diverse, competing discourses about the best way forward to develop Africa's mining sectors and are through this engaged in processes of negotiation that generate new forms of stateness as co-produced projects of economic development and integration into world markets.

Resource curse/resource conflicts

One of the dominant paradigms to explore the impact of natural resource extraction in Africa is the notion of the resource curse, with the resource conflicts hypothesis as one prominent subcategory. The concept of the resource curse has gained much traction in the media, policy and scholarship. It is a tale of greed, corruption and squandered billions, with countries like Gabon, Nigeria, Equatorial Guinea and Angola cited as prime examples of everything that can go wrong in an oil-rich country. The paradigm postulates that 'countries highly dependent on revenues from exports of non-renewable natural resources tend to be characterized by poorer economic performance, lower levels of human development, and higher levels of inequality and poverty' (Williams and Le Billon 2017, 10). Though some authors (e.g. Ross 2012) advise against asserting a systematic relationship, most cite statistics in their efforts to demonstrate a correlation between the incidence of capital-intensive natural resource extraction and poor governance (Leite and Weidmann 1999). Proponents of the resource curse advance the notion of a strong correlation between natural resource wealth and 'undemocratic and illegitimate governance ... high levels of public sector corruption ... [and] greater risk of civil conflict' (Mailey 2015, 1). Resource booms, in this perspective, promote fiscal indiscipline and undermine the functioning of state apparatus (Karl 1997). Bolstered by statistics, authors claim, 'Empirical support for the curse of natural resources is not bulletproof, but it is quite strong' (Sachs and Warner 2001, 828).

This argument is partly based on a reading of macroeconomic indicators as signals of the 'Dutch disease', whereby 'an increase in revenues from natural resources appreciates the exchange rate and makes other sectors less competitive ... [crowding] out manufacturing and agriculture' (Amundsen 2017, 18); while local food production is devaluated, workers are attracted away from agriculture and manufacturing (Yates 2014, 60). However, although countries that rely on the export of one primary commodity do indeed become exposed to volatile world market prices, there are a few problems with this analytic, principally the error of mistaking correlation for causality. This problem seems to puzzle even ardent supporters of the resource curse thesis, although it rarely causes them to reassess the validity of the thesis itself. Once one is willing to acknowledge that 'resource rents lead to an increase in corruption if the quality of the democratic institutions is relatively poor, but not otherwise' (Bhattacharyya and Hodler 2010, 608), that 'the impacts [of the resource curse] are worse in poor countries than in rich countries ... [I]f there is a resource curse, it probably lies in the deeper political economy of institutions, rather than in economic management per se' (Hendrix and Noland 2014, 7), or that 'in most of Africa's resource-rich states, the corrosive political dynamics associated with the resource curse actually pre-date the discovery of oil or minerals' (Mailey 2015, 7), it would appear that natural resources, in these studies, are just proxies for 'politics in messy African states'. Apart from the fact that most of these studies are premised on a rather normative understanding of statehood, we align with critics who argue that, in such a perspective, oil is just an 'idiom for doing politics ... inserted into an already existing political landscape of forces, identities, and forms of power' (Watts 2004, 76). Moreover, laying the blame for the worsening of social indicators in resource-extracting countries exclusively on institutional practices undermined by corruption silences structural and global power inequalities that are central to issues of the governance of natural resources in Africa (Grant et al. 2014c, 278). Rather than using natural resources as the single determining variable to explain governance failures in African states, analyses should aim to be context-specific, taking into account local political and societal dynamics, and how these are reshaped by transnational resource extraction (see Le Billon 2004).

The resource conflict theory, a subcategory of the resource curse theory, similarly gained much traction from the 1990s onwards, as rational choice theorists sought to develop an alternative to the 'new barbarism' approach of theorists such as Robert D. Kaplan[4] to explain the 'new wars' in Africa following the end of the bipolar world order (Kaldor 1999). In their view, conflicts, especially in Africa, are 'resource based' and almost proverbially driven by 'greed, not grievance' (Collier and Hoeffler 2000). Grievances are always present, so the argument goes, but the material conditions for rebellion are not. In resource-rich countries that are already (as per the resource curse theory) afflicted by weak state institutions, poor governance and unsound economic behaviour, the availability of resources gives strong incentives for armed rebellion and plunder, especially in Africa, where many youths are unemployed and poverty is rampant. A variant of the notion that resource abundance causes conflict is what Richards (2005) has termed 'Malthus with guns': that is, the idea that competition over scarce resources results in conflict. Some of these arguments are not entirely without merit. It makes sense to include the political economy of conflict when attempting to understand the factors that drive it. Le Billon's (2001) matching of resource type to type of conflict, for example, is useful and convincing. However, there is still a whiff of resource determinism to the resource curse theory, and a tendency to monocausal explanations. As Englebert and Ron (2004, 61) state in their critique of the resource conflict theory, 'Politics should be privileged over economic determinism, because resources are unlikely to trigger civil war in a stable political environment.' Some authors have successfully integrated oil as a complicating factor in internationally entangled local political struggles in their *longue durée* (e.g. Behrends 2011). Overall, however, we see problems with more monocausal proponents of the resource conflict hypothesis that are similar to those identified above for the resource curse theory: it reduces the role of the state, overplays the role of resources as the sole determining factor and pays insufficient attention to politics.

The limits of the argument become even more evident when it is applied to interstate conflicts. In a particularly egregious example, captured in the catchy title *Petro-Aggression: When Oil Causes War*, Jeff Colgan (2013, 4) argues that oil wealth allows political leaders to take risks, 'including those involved in aggressive foreign policy adventurism'. Apart from taking US foreign policy interests almost entirely out of the equation, Colgan's book argues that 'revolutionary regimes' like Iran and Venezuela are more likely to initiate conflict than more stable polities, which strongly calls into question the explanatory power of oil as *the* determining variable to predict conflict.

In addition to epistemological and methodological problems, there is a political critique to be made against the resource conflict theory, as Jon Barnett (2000, 274) convincingly argues in his appraisal of the environment-conflict hypothesis:

> the environment-conflict literature is almost entirely premised on the ethno-centric assumption that people in the South will resort to violence in times of resource scarcity. Rarely, if ever, is the same argument applied to people in the industrialized North. There is continued

scripting of people from the South as barbaric, strongly implying that those in the North are more civilized.

Overall, we can say that the resource curse theory mistakes correlation for causality, depoliticises political issues, explains violence as 'rational' and, with few exceptions, denies the responsibility of industrialised countries for resource exploitation. Nevertheless, it is a powerful idea that, regardless of the supposed direction of causality, ends up shaping policy decisions, including, as mentioned above, some that are taken with the specific aim of preventing it (Donner 2009; Weszkalnys 2014). 'Through associated policy prescriptions and interventions, the resource curse thesis has power not only as a set of management norms, but as an economic device that shapes how resource development is constructed' (Phillips et al. 2016, 27). The idea is also so pervasive and evocative that it informs understandings of politics across a wide range of actors. Authors of a World Bank study, for example, state that, from a policy perspective, it is 'important to know the mechanism by which [the resource curse] casts its spell … [to] allow a better stab to be made at prescription' (Sala-i-Martin and Subramanian 2003, 5). More surprisingly, perhaps, in Englebert and Ron's (2004, 61) study of rebellions in the Republic of Congo (Brazzaville), 'the authors' informants uniformly believe[d] that greed for petroleum rents in a new and uncertain political context was a major motivation for the war'. Rather than dismissing it entirely, we therefore suggest studying the resource curse as one of several powerful discourses currently in circulation that relate to the ways in which African states should manage their extractive resource wealth. These discourses shape the outcomes of negotiations between unequal actors that jointly produce stateness.

Good governance

Owing to the impact of the resource curse thesis, a second strand of literature on natural resource extraction in Africa is chiefly concerned with the good governance of the sector, or lack thereof. In fact, it would appear that the focus of most studies on extractive industries in Africa tends to be on resource governance and the correlated issues of setting normative standards and enforcement mechanisms within a multi-stakeholder collaborative framework as a means to mitigate or eliminate the prolific structures and incidents of resource-based conflict. There have been some important conceptual advances in this field, chiefly a move away from viewing state actors as the main actors of governance to an acknowledgement of 'the powerful role of non-state actors such as multinational corporations and civil society organizations in the governance process' (Grant et al. 2014b, 3). However, although the conception of 'governance' has been substantially broadened by including the 'institutional conditions, the historical and decision-making processes and … the power relations' that shape governance practices in the larger sense (Campbell 2013, 3), and authors increasingly reject presumably universally valid criteria of measurement, their objective often remains prescriptive in the sense that their research on natural resource governance aims to

> contribute to the improved understanding of the consequences of investment in the mining sector in Africa, notably with regard to revenue flows and the conditions which might allow the sector to further the developmental and poverty reduction objectives of the countries.
> (Ibid.)

For example, in Grant *et al.*'s influential *New Approaches to the Governance of Natural Resources: Insights from Africa* (Grant *et al.* 2014a), contributors Dashwood and Puplampu's case-study of the Ghanaian mining sector is chiefly interested in how far 'multi-stakeholder partnerships have the potential to address institutional weaknesses, governance gaps and the high poverty levels typical of rural Ghana where mining takes place' (Dashwood and Puplampu 2014, 131). Similarly, in the same volume, du Preez acknowledges that 'good governance' is not a panacea, but insists that governance still has an important role to play in ensuring that 'the continent's population benefit optimally and sustainably from its abundant resources' and therefore suggests 'replacing the idea of blanket "good governance" with that of "context-specific governance"' (du Preez 2014, 39). However, 'as analysis [*sic*] of profitable oil ventures in Nigeria or Angola demonstrates, it is problematic to assume that political instability hinders capital accumulation or indeed that good governance enables it' (Phillips et al. 2016, 37).[5] Moreover, critical scholarship has rightly noted that such 'good governance' interventions serve primarily to make countries 'fit for foreign investment' (Sabaratnam 2017), that resource-based economic growth perpetuates historic patterns of dependency and deepens inequalities (Taylor 2016), and that statistics relating to the economic wellbeing of African countries are notoriously unreliable (Jerven 2013). A more open-ended, non-deterministic understanding of governance would seek to analyse it as the imposition of rules and the regulation of access, and the logics and norms that organise the delivery of collective goods (Olivier de Sardan 2011, 22). This then raises the question of who devises these regulations or institutions and who has the power to influence them on multiple scales (Haller et al. 2007; Haller 2010; Niederberger et al. 2015).

Politically, we do evidently share the opinion that it would be preferable if most of the revenues from resource extraction benefited the actual populations (see Schubert 2017, 14); analytically, however, while we share an attention to social, political and historical context, as well as an interest in 'the local and global norms and structures through, and within, which these various stakeholders operate' (Grant et al. 2014b, 3), we reiterate our insistence on a non-normative, processual take on stateness that will also allow us to understand the deployment of 'good governance' in the constant negotiations of stateness in contemporary African states. Indeed, as 'good governance' is an extremely versatile term which ensures that 'debates over resource management will be couched in such terms for years to come' (Phillips et al. 2016, 39), we suggest looking at which ideas and discourses of 'best practice' or 'good governance' in the natural resource sector are mobilised, by whom and to what end.

Extractive industries as co-constitutive of states

A more promising perspective has been to look at the ways in which extractive industries have shaped politics beyond more normative issues of corruption or state failure. A prime example of such an approach is Timothy Mitchell's *Carbon Democracy* (Mitchell 2009, 2011), which looks at how the technicalities and modes of production (technologies, organisation of labour and capital) of oil have produced certain forms of political authority:

> political possibilities were opened up or narrowed down by different ways of organizing the flow and concentration of energy, and these possibilities were enhanced or limited by arrangements of people, finance, expertise and violence that were assembled in relationship to the distribution and control of energy.
>
> (Mitchell 2009, 401)

Stefan Andreasson (2015, 311) also points to how the mining industry and the nation's fortunes have been historically intertwined in South Africa, and how, until today, 'the mining industry remains a key dimension of the shifting tides of political power'. And Michael Watts (2011, 67), writing about Nigeria, notes how contestations around issues of the equitable distribution of oil revenues and the environmental burden of oil production have led to the 'political fragmentation of the national space called Nigeria – characterised by the emergence of highly contentious and insurgent political (and criminal) spaces, rather than a robust sense of nationalism and a modern petro-state'.

A more anthropologically oriented strand of such scholarship is concerned with how mining or oil companies and local communities interact (e.g. Hönke 2012, 2013). This can also take the form of a somewhat more activist stance, focusing on the 'negative impact on local livelihoods' by detailing the 'traditional resource use' of 'the indigenous peoples' and their 'reactions and strategies' against the 'environmental and social impact' of hydrocarbons extraction in the areas where they live, as well as the strategies of corporations to minimise (or at least give the impression of minimising) their negative impact among local communities (Haller et al. 2007). Others, however, have privileged an approach that seeks to study the corporations and states involved in mineral extraction as a series of shifting – sometimes cooperating, sometimes conflicting – institutions and assemblages (Welker 2014), and show how 'the mining company' and 'the local community' are mutually constitutive (Golub 2014; Kirsch 2014). In a similar vein, Andrew Barry

(2006, 243) has suggested studying the oil industry as a technological zone, a framing device or 'an abstraction which draws attention to certain features of the social landscape and its spatial forms which may otherwise go unnoticed'. From this, we heed the call to move beyond binaries of resistance or accommodation and look at the co-production of stateness through the negotiations around the activities of extractive industries.

Our approach: changing stateness under the impact of extractives

Our approach is therefore premised on four interlinked lines of enquiry. First, who are the actors? Here, the challenge is to account for the multiplicity of actors, but also their internal diversity. From this, we can then ask concretely what instruments for the governance of extractive industries are being elaborated and implemented, by whom and at what levels (national legislation, national regulatory bodies, regional/continental strategies). How do these levels interact and impact upon the negotiations and implementation of projects at national and local levels?

Second, which discourses do they deploy around the implantation, development or implementation of extractive industry activities? 'Change', 'development' and 'growth' are not just empty buzzwords deployed by armies of consultants; they are also potent socio-political imaginaries (Hansen and Stepputat 2001; Mbembe 2001; Karlström 2003) that have efficacy beyond the confines of strategy papers and memoranda of understanding, and are generative of new ideas and practices of stateness. They are culturally resonant templates for thought and action (Gaonkar 2002; Taylor 2002; Bertelsen et al. 2014; Nielsen and Pedersen 2015; Schubert 2016) that can be deployed strategically by a variety of actors to make claims on the state and the society in which they live. We therefore suggest that we need to pay attention to the productive and performative dimensions of such imaginaries. How are ideas of change, development and growth, which we often tend to associate instinctively with a top-down, state/corporate development project, invested with meaning and invoked by different actors? What leeway do these various actors have to promote their agendas within, for example, a 'good governance of extractive resources' framework? How are ideas and ideals of the state played out and renegotiated in these interactions of national politics and globalised capital? And how do such – admittedly global – imaginaries of the common good, globalised modernity and inclusive development latch on to and resonate with – local – historical and cultural contexts (Geschiere and Jackson 2006, 3)? We hold that it is of analytical interest to chart how programmatic buzzwords like 'growth', 'redistribution', 'transparency' and 'responsibility' or potent political imaginaries such as 'good governance' and the 'resource curse' are invoked, reinterpreted and invested with meaning by the various actors engaged in making resource extraction profitable, beneficial and socially 'thick'.

Third, what is the contingency of these negotiations? That is, in what ways are they dependent on specific histories of public authority, economic exploitation and boom-and-bust cycles? What happens, for example, to states that rely on revenues from extractive industries after ten years of bonanza in the current period of commodity slump? Also, though, how do country-specific political economies (the capture of strategic economic sectors by political elites, for example) influence these negotiations in ways that were perhaps unforeseen by proponents of a more normative 'good governance' approach?

Finally, as a result, what are the outcomes of these negotiations? How do they reshape relations between the state, society and corporations? Do they, for example, offer inroads for 'civil society' actors to push their agendas, or for state administrations to transform their ways of working? And how are ideas and practices of the state reconfigured through these interactions? Focusing on co-production does not mean closing our eyes to the very real power inequalities that shape the encounters between such varied actors, or to the disciplining power of neoliberal 'development interventions' (see Macamo 2003) – quite the contrary. However, equally, we should not assume that these forms of political authority that emerge from the imbrication of corporate investments and state power are simply a top-down process imposed on 'weak' African public administrations or supine populations.

The zoning-off of communal lands for a logistics base, the destruction of communal fishing grounds by oil extraction, or the displacement of local residents to make way for a coal mine are often accompanied by real violence, yet these are not complete, totalising projects. Stateness is a process, always incomplete and evolving, and even in the most exploitative, unequal settings, 'political power is far more dispersed and transactional than is most often assumed' (Krohn-Hansen 2008, 8–9).

How, then, can we understand empirically how social actors engage and subvert, or endorse and align with, the projects of extractive industries, and how do they use this avenue to press claims on the state in which they live or pursue avenues for individual or collective social improvement? By revealing the tensions *and* the multiple linkages between spheres commonly held as separate or even oppositional, we may think beyond stories of resistance and struggling grassroots communities pitted against (or accommodating) global corporate overlords. This idea of co-production, which goes beyond totalising state control or the cultivation of consent by the dominant, should allow us to draw out subtler accounts of the role of extractive industries in the reshaping of political authority, public institutions and ideals of stateness in contemporary Africa.

Structure of the book

The contributors to this volume therefore investigate the different areas in which resource extraction and the interactions around these activities are reshaping the ideas and practices of African states. One of the recurring themes is that grand visions of extractive-driven development through large-scale investments in infrastructure are far from confined to the past; rather, such political visions gained a new lease of life with the return to extractivism in the mid-2000s, even though the language deployed shifted from state-led modernisation to market-efficient development and growth. The first three chapters are directly concerned with these competing visions of development, and how these may or may not be influenced by the boom-and-bust cycle of extractive industries over recent years. The five case-studies that follow then map in detail how the interplay between state, corporate and civil society actors reshapes ideas and practices of the state and development through extractive industries in specific cases.

The first two chapters, by Paul Nugent and Jana Hönke, respectively, look at the building of transport infrastructures and the different ways in which the activities of extractive industries have – or have not – contributed to the development of transport corridors and hubs, and the development of state capacities with regard to the levying of customs duties. Chapter 1 maps the changing patterns as well as the principal actors in Africa's recent infrastructure boom, with a view to assessing how far the needs of the extractive industries are driving and shaping these investment flows. By historicising the 're-enchantment' with infrastructure investments, Nugent paints a differentiated picture that questions the ability of extractive industries to shape infrastructural provision. These different drivers of the infrastructural 'big push' then have uneven implications for African governments' ability to shape the development agenda and for state bureaucracies' capacity to undertake their (partially reconfigured) functions.

Chapter 2, on infrastructure investments in Tanzania, deepens this line of argument. Hönke carefully explains that the assumption that much of Africa's infrastructure boom is driven by resource extraction does not entirely stand up to scrutiny, especially when China is the principal investor. She traces the deployment of competing, new and old imaginaries of development by actors involved in making the new transport corridors work, including China and the Gulf states. These imaginaries, she demonstrates, inform how 'states' are performed alongside transnational political geographies, and point to the political potency of alternatives to the liberal–capitalist models of development.

In Chapter 3, Ulf Engel looks at the nascent 'blue economy' in South Africa, which pulls together the exploration of submarine minerals and offshore hydrocarbons, aquaculture and marine protection, and maritime commerce and manufacturing in one common imaginary and policy framework that is intended to 'unlock' South Africa's development potential. He shows how a cultural transfer of a great economic leap forward from Malaysia has been adapted to the local context, thereby reconfiguring the governing ANC's role in shaping a vision for South Africa's development.

In Chapter 4, Erika Tchatchouang investigates the development of participatory mining legislation in Cameroon. Based on extensive interviews with the actors involved in the process of reforming the country's mining code and documentary research, she analyses the dynamics and processes involved in the emergence of participatory codes by highlighting their advantages and limitations with respect to the clearly stated objective of capitalisation of foreign direct investment. It seems that the current generation of participatory mining codes is attractive, at least in theory, to local and foreign investors, optimises state revenues *and* helps to protect people's fundamental rights and the environment. However, it remains to be seen whether this more participatory approach to legislation will generate the desired outcomes.

In Chapter 5, Padil Salimo looks at the reshaping of state–community relations at the local administrative level brought about by the advent of onshore liquefied natural gas (LNG) extraction in the Rovuma Basin in northern Mozambique. The political-economy dynamics related to these investments have resulted in extraordinary demands for land by multinational oil companies and ruling elite actors in the private sector, putting pressure on the local government to manage land acquisitions. Thus, insecurity of land tenure for local communities has become a serious concern as their interest in 'securing a good deal' is threatened by the competing interests of multinational oil companies and ruling elites. Salimo argues that the bargaining power of local government is too weak to secure the interests of local communities when pitted against the competing interests of multinational oil companies and ruling elites. In consequence, the rights of local communities to land and fair compensation are at risk.

In Chapter 6, Sonwabile Mnwana analyses the ways in which the power of traditional authorities has been reconfigured through platinum mining in South Africa's North-West Province. He demonstrates how South Africa's post-apartheid state's mineral policy reform, particularly its redress mission, has been significantly compromised by the local institutions that shape the structure of power at the local level. Although the 'new' mineral policy has nationalised all minerals rights and placed them under state custodianship, rural land in the former 'homelands' remains largely under the control of traditional authorities. The rural expansion of the platinum industry coincides with post-apartheid legislation's attempts to redefine residents in these communal areas as 'traditional communities' (or 'tribes'), under local chiefs. Subsequently, they have become the mediators of mineral-led development and conflictive mining deals.

In Chapter 7, Rita Kesselring looks at how the entry of a new economic actor – the copper mine – transforms the relationships between local government and residents in Zambia's 'New Copperbelt' in the context of post-structural adjustment reforms and the global commodity slump. She carefully details how the presence of the mine in Solwezi has had an impact on revenue collection, urban planning and administrative capacities and, ultimately, voting patterns at the local level, thereby demonstrating how the capacities of the local state are indeed changing, though not for the reasons typically advanced by the resource curse literature.

In Chapter 8, Monica Skaten investigates 'petroleum legacies' in Ghana's domestic politics. As she details, development through domestic hydrocarbons production and refining has been a core element of the political vision of Ghana's development since independence under Kwame Nkrumah. This gives the Tema Oil Refinery enduring political weight beyond the successive regime and government changes since that time. In contrast to oil-rich, dominant-party regimes such as Angola and Equatorial Guinea, Ghana's competitive democracy means that the two main parties, which have been alternating in power since 1992, both seek to bolster their fortunes by claiming credit for the development of the 'new' oil sector while at the same time accusing their rival of mismanaging the sector.

Finally, the Conclusion pulls these diverse case-studies into focus under the heading 'The Political Ecology of the State' and links them back to the common theme and the overarching research question: how are extractive industries reshaping political authority, public institutions and ideals of stateness in contemporary Africa?

Notes

1 For the 'lost decade' trope, see various reports from such organisations as the NCPA (www.ncpa.org/sub/dpd/index.php?Article_ID=4167, accessed 3.10.2017) and the UN ESA (www.un.org/esa/socdev/csd/2006/PressReleases/Development-The LostDecade.pdf, accessed 3.10.2017).
2 www.africaminingvision.org/about.html.
3 See, for example, Moçambique para todos, 'O regime especial para gás da Bacia do Rovuma' (http://macua.blogs.com/moambique_para_todos/2014/12/o-regime-especial-para-g%C3%A1s-da-bacia-do-rovuma.html, accessed 24.2.2017); Reuters, 'Chevron, Angola government in tax, investment talks' (www.reuters.com/article/us-chevron-angola-idUSKBN16113N, accessed 24.2.2017).
4 See his 1994 article at: www.theatlantic.com/magazine/archive/1994/02/the-coming-anarchy/304670/, accessed 26.2.2018.
5 Though policy reports such as UNECA's *African Governance Report IV* (2017) or the final report of the Tana High-Level Forum on Security in Africa (2017) tend to reproduce such tropes.

References

Allen, C. 1999. Warfare, Endemic Violence and State Collapse in Africa. *Review of African Political Economy*, 26(81), 367–384.

Amundsen, I. 2017. Nigeria: Defying the Resource Curse. In D.A. Williams and P. Le Billon, eds, *Corruption, Natural Resources and Development: From Resource Curse to Political Ecology*. Cheltenham and Northampton, MA: Edward Elgar Publishing, 17–27.

Andreasson, S. 2015. Varieties of Resource Nationalism in Sub-Saharan Africa's Energy and Minerals Markets. *Extractive Industries and Society*, 2(2), 310–319.

Barnett, J. 2000. Destabilizing the Environment-Conflict Thesis. *Review of International Studies*, 26(02), 271–288.

Barry, A. 2006. Technological Zones. *European Journal of Social Theory*, 9(2), 239–253.

Bayart, J.-F., S. Ellis and B. Hibou. 1999. *The Criminalization of the State in Africa*. Oxford and Bloomington, IN: James Currey, Indiana University Press.

Behrends, A. 2011. Fighting for Oil When There is No Oil Yet: The Darfur–Chad Border. In A. Behrends, S. Reyna and G. Schlee, eds, *Crude Domination: An Anthropology of Oil*. New York and Oxford: Berghahn Books, 81–106.

Bertelsen, B.E., I. Tvedten and S. Roque. 2014. Engaging, Transcending and Subverting Dichotomies: Discursive Dynamics of Maputo's Urban Space. *Urban Studies*, 51(13), 2752–2769.

Bhattacharyya, S. and R. Hodler. 2010. Natural Resources, Democracy and Corruption. *European Economic Review*, 54(4), 608–621.

Bierschenk, T. and J.-P. Olivier de Sardan, eds. 2014. *States at Work: Dynamics of African Bureaucracies*. Leiden and Boston, MA: Brill.

Büscher, Bram. 2015. Investing in Irony? Development, Improvement and Dispossession in Southern African Coal Spaces. *European Journal of Development Research*, 27(5), 727–744.

Campbell, B., ed. 2013. *Modes of Governance and Revenue Flows in African Mining*. Houndmills and New York: Palgrave Macmillan.

Chabal, P. and J.-P. Daloz. 1999. *Africa Works: Disorder as Political Instrument*. Oxford and Bloomington, IN: James Currey, Indiana University Press.

Colgan, J.D. 2013. *Petro-aggression: When Oil Causes War*. Cambridge: Cambridge University Press.

Collier, P. and A. Hoeffler. 2000. *Greed and Grievance in Civil War*. Oxford: University of Oxford, Institute of Economics and Statistics, Centre for the Study of African Economies.

Cooper, F. 2002. *Africa since 1940: The Past of the Present*. Cambridge and New York: Cambridge University Press.

Dashwood, H.S. and B.B. Puplampu. 2014. Multi-stakeholder Partnerships in Mining: From Engagement to Development in Ghana. In J. Grant, W. Compaoré and M. Mitchell, eds, *New Approaches to the Governance of Natural Resources: Insights from Africa*. Houndmills andNew York: Palgrave Macmillan, 131–153.

Davis, G.A. and J.E. Tilton. 2005. The Resource Curse. *Natural Resources Forum*, 29(3), 233–242.

Donner, N. 2009. The Myth of the Oil Curse: Exploitation and Diversion in Equatorial Guinea. *Afro-Hispanic Review*, 28(2), 21–42.

du Preez, M.-L. 2014. Interrogating the 'Good' in 'Good Governance': Rethinking Natural Resource Governance Theory and Practice in Africa. In J.A. Grant, W.R.N. Compaoré and M.I. Mitchell, eds, *New Approaches to the Governance of Natural Resources: Insights from Africa*. Houndmills andNew York: Palgrave Macmillan, 25–42.

Engel, U. 2009. Die Neuordnung Afrikas – Souveränität im Wandel. *Politik und Zeitgeschichte*, 34–35, 7–12.

Engel, U. and P. Nugent, eds. 2010. *Respacing Africa*. Leiden and Boston, MA: Brill.

Englebert, P. and J. Ron. 2004. Primary Commodities and War: Congo-Brazzaville's Ambivalent Resource Curse. *Comparative Politics*, 37(1), 61–81.

Erdmann, G. and U. Engel. 2007. Neopatrimonialism Reconsidered: Critical Review and Elaboration of an Elusive Concept. *Commonwealth & Comparative Politics*, 45(1), 95–119.

Ferguson, J. 2010. The Uses of Neoliberalism. *Antipode*, 41, 166–184.

Gaonkar, D.P. 2002. Toward New Imaginaries: An Introduction. *Public Culture*, 14(1), 1–19.

Geschiere, P. and S. Jackson. 2006. Autochthony and the Crisis of Citizenship: Democratization, Decentralization, and the Politics of Belonging. *African Studies Review*, 49(2), 1–7.

Golub, A. 2014. *Leviathans at the Gold Mine: Creating Indigenous and Corporate Actors in Papua New Guinea*. Durham, NC: Duke University Press.

Grant, J., W. Compaoré and M. Mitchell, eds. 2014a. *New Approaches to the Governance of Natural Resources: Insights from Africa*. Houndmills and New York: Palgrave Macmillan.

Grant, J.A., W.R.N. Compaoré, M.I. Mitchell and M. Ingulstad. 2014b. 'New' Approaches to the Governance of Africa's Natural Resources. In J.A. Grant, W.R.N. Compaoré and M.I. Mitchell, eds, *New Approaches to the Governance of Natural Resources: Insights from Africa*. Houndmills andNew York: Palgrave Macmillan, 3–24.

Grant, J.A., W.R.N. Compaoré, M.I. Mitchell, and T.M. Shaw. 2014c. Prospects and Trends in the Governance of Africa's Natural Resources: Reflections on the Role of External and Internal Actors. In J.A. Grant, W.R.N. Compaoré and M.I. Mitchell, eds, *New Approaches to the Governance of Natural Resources: Insights from Africa*. Houndmills andNew York: Palgrave Macmillan, 267–284.

Hagmann, T. and D. Péclard. 2010. Negotiating Statehood: Dynamics of Power and Domination in Africa. *Development and Change*, 41(4), 539–562.

Haller, T., ed. 2010. *Disputing the Floodplains: Institutional Change and the Politics of Resource Management in African Floodplains*. Leiden and Boston, MA: Brill.

Haller, T., A. Blöchlinger, M. John, E. Marthaler and S. Ziegler, eds. 2007. *Fossil Fuels, Oil Companies, and Indigenous Peoples: Strategies of Multinational Oil Companies, States, and Ethnic Minorities*. Wien: Lit-Verlag.

Hansen, T.B. and F. Stepputat, eds. 2001. *States of Imagination*. Durham, NC: Duke University Press.

Hendrix, C.S. and M. Noland. 2014. *Confronting the Curse: The Economics and Geopolitics of Natural Resource Governance*. Washington, DC: Peterson Institute for International Economics.

Herbst, J. 1996. Responding to State Failure in Africa. *International Security*, 21(3), 120–144.

Hönke, J. 2012. Multinationals and Security Governance in the Community: Participation, Discipline and Indirect Rule. *Journal of Intervention and Statebuilding*, 6(1), 57–73.

Hönke, J. 2013. *Transnational Companies and Security Governance: Hybrid Practices in a Postcolonial World*. London: Routledge.

Jackson, R.H. and C.G. Rosberg. 1982. Why Africa's Weak States Persist: The Empirical and the Juridical in Statehood. *World Politics*, 35(1), 1–24.

Jacobs, J. 2013. An Overview of Revenue Flows from the Mining Sector: Impacts, Debates and Policy Recommendations. In B. Campbell, ed., *Modes of Governance and Revenue Flows in African Mining*. Houndmills and New York: Palgrave Macmillan, 16–46.

Jerven, M. 2013. *Poor Numbers: How We Are Misled by African Development Statistics and What to Do about It*. Ithaca, NY: Cornell University Press.

Jones, S. 2008. *Sub-Saharan Africa and the 'Resource Curse': Limitations of the Conventional Wisdom*. DIIS Working Paper No. 2008/14. Copenhagen: Danish Institute for International Studies.

Kaldor, M. 1999. *New and Old Wars: Organized Violence in a Global Era*. Stanford, CA: Stanford University Press.

Karl, T.L. 1997. *The Paradox of Plenty: Oil Booms and Petro-states*. Berkeley: University of California Press.

Karlström, M. 2003. On the Aesthetics and Dialogics of Power in the Postcolony. *Africa*, 73(1), 57–67.

Kirsch, S. 2014. *Mining Capitalism: The Relationship between Corporations and Their Critics*. Oakland: University of California Press.

Koechlin, L. 2013. *Corruption as an Empty Signifier: Politics and Political Order in Africa*. Leiden and Boston, MA: Brill.

Krasner, S.D. and T. Risse. 2014. External Actors, State-building, and Service Provision in Areas of Limited Statehood: Introduction. *Governance*, 27(4), 545–567.

Krohn-Hansen, C. 2008. *Political Authoritarianism in the Dominican Republic*. New York: Palgrave Macmillan.

Lange, S. 2011. Gold and Governance: Legal Injustices and Lost Opportunities in Tanzania. *African Affairs*, 110(439), 233–252.

Le Billon, P. 2001. The Political Ecology of War: Natural Resources and Armed Conflicts. *Political Geography*, 20(5), 561–584.

Le Billon, P. 2004. The Geopolitical Economy of 'Resource Wars'. *Geopolitics*, 9(1), 1–28.

Leite, C. and J. Weidmann. 1999. *Does Mother Nature Corrupt? Natural Resources and Economic Growth*. IMF Working Paper No. WP 99/85. Washington, DC: IMF.

Macamo, E. 2003. How Development Aid Changes Societies: Disciplining Mozambique through Structural Adjustment. Presented at the CODESRIA General Assembly, Maputo, 6–10.12.2003.

Mailey, J.R. 2015. *The Anatomy of the Resource Curse: Predatory Investment in Africa's Extractive Industries*. ACSS Special Report No. NDU/ACSS-SR-3. Washington, DC: Africa Center for Strategic Studies.

Mamdani, M. 1996. *Citizen and Subject: Contemporary Africa and the Legacy of Late Colonialism*. Princeton, NJ: Princeton University Press.

Mbembe, A. 2001. *On the Postcolony*. Berkeley, Los Angeles and London: University of California Press.

Melber, H. 2015. Where and What (for) is the Middle? Africa and the Middle Class(es). *European Journal of Development Research*, 27(2), 246–254.

Migdal, J. and K. Schlichte. 2005. Rethinking the State. In K. Schlichte, ed., *The Dynamics of States: The Formation and Crises of State Domination*. Aldershot: Ashgate Publishing, 1–40.

Mitchell, T. 2009. Carbon Democracy. *Economy and Society*, 38(3), 399–432.

Mitchell, T. 2011. *Carbon Democracy: Political Power in the Age of Oil*. London: Verso.

Niederberger, T., T. Haller, H. Gambon, M. Kobi and I. Wink, eds. 2015. *The Open Cut: Mining, Transnational Corporations and Local Populations*. Wien: Lit-Verlag.

Nielsen, M. and M.A. Pedersen. 2015. Infrastructural Involutions: The Imaginative Efficacy of Collapsed Chinese Futures in Mozambique and Mongolia. In M. Harris and N. Rapport, eds, *Reflections on Imagination: Human Capacity and Ethnographic Method*. Aldershot and London: Ashgate Publishing, 237–262.

Olivier de Sardan, J.-P. 2011. The Eight Modes of Local Governance in West Africa. *IDS Bulletin*, 42(2), 22–31.

Phillips, J., E. Hailwood and A. Brooks. 2016. Sovereignty, the 'Resource Curse' and the Limits of Good Governance: A Political Economy of Oil in Ghana. *Review of African Political Economy*, 43(147), 26–42.

Reno, W. 2000. Shadow States and the Political Economy of Civil Wars. In M. Berdal and D.M. Malone, eds, *Greed and Grievance: Economic Agendas in Civil Wars*. Boulder, CO: Lynne Rienner Publishers, 43–68.

Richards, P., ed. 2005. *No Peace, No War: An Anthropology of Contemporary Armed Conflicts*. Athens: Ohio University Press.

Ross, M.L. 2012. *The Oil Curse: How Petroleum Wealth Shapes the Development of Nations*. Princeton, NJ, and Oxford: Princeton University Press.

Sabaratnam, M. 2017. *Decolonising Intervention: International Statebuilding in Mozambique*. London and Lanham, MD: Rowman & Littlefield International.

Sachs, J.D. and A.M. Warner. 2001. The Curse of Natural Resources. *European Economic Review*, 45(4), 827–838.

Sala-i-Martin, X. and A. Subramanian. 2003. *Addressing The Natural Resource Curse: An Illustration from Nigeria*. Washington, DC: IMF.

Schubert, J. 2016. 'A Culture of Immediatism': Co-optation and Complicity in Post-war Angola. *Ethnos*, 83(1), 1–19.

Schubert, J. 2017. *Working the System: A Political Ethnography of the New Angola*. Ithaca, NY and London: Cornell University Press.

Taylor, C. 2002. Modern Social Imaginaries. *Public Culture*, 14(1), 91–124.

Taylor, I. 2016. Dependency Redux: Why Africa Is Not Rising. *Review of African Political Economy*, 43(147), 8–25.

Van Gyampo, R.E. 2011. Saving Ghana from Its Oil: A Critical Assessment of Preparations so Far Made. *Africa Today*, 57(4), 49–69.

von Schnitzler, A. 2016. *Democracy's Infrastructure: Techno-politics and Protest after Apartheid*. Princeton, NJ: Princeton University Press.

Wai, Z. 2012. Neo-patrimonialism and the Discourse of State Failure in Africa. *Review of African Political Economy*, 39(131), 27–43.

Watts, M. 2004. Resource Curse? Governmentality, Oil and Power in the Niger Delta, Nigeria. *Geopolitics* 9(1), 50–80.

Watts, M. 2011. Blood Oil: The Anatomy of a Petro-insurgency in the Niger Delta, Nigeria. In A. Behrends, S. Reyna, and G. Schlee, eds, *Crude Domination: An Anthropology of Oil*. New York and Oxford: Berghahn Books, 49–80.

Welker, M. 2014. *Enacting the Corporation: An American Mining Firm in Post-authoritarian Indonesia*. Berkeley: University of California Press.

Weszkalnys, G. 2014. Anticipating Oil: The Temporal Politics of a Disaster Yet to Come. *Sociological Review*, 62, 211–235.

Williams, A. and P. Le Billon, eds. 2017. *Corruption, Natural Resources and Development: From Resource Curse to Political Ecology*. Cheltenham and Northampton, MA: Edward Elgar Publishing.

Yates, D.A. 2014. The Rise and Fall of Oil-rentier States in Africa. In J.A. Grant, W.R. N. Compaoré and M.I. Mitchell, eds, *New Approaches to the Governance of Natural Resources: Insights from Africa*. Houndmills andNew York: Palgrave Macmillan, 45–64.

Zartman, I.W. 1995. *Collapsed States: The Disintegration and Restoration of Legitimate Authority*. Boulder, CO: Lynne Rienner Publishers.

1 Africa's re-enchantment with big infrastructure

White elephants dancing in virtuous circles?

Paul Nugent[1]

When it comes to Africa, the capacity of international organizations to champion that which they previously disavowed is nothing less than remarkable. At the present time, all the principal actors – African governments, corporate investors and the international agencies themselves – are fixated upon the transformative potentialities of infrastructure, by which they mostly mean 'big infrastructure'. This is intriguing, given that Africa has been through previous iterations of much the same thing. During the late 1940s and 1950s, when the modern idea of development was born, overwhelming emphasis was placed upon the catalytic effects of infrastructure, and to that end unprecedented levels of investment were channelled into the construction of ports, roads and railways (Hoyle and Hilling 1970). When the results proved disappointing, enthusiasm waned; and when the money dried up in the late 1970s, a steady process of attrition ensued. The decline of Africa's railway systems is merely the most striking example of a technology that had come to be regarded as too expensive and unsuited to African requirements. A residual scepticism about big infrastructure remained firmly entrenched during the heights of structural adjustment. Hence, the *Berg Report*, for example, devoted an entire chapter to agriculture, but a modest ten pages to transport and communications, which were subsumed within a chapter entitled 'Other Productive Sectors' that bundled together industry, mining and energy. It specifically advised caution with respect to 'large-scale capital-intensive projects' and proposed that the accent should be placed on the maintenance and renewal of existing roads (World Bank 1981, 106). World Bank documents today devote most of their attention to championing substantial new investments in transport and energy, which are regarded as the drivers of economic change. Clearly, there has been nothing less than a paradigm shift and this is reflected in the places where international agencies place their money.[2] If economic development has become a kind of modern religion, infrastructural investment is once again its most potent fetish.

In this chapter, I set out to do two things. First, I address the question of how far these investments are driven by the requirements of the extractive industries. This has a bearing on the likely consequences of lower commodity prices for the more ambitious plans to 'respace' the African continent in the future (Engel and Nugent 2010). In the second section, I consider some implications for the institutional capacity of African states and raise the question of whether the current patterns are sustainable.

The big fix: regional variations in infrastructural expenditure patterns

The re-enchantment with infrastructure arises out of a conjuncture of a number of elements that came into play around the start of the millennium. The first is the rediscovery of regional integration as a platform on which to build complementarities between African economies (Bach 2016). Whereas economic policies after independence tended to mirror each other, and to be competitive in their effects, regional integration today aims to create a common market for goods produced locally as well as more advantageous conditions for Africa's integration into the global marketplace. This is clearly an imperative for the countries with large mining sectors as well as for land-locked states – and all the more so for those that fall into both categories, such as Zambia and Niger. But the expectation is that regional integration will also grow the market for countries with substantial manufacturing sectors (like Nigeria) or with potential for exporting their agricultural surpluses (like Uganda). Within this schema, transport corridors are conceived of as the veins and arteries that circulate goods between coastal ports, urban markets and mining hubs. The second factor is a decade of sustained economic growth underpinned by high primary commodity prices. This led to renewed interest in Africa on the part of global corporations, and emboldened African leaders to anticipate a qualitative transformation on the back of targeted investments. It is no exaggeration to say that the notion of a 'big push' (Killick 1978), which was current in development thinking in the early 1960s, is back in vogue, if not in name. The third element is the rapid elaboration of new information technologies that create the 'smart' systems that potentially enable big infrastructure, for example at seaports, to be deployed in much more efficient ways. Finally, there is a shift in the consensus towards what is sometimes called 'neoliberal governance', in which the boundary between the public and private domains has become blurred (Ferguson 2006; Chalfin 2010). To some extent, this represents a hangover from the era of structural adjustment, but it also reflects a curious convergence of governance trends in Europe and the mixture of public and private interests in China. Given that the European (EU) and China are amongst the most important players in the infrastructural game, this context clearly matters. All of this has enabled some of the grander visions to seem credible in areas where state-led development fell short in the past. These four trends reinforce each other in multiple ways to the point that they can often seem like a single package. However, each of these elements embodies its own internal tensions, and to that extent the relationships between them are also inherently unstable.

It is a recurring theme in policy documents, most notably those produced by the World Bank and the African Development Bank (AfDB), that what is holding Africa back is its severe infrastructural deficit. A particular emphasis is placed on seaports, which are characterized as chronically congested and lacking overall capacity. The problem is attributed to a combination of geographical circumstances, especially the scarcity of natural deep-water harbours, and historical legacies arising from decades of economic failure. However, it is also attributed to the more heartening reality that in the first decade of the new millennium the volume of trade passing through Africa's ports tripled (African Development Bank 2010, 32). The existing seaports were only constructed to handle general cargo and were unable to accommodate the latest generation of container ships, the so-called 'Panamax' and 'Post-Panamax' vessels. Port investments across Africa are largely about bridging the gap with other parts of the maritime world.

The cost of transporting goods is commonly said to be the most serious constraint upon Africa's trade with the rest of the globe. The greatest single factor is the amount of time that it takes for ships to be turned around. A report from 2005 estimated that the time spent on average in East Asian ports amounted to 20 per cent of the total transport time, whereas in Africa this rose to as much as 80 per cent (African Development Bank 2010, 48). The 'dwell time' in African ports ranged from 4 days in Durban and 5 days in Mombasa to 25 days in Tema and 28 days in Port Sudan. The costs also varied wildly with Luanda recording an average handling cost of $320 per TEU (twenty-foot equivalent unit) by comparison with an average of $90 in Mombasa and $121 in Durban (African Development Bank 2010, 47). In addition, the neglect of the continent's rail network has meant that it has not always been possible to follow the shortest route to the coast. Because more traffic is forced onto the roads as a consequence, this contributes to the wider problems of congestion and delay. The fact that most Zambian copper can no longer be dispatched along the Tanzania–Zambia railway (instead, it is transported by truck to Durban and Dar es Salaam) is considered symptomatic of the wider problem (Raballand and Whitworth 2014, 4). In colonial East Africa, an earlier version of the regional integration agenda placed overwhelming emphasis on the railway from the port of Mombasa to the Uganda border. Today, the Rift Valley Railway carries only 5 per cent of the freight from Mombasa's port, although it is currently in the process of being upgraded (World Bank 2014, 82). Finally, one should mention the parlous state of some of Africa's main roads, which represent continental 'highways' in name only. Along the Abidjan–Lagos Corridor (ALCO), for example, only 51 per cent of the roads were classed as 'good' in 2010, with 28 per cent categorized as 'fair' and 21 per cent as 'poor'. Meanwhile, along the Cotonou–Niamey Corridor, as many as 42 per cent of the roads were classed as 'poor' (Deen-Swarray *et al.* 2014, 45).

The shifting configuration of financing is based on the premise that the infrastructural deficit is beyond the financial capacities of African governments, even when they pool their resources. The AfDB has, for example, taken the lead in financing the Trans-African Highway Project, which is a priority of the African Union. The World Bank has greatly increased its own commitments to transport infrastructure, abandoning the scepticism of the relatively recent past. This in part reflects a retreat from the narrowly economistic prescriptions of the structural adjustment era, which produced disappointing results across much of Africa. In addition, development banks, bilateral donors and the private sector all play important roles. Along any given transport corridor, there is typically a multiplicity of projects that bring together different combinations of actors, while the usual corporate suspects, such as Bolloré, turn up in several locations at once. There is a certain structural logic that favours big infrastructure, for the reason that it is often easier for African governments to access external funds to cover large investments than to find money for more modest projects. For politicians whose reputations rest on their ability to point towards 'development', there is an additional incentive to favour big infrastructure because it tends to be highly visible. The electoral cycle plays its own part as incumbent politicians feel the need to be seen commissioning or championing new projects in advance of going to the polls. Regimes may also seek to secure political support by devolving some of the work to local contractors.

Let us now consider the patterns of infrastructural expenditure in more detail before assessing the relative importance of the various actors. The Infrastructure Consortium for Africa (ICA), which brings together the G8 countries, the World Bank, the EU, the AfDB and some others, publishes an annual report on infrastructural financing. It distinguishes between investments in transport, energy, water and information and communications technologies (ICT). In 2013, the report revealed that ICA members invested considerably more in energy than transport infrastructure, whereas other external investors leaned the other way (Infrastructure Consortium for Africa 2014). In 2015, energy and transport accounted for 43.5 per cent and 34.1 per cent of ICA financing, respectively (Infrastructure Consortium for Africa 2016, 24). However, if the investments in energy in South Africa and North Africa are removed from the equation, transport comes out ahead across the other regions of Africa. It will come as little surprise to learn that China was by the far the largest bilateral investor, accounting for 25 per cent of all infrastructural financing in 2015, or that it has specifically targeted transport infrastructure. But the data also highlights two other patterns that are worthy of note. First, private investment in infrastructure has been unevenly distributed, with a strong bias towards energy in South Africa, but it has contributed far less than the ICA and other public investors – in fact, a mere 8.9 per cent of the total in 2015 (Infrastructure Consortium for Africa 2016, 15). Second, African governments finance slightly more than half of the expenditure commitments, typically placing their own money into transport rather than energy. In addition, African governments incur the obligations that come with external lending. In 2015, as much as 72.9 per cent, or $14.25 billion, of ICA funding commitments were in the form of loans, whereas grants accounted for only $2.35 billion and 'blended' funding a mere $1.10 billion (Infrastructure Consortium for Africa 2016, 26). This suggests that African states are far more engaged with the infrastructural 'big push' than is commonly assumed.

A separate report by Deloitte (2015), which deals with recent trends in large construction projects valued at over $50 million, tells a broadly similar story. However, it uses a different breakdown of expenditure and only deals with newly activated projects. It reveals that transport gained ground relative to energy between 2013 and 2015 in terms of the number of projects, and accounted for substantially more in terms of the total value of expenditure. Whereas mining investment fell back, the oil and gas sector underwent significant growth. The report is also of interest for what it reveals about public–private partnerships (PPPs), which the World Bank has been especially keen to promote (World Bank 2014). It revealed that between 2013 and 2015, public investment projects increased from 181 to 205, private projects fell from 127 to 57, and PPPs increased from 14 to 39. The uptake of PPPs seems, therefore, to have come at the expense of private projects rather than public financing. Somewhat surprisingly, PPPs have had the greatest purchase in West Africa, followed by Southern Africa (Deloitte 2015, 5–6). This data therefore indicates that the progress in implementing PPPs has been incremental as well as uneven.

This brings us to the question of how far resource extraction is shaping the pattern of infrastructural investment. Some of the extractive industries clearly make their own investments, but they also depend on connective infrastructure such as ports, roads and railways. Diamonds are mostly flown out, but mining equipment has to be brought in the hard way (African Development Bank 2010, 10). In the case of oil that is produced away from

Table 1.1 Infrastructure commitments by sector and source, 2015 ($ million)

Source	*Transport*	*Water*	*Energy*	*ICT*	*Multi-sector*	*Other*	*Total*
ICA	6,770.9	3,184.3	8,635.0	626.0	634.4	–	19,840.7
ACG	2,071.7	377.8	1,554.9	16.5	391.5	–	4,412.4
RDBs	173.7	47.6	95.0	76.4	25.5	–	418.2
China & others	9,932.2	268.4	10,747.5	1,032.1	–	–	21,980.1
Non-ICA Europe	345.5	–	458.2	72.5	–	–	876.2
African governments	15,278.3	4,124.8	5,692.0	705.2	1,164.7	1,1167.3	28,402.3
Private	113.5	114.0	7,214.8	–	–	–	7,442.3
Total	34,658.8	8,116.8	34,667.5	2,518.8	2,216.1	1,167.3	83,372.3

Source: Infrastructure Consortium for Africa 2016, 89

Notes: These figures refer to commitments rather than disbursements. ACG = Arab Coordination Group, RDB = regional development banks.

Table 1.2 Construction projects in 2015 valued at above $50 million

Type of project	*Value of projects ($ million)*	*Number*	*Percentage of all projects (%)*
Education	131	2	0.66
Energy and power	95,555	85	28.24
Healthcare	561	4	1.33
Manufacturing	2,000	1	0.33
Mining	39,776	22	7.31
Oil and gas	81,558	18	5.98
Real estate	12,522	18	5.98
Shipping and ports	1,035	1	0.33
Social development	3,305	12	3.99
Telecommunications	567	2	0.66
Transport*	131,664	111	36.88
Water	6,736	25	8.31
Total	375,410	301	100

Source: Adapted from Deloitte 2015, 5

Note: * A considerable amount of port development is included within the 'Transport' category rather than under 'Shipping and ports'.

the coastline, there is a preference these days for underground pipelines that are linked to dedicated oil terminals at the coast. To that extent, oil does not merely create an enclave effect where it is drilled, but also in the locations from where it is shipped. The same applies perforce to natural gas. By contrast, other mining operations tend to rely on infrastructure that is shared with other users. Historically, one form of subsidy to the mining industry resided in the construction of railways followed by the creation of monopolies that forced all transporters onto the tracks. By spreading the cost among multiple users, the freight charges to the mining sector were reduced. These days, such monopolies are frowned upon, which means that the railways have to attract willing customers by offering faster and more reliable services. One argument in favour of railways is that they reduce wear and tear on the roads, which ought to benefit those engaged in the haulage of other commodities. Whether this is optimal for the mining industry depends on the nature of what is being transported and other associated costs. In many parts of the world, copper is transported by rail, and it is likely that, all else being equal, this would be the preferred mode among mining companies in Central Africa. But because the real cost of road maintenance is not borne by those who transport copper, and because the labour of truck-drivers is so cheap,[3] there is presently little incentive to alter existing practices. Aside from railways, ease of shipment through the seaports is of fundamental importance to the mining industry, especially in this era of containerization. This brings us back to the cost and speed of handling through the various ports.

In practice, the extractive industries carry very different weight in the various regions. This is reflected in the design of the transport corridors that the regional economic communities (RECs) have been promoting for some years now (Söderbaum and Taylor 2008). In the case of East Africa, the discovery of oil and gas deposits has brought an appreciation of the need for new pipeline projects, but as of 2015 most of the work was no more than incipient. The main focus of the East African Community (EAC) has been on removing trade barriers within the designated Single Customs Territory (SCT) and attempting to facilitate regional access to global markets. For landlocked countries such as Rwanda, Burundi and Uganda, the ports of Mombasa and Dar es Salaam are the entry points for petroleum imports (all of which are currently transported by road) and manufactured goods (which come largely from Asia). The current focus is on making substantial improvements to existing ports as well as constructing some entirely new ones; upgrading rail links; and improving the roads along the corridors. Given that the EAC has few minerals outside of Tanzania, it cannot be said that either the Northern Corridor from Mombasa or the Central Corridor through Dar es Salaam is driven by an extractive logic. It is revealing that the most expensive construction projects in 2015, in order of importance, were the East African Railway, the new port development at Bagamoyo, the Grand Ethiopian Renaissance Dam, the Djibouti–Ethiopia Railway and the Mombasa–Malaba Railway. The only straightforwardly extractive investment was a railway to transport potash in northern Ethiopia.

In West Africa, the picture is more mixed. The Economic Community of West African States (ECOWAS) has indicated that its priority is to promote ALCO, with a view to exploiting the possible agglomeration effects of Africa's most densely populated zone in a belt that stretches along the coastline from Lagos to Accra (World Bank 2009; OECD/SWAC 2017, 134–136). There are limited mineral resources along the coastal corridor, and the expectation is that most of the traffic will involve goods produced within the region, including manufactures and agricultural produce. At present, the most visible item of trade is Nigerian cement, which has found a ready market in Ghana. The expansion of the ports that are dotted along the coastline, notably at Abidjan, Tema, Lomé and Cotonou, is intended to facilitate access to the global market for the Sahelian countries. Burkina Faso depends on the road corridors through Ghana and Togo for many of its manufactured imports, whereas the mining industry makes use of the Abidjan–Ouagadougou railway. In 2014, when the existing management contract expired, the major stake in the operation of the railway was taken on by Pan-African Minerals, which announced plans to extend the line to its manganese mine in north-eastern Burkina Faso.[4] In West Africa, some of the largest infrastructural investments involved extractive industries. Oil and gas projects, such as the Nigeria–Algeria pipeline project, accounted for five of the ten most expensive projects in the region in 2015. However, the Simandou iron-ore project in Guinea topped the list, while a bauxite/alumina project was ranked fifth. The construction of a partially new rail link between Niamey (Niger) and Cotonou (Benin), which was assigned to Bolloré, is another example of the linkage between mining (in this case uranium) and railway investments in the Sahel, although work ground to a halt following a legal challenge in Benin in 2015.

In West–Central Africa, the picture is different again. Here, the overall level of infrastructural investment has been considerably smaller, but it has certainly been pursued with a view to facilitating mineral exports. The Kribi–Edea railway, which is geared to the development of iron-ore and bauxite exports from Cameroon, was the largest project in the region in 2015. There has also been major investment in seaports, especially at Kribi. However, the many delays to the expansion of the port have meant that the transport corridor to neighbouring countries is poorly developed.[5]

In Southern Africa, which was the largest recipient of new investment by some margin, there has been a much greater focus on power generation, some of which serves the mining industry but is clearly also driven by rising consumer demand. By far the largest construction project in Southern Africa in 2015, at a cost of $22.5 billion, was the redevelopment of the port of Durban. Already the continent's second-busiest port, Durban hopes to quadruple its capacity in the coming years. Part of the rationale is that the copper industries of Zambia and the DRC will continue to patronize the port, but it is also intended to cater to South Africa's own requirements.

Finally, there is much less evidence of an extractive logic at work in North Africa, which accounted for only around 10 per cent of all new investments. In 2015, the largest project was the Tangier–Casablanca high-speed rail project in Morocco, which is oriented towards passenger traffic. The other major investments were concerned with power generation of various kinds, including the development of the Nador West Port in Morocco, which is connected to plans for a thermal energy project. The other rationale behind this port development is that it will enable Morocco to bid for cargo traffic in the western Mediterranean.[6]

In general, therefore, we may conclude that infrastructural investments are only partially justified with reference to the requirements of the mining industry, whereas the more specific needs of the oil and gas sectors are often prioritized. In East Africa, the main transport corridors are intended to facilitate the flow of Asian manufactures and petroleum imports, and to increase regional trade. In West Africa, the case for ALCO has been advanced on the basis of developing the internal market, whereas the corridors that run from the ports to the Sahelian countries are intended to facilitate both the import of consumer goods and the export of minerals. In West–Central Africa and Southern Africa, mining logics play a more significant role. In North Africa, however, the extractive industries are confined to a handful of oil and gas projects. Given this highly variegated picture, it is clearly very difficult to generalize for the continent as a whole, but the overall picture is that 'internal' needs – for cheap electricity, faster travel and cheaper consumer goods – are at least as important as 'external' drivers. In the context of less favourable international prices for minerals, one would expect the relative balance of investments to shift – as indeed it has in recent years –albeit without significant effect on the overall momentum behind infrastructural investments. China's interests are not confined to the extractive industries, and one would expect its broader interest in infrastructure to continue for as long as it is able to sustain its own growth trajectory. As for the development banks, they exhibit an undiminished enthusiasm for investments in big infrastructure and this is unlikely to change any time soon. A retreat from big infrastructure would require a paradigm shift, and this is not currently on the horizon.

Infrastructure and state capacities

When we consider the impact of all this investment upon state capacities, a fundamental distinction needs to be drawn between the ability of African governments to shape the developmental agenda and their capacity to complete administrative functions with a modicum of efficiency. A moment's reflection would indicate that these are not necessarily congruent, because the assertion of (multi-)state ownership over the project for respacing Africa might well be associated with greater bureaucratic confusion.

As far as the first criterion is concerned, it sometimes seems as if the agenda is being driven by external actors and that African governments simply tag along. But much as statist versions of development in the 1960s and 1970s were hegemonic, so current versions of development through 'infrastructuring' are based on a consensus that is shared by all the principal actors – ranging from the World Bank, to Bolloré, to African governments themselves. I have already indicated that the latter have manifested a high level of commitment by financing much of the infrastructure, but it is also noteworthy that these states have retained a considerable measure of control over the way in which infrastructure is rolled out and operationalized. An obvious place to start is with corridor management, which is a complex field because it necessarily involves government agencies across multiple countries as well as non-state agencies operating at the regional and national levels. The task of coordinating all of this complexity should not be underestimated.

The corridors themselves are constituted in very different ways. The Walvis Bay Corridor Group, which is responsible for four transport corridors, has made a formal attempt to be inclusive. Its members include four Namibian ministries, the Road Authority, the Namibian Ports Authority (NAMPORT), the Walvis Bay municipality and six business, logistics and transport associations. Non-Namibian companies are permitted an associated status, which is indicative of the measure of control that the Namibian state prefers to retain.[7] By contrast, ALCO was established by the five states along the corridor with the support of the World Bank and UNAIDS, and with additional input from ECOWAS, UEMOA, USAID, the Global Fund and other international organizations.[8] Unusually, AIDS and malaria prevention has shared the limelight with trade facilitation, which reflects some donor preferences. Importantly, ALCO remains an intergovernmental initiative, with no direct input from the private sector.[9] It has, however, engaged with the West Africa Trade Hub, which was established as an initiative of USAID. Over several years, the Hub generated valuable field data on checkpoints and bribes demanded per kilometre along the corridors. Although USAID funding for this work has now ceased, the Borderless Alliance continues to provide a forum through which state agencies and private businesses can work together to minimize transport delays.

In East Africa, the pattern is somewhat similar. The Northern Corridor Transit and Transport Coordination Authority (NCTTA) is operated by the Ministries of Transport in the member countries. The input of the private sector is confined to a Stakeholders Forum that convenes from time to time.[10] However, TradeMark East Africa (TMEA), a non-profit organization, has served as the conduit for much of the donor funding that has gone into the construction of roads and one-stop border posts (OSBPs). TMEA has been closely involved in upgrading computer systems for Customs and promoting trade facilitation. It also acts as something of a lobbyist for the private sector, promoting the interests of corporate actors and small-scale traders alike.[11] The overall pattern, therefore, is one in which state agencies have remained in control, but have looked for common ground with non-state actors that have stakes in trade and transport.

International corporations are playing a critical role in the construction of port facilities, but African governments have resisted any move towards wholesale privatization. At Walvis Bay, a decision was taken to upgrade the existing port with a large tranche of funding from the AfDB, but without any private sector involvement. The solid governance record of the Namibian state, and the relative efficiency of the port, made the AfDB more than usually accommodating (African Development Bank 2013). In this way, the Walvis Bay port was retained firmly within the public domain, although the actual construction was put out to tender. In most cases, governments have established port authorities (PAs) that are granted a high degree of autonomy and maintain overall regulatory oversight. It is customary to distinguish between three models of port management: namely, landlord ports, in which the infrastructure (berths, docks and roads) is owned and operated by the PA, while the superstructure (cranes, sheds and so on) is owned by private operators; tool ports, in which private companies manage the infrastructure and superstructure on behalf of the PA; and service ports, in which the PAs remain fully in control of operations (Trujillo and Nombela 1999, 11–12). In a survey of trends up to 2010, the AfDB indicated that the landlord model found little favour, and was confined to Ghana and Nigeria. Versions of the service port were very common across Africa, but with concessions often granted to private companies to manage part of the operations (African

Development Bank 2010, 82–85). In that way, the PAs managed to retain ownership of the hard infrastructure. In recent years, new container terminals have been leased as concessions to corporate giants such as Dubai Port World (DPW) and Bolloré.[12]

However, governments have also driven hard bargains. A case in point is the port of Djibouti, which granted the concession for a new container terminal to DPW before revoking it in 2014.[13] In Tema, a hybrid configuration is unfolding. The current expansion project entails the investment of $1.5 billion to construct a port that will be equipped to handle container ships that are three times the size of those currently using the facilities.[14] The container port is operated by Meridian Port Services (MPS), a joint venture between the Ghana Ports and Harbours Authority (GPHA) and Meridian Port Holdings, in which APM Terminals (part of the Maersk group) and Bolloré are the main shareholders. Therefore, the GPHA has not relinquished control; rather, it has sought to remain fully embedded in port management.

The AfDB attributes governments' reluctance fully to privatize port operations to their desire to use the income from the ports to cross-subsidize other sectors (African Development Bank 2010, 84). But there is another consideration: namely, in the context of regional integration, Customs revenues are attributed to the country of final destination for imports. This comes at the expense of the countries that own the ports. In Ghana, a representative of a major international organization confided that while the incoming Kufuor government loudly trumpeted its plans to improve operations at Tema, the assumption is that the port's principal purpose is to generate revenue. In his view, Tema is, to all intents and purposes, a tool port, subordinating operational efficiency to the revenue imperative.[15] In many countries, ownership is a politically charged issue that ties the hands of government. In Kenya, rumours that the authorities planned to privatize the port of Mombasa caused an uproar that led to a hasty retreat in 2012. The government subsequently announced that a newly built second container terminal would be operated by a private company after a competitive tendering process. In 2016, the tendering was itself suspended following legal challenges and claims of questionable dealing, as a result of which the Kenya Ports Authority assumed direct control of the terminal.[16]

In contrast with the ports, governments exhibit less sensitivity about railways, many of which are being constructed and upgraded with external financing and operated by private companies. Governments seem to view more efficient railways as crucial elements in improving trade flows rather than milch-cows in their own right. Roads are different again in that there is an increasing tendency for construction and maintenance to be contracted out to private companies that assume responsibility for particular sections. Although there is a proliferation of tollbooths along the transport corridors, such as ALCO, these do not, in themselves, generate any financial rewards for the state, which can therefore afford to be more sanguine about hiving off de facto control.

Finally, although Customs ostensibly has little to do with big infrastructure, physical enlargement of the seaports and the construction of OSBPs are closely associated with upgrades to information systems and the respacing of Customs work with donor support. Customs reforms are part of a global trend, and reflect the fact that almost all African countries are members of the World Customs Organization (WCO) and have either already joined, or are in the process of entering, the World Trade Organization (WTO). This, in itself, presupposes compliance with international norms and procedures. Whereas most countries have historically been characterized by rather limited integration between government agencies, the shift towards variants of single window means that it is possible for various agencies within a single country to access the same computer records. This is being strongly driven by an integrated border management (IBM) agenda (Siva 2011), but it has implications for other branches of the bureaucracy (Nugent 2016). At the same time, IBM is supposed to facilitate the sharing of data across borders, which is a challenge because of language differences and entrenched institutional cultures. As many countries have migrated to versions of the ASYCUDA (Automated System for Customs Data) Customs system, which is championed by UNCTAD, revenue authorities are increasingly able to access one another's entries (Cantens *et al.* 2010). For imports transiting through Mombasa, a single Customs entry is made in the country of final destination, which may be Rwanda or Uganda. Along with the rolling out of an electronic cargo tracking system (ECTS) in 2017, this circumvents the need for physical inspection of transit goods and thereby contributes to an overall reduction in delays.

This is also a domain in which states are actively seeking to reclaim the agenda. In a number of countries, aspects of Customs work – most notably valuation and inspection – were initially subcontracted to international companies in the name of greater efficiency (Chalfin 2010, 107–108, 171–184). At the same time, Customs departments in many countries were restructured and folded into semi-autonomous revenue authorities (RAs). There were fourteen of these RAs in 2009, mostly of them in Anglophone countries, with more expected to follow (Fjeldstadt and Moore 2009, 2). A recent trend has been for RAs to claw back control of valuation from private companies and to centralize their activities in the capital city. This restructuring was implemented in both Uganda and Ghana in 2017.[17] The centralization of Customs operations conforms to a larger pattern in which states seek to remain in the driving seat. Given that RAs furnish the revenues that enable the rest of the state to function, this has the potential to give them a much greater voice within the state bureaucracy. This, in turn, has implications for the extractive industries, given a context in which there is much debate about whether mining companies are paying their way.

This brings us to the second question of whether the infrastructural big push is helping to enhance the administrative performance of African states.

One critique of 'neoliberal governance' reforms is that they risk creating islands of effectiveness amidst large swathes of institutional incoherence. Here I will confine myself to a consideration of performance along the transport corridors and the implications for the extractive industries. The re-enchantment with railways is relatively recent, and as yet there is insufficient evidence to judge whether there has been a significant improvement – although, given the decrepit state of the existing networks, one would expect fresh investments to bring rapid returns. I will therefore focus on long-distance trucking routes and seaports. In each case, a great deal of donor effort has gone into calibrating the effects of infrastructural improvements on transit times – and hence on transport costs. The data that is freely available presents a mixed picture.

The condition of the roads along any corridor clearly affects journey times, but one of the greatest impediments has been the quality of the border crossings, where literally creaking infrastructure (degraded roads and bridges) and duplicated border formalities have led to lengthy delays along the main trucking routes. A case in point is the section of corridor between the Congolese/Zambian Copperbelt and the port of Durban. The crossing from the DRC to Zambia at Kasumbalesa is notoriously slow, and it has been repeatedly blockaded by drivers protesting against chronic insecurity. There have also been acute delays at Chirundu on the Zambia/Zimbabwe border and at the Beit Bridge crossing between Zimbabwe and South Africa. According to one estimate, a third of the total transport time along the corridor was spent waiting at the border crossings (Curtis 2009, xv). In an effort to address this serious problem, the governments of Zimbabwe and Zambia decided to construct an OSBP at Chirundu, an initiative that was subsequently adopted by COMESA. The OSBP, which was the first of its kind in sub-Saharan Africa, became partly operational in 2007 and was formally opened in 2009. At that point, it took a vehicle thirty-nine hours to transit northbound and fourteen hours to move southbound through Chirundu (Curtis 2009, 20). At Beit Bridge, the equivalent delays were thirty-four and eleven hours, respectively. Assessments indicated that some of the most stubborn challenges related to coordinating the activities of around twenty government agencies on the two sides of the border, sharing Customs information and persuading officials that greater efficiency was in their best interests (OECD/WTO 2011, 7–8). After several years, the flow of traffic through Chirundu improved, with copper accounting for most of the southbound traffic. However, in 2017, there were reports of vehicles stranded at Chirundu for days amidst allegations of corruption and bureaucratic obstacles. In West Africa, a series of OSBPs has been constructed along ALCO, but they are standing empty because officials on either side have not been able to agree on the modalities for opening them. There have been some improvements to crossing times since 2014, but from a very low base: for example, the average time for a truck crossing from Kraké in Benin to Seme in Nigeria fell from sixty-three to twenty-seven hours between 2014 and 2016 (ALCO 2016). As in Chirundu, border officials who have not bought into the official rhetoric on the advantages of the frictionless border have found ways to slow down the system.

The greatest successes have been chalked up in East Africa, along the Northern and Central Corridors, which, as I have indicated, are of marginal significance to the extractive industries. The lessons here are that the involvement of external actors in the design of OSBPs may facilitate coordination between state agencies. TMEA has been involved in the construction of thirteen OSBPs, ten of which are now complete. The landlocked states of Rwanda and Uganda have displayed particular interest in creating purpose-built facilities and rendering clearance procedures as smooth as possible, whereas in Kenya there has been much greater institutional competition and bureaucratic inertia. Along the Northern Corridor, the Malaba and Busia OSBPs are operational on a twenty-four-hour basis, but the inherited infrastructure and institutional communications on the Kenyan side are noticeably less conducive to making rapid strides. Where the OSBPs have become fully operational, the results have been significant. At Busia, the long queues of trucks that were apparent in 2014 had largely disappeared by 2017. In 2011, the average crossing time at Busia was 14.3 hours, but this had been reduced to just 3.6 hours by 2017 (Soi and Nugent 2017, 546–547). An even more dramatic improvement was recorded at the Mutukula OSBP on the Uganda/Tanzania border, which was formally opened by the two countries' presidents in November 2017.

At the ports, the picture is somewhat similar. Many of the PAs have been accused of chronic inefficiency and everyday corruption, and they have come under government pressure to boost their performance. These days, most PAs post online statistics on volumes of cargo handled and waiting times, so progress may be monitored and port trajectories compared. A number of ports have produced evidence to back up their claims of improved performance. The website of the port of Djibouti, for example, claims an increase in container traffic from 424.9 thousand TEUs in 2010 to 910.2 thousand TEUs in 2015. Over the same period, it reported that non-containerized traffic almost doubled.[18] The port of Mombasa similarly claims a substantial increase in container traffic – from 770.8 thousand TEUs in 2011 to 1.1 million TEUs in 2015.[19] While the advocates of state withdrawal from port management maintain that the current arrangements remain sub-optimal, the evidence of incremental improvement means it is easier to make the case for continued public control. Clearly, though, qualitative shifts in the performance of seaports and OSBPs alike will depend on transforming institutional cultures – and this still has some way to go. While the RAs have seen some significant changes in the way staff relate to their work in a country like Uganda or Ghana, it is the most laggardly agency that typically dictates the pace at the ports and the OSBPs. Moreover, the experience of many of the OSBPs is that better flows at the border crossings are often accompanied by a proliferation of informal checkpoints – erected by the police and a range of other state agents – along other sections of the corridors. This has the effect of simply transplanting the transport delays to different locations.

Finally, it should be mentioned that there is a risk of African countries overreaching themselves at a time when the global economic environment is no longer particularly favourable. Although regional integration initiatives are proceeding apace, it is difficult to point to a coordinated regional strategy when it comes to big infrastructure. On a more modest scale than in South-East Asia, but following a similar zero-sum logic, governments seek to entice trade to their ports to the detriment of their neighbours (Fau 2014, 58–63). Some irony resides in the fact that, while the coastal states are making the greatest investments, the landlocked countries are incurring fewer risks and reaping more of the benefits as a consequence. On the one hand, as part of the creation of free-trade zones and the imposition of a Common External Tariff (CET), the poorer landlocked countries receive manufactured goods at lower costs as well as Customs revenue on imported goods. On the other hand, the competitive investment in ports and railways enables them to shop around for the best deals, potentially leaving the littoral states high and dry. As I have indicated, most of the copper from Zambia and southern DRC travels to the seaports by road. The expansion of the port of Durban is intended to consolidate the niche that it has carved for itself. However, at the same time, the bridging of the Zambezi River and the promotion of the Walvis Bay–Ndola–Lubumbashi Development Corridor, as it is now called, is intended to provide an alternative outlet to the sea. The governments of Zambia, the DRC and Namibia have formally committed themselves to promoting this corridor as a conduit for materials used in mining and for the export of copper.[20] Yet, the Congolese authorities have also been receptive to plans to develop the Angolan port of Lobito as an alternative outlet for their exports. Therefore, *three* expensive port developments are pinning their hopes on assumptions about the direction that copper exports will take in the future. Similarly, the ports of Abidjan, Tema, Lomé and Cotonou are formally partners in ALCO, but they stand in a competitive relationship with respect to the transit trade with the landlocked countries of the Sahel.

Another striking example is LAPSSET (the Lamu Port–South Sudan–Ethiopia Transport Corridor), which Kenya has been aggressively promoting. It is supposed to cater to the landlocked countries of Uganda, South Sudan and Ethiopia and to promote development in the poorest parts of northern Kenya by means of rail, road, air and fibre-optic-cable links. The centrepiece is a new port at Lamu that a Chinese company is constructing. However, Ethiopia has already chosen to prioritize a new rail link to the port of Djibouti, possibly because it is less susceptible to terrorist attacks by al-Shabaab. To compound matters, the projected oil pipeline from northern Uganda to Lamu has been abandoned in favour of a route to the port of Tanga in Tanzania. With the latter country also planning to open a new port at Bagamoyo, Kenya's heavy investment in seaports suddenly seems to be a dangerous gamble. The downstream consequences of overreach are apparent when one recalls that African governments channel many of their scarce resources into infrastructural development. Indeed, one recent study suggests that African governments fund as much as 65 per cent of infrastructural expenditure from the general budget (Guttman *et al.* 2015, 3). This inevitably means that resources are diverted away from competing priorities, such as urban water supply and power generation, which may be more pressing needs. Kribi has often looked like turning into a white elephant, although it will probably come to fruition – albeit at great expense and long behind schedule – because of its strategic importance to neighbouring countries. However, the port of Lamu seems unlikely ever to pay its way, and many other infrastructural investments may go the same way in the future.

Conclusions

In this chapter, I have addressed two fundamental issues concerning infrastructural investment in Africa. First, I have mapped the changing patterns as well as the principal actors, with a view to assessing how far the needs of the extractive industries are driving and shaping investment flows. It is striking that investments in big infrastructure – especially in seaports and railways – are back in vogue amongst donors, investors and African governments alike. One significant finding is that African governments finance much of the infrastructure both directly and through loans. Another is that, whereas the oil and gas sector has tended to benefit from investments in pipelines across the regions, the ability of mining to shape infrastructural provision has varied considerably. Some transport corridors, most notably in East Africa and coastal West Africa, are geared towards facilitating the flow of imported and domestically produced commodities rather than easing the export of minerals. It is really only in Southern Africa and parts of West Africa that infrastructural investments are driven by mining logic.

Second, I have weighed up the implications of the infrastructural 'big push' for the ability of African governments to shape the agenda and for the capacity of bureaucracies to undertake their (partially reconfigured) functions. African governments have retained a surprising degree of control over the process, as is reflected in the stubborn persistence of PAs and public management of the transport corridors. Through a closer examination of OSBPs and seaports, I have concluded that the record of bureaucratic implementation remains patchy. Although performance indicators mostly point to demonstrable improvements, the patterns are highly uneven, especially with respect to OSBPs. The results have been encouraging where there has been significant harmonization of information systems and procedures, and where a range of state agencies has displayed commitment to the process of reform. East Africa is forging ahead by comparison with the other regions. However, across much of the continent, the big infrastructure is still waiting for the rest of the institutional bandwagon to catch up. Be that as it may, I have found little evidence to support the claim that 'infrastructuring' has contributed to greater institutional coherence, even though a bewildering array of actors is now involved.

Finally, I have concluded this chapter on a cautionary note. Precisely because infrastructural investments are not driven by a purely extractive logic, they are more likely to proceed apace irrespective of lower commodity prices. But herein lies a danger that African countries will overreach themselves and be saddled with a series of white elephants that will be held under state ownership. It would be profoundly ironic if history ended up repeating itself.

Notes

1 The research for this chapter was facilitated by a European Research Council (ERC) advanced grant for the project entitled 'African Governance and Space: Transport Corridors, Border Towns and Port Cities in Transition' (AFRIGOS; ADG-2014–670851), of which I am the principal investigator. I would like to thank Isabella Soi and the editors for their comments on the draft and Hugh Lamarque, Jose-Maria Muñoz, Sidy Cissokho and Wolfgang Zeller for their insights on specific points. I am very grateful to Michael Ojatum of TradeMark East Africa for granting me access to performance data on one-stop border posts.

2 For a graph that plots the shift in World Bank investments in transport infrastructure, see http://projects.worldbank.org/search?lang=en&searchTerm=infrastructure, accessed 28 December 2017.

3 This is an aspect that Wolfgang Zeller has been considering as part of the AFRIGOS project.

4 See www.reuters.com/article/ivorycoast-burkina-railway/burkina-ivory-coast-hand-control-of-railway-to-mining-firm-pm-idUSL5N0L70J720140204, accessed 28 December 2017.

5 I am grateful to Jose-Maria Muñoz for his insights into the reasons why progress at Kribi has been so slow.

6 See www.afdb.org/fileadmin/uploads/afdb/Documents/Environmental-and-Social-Assessments/Maroc_-_Projet_de_construction_du_complexe_portuaire_Nador_West_Med_%E2%80%93_PCR_-_OITC_%E2%80%93_03_2015.pdf, accessed 28 December 2017.

7 See www.wbcg.com.na/members/our-members.html, accessed 28 December 2017.

8 See www.corridor-sida.org/?Institutional-arrangement, accessed 28 December 2017.

9 Interview with Edy K. Anthony, Abidjan–Lagos Corridor Group, Cotonou, 21 August 2017.

10 See www.ttcanc.org/page.php?id=16, accessed 28 December 2017.

11 See www.trademarkea.com/who-we-are/our-organisation/, accessed 28 December 2017.

12 DPW, based in the Emirates but a truly global operator, took over a concession for the existing container terminal in Dakar in 2007. It also held the concession at Djibouti port between 2000 and 2011, when the arrangement was terminated, as well as concessions in Algiers and Maputo. Bolloré holds a concession at Douala and leads a consortium for a terminal at Kribi, which is not yet operational. Other significant players are AP Møller (for Walvis Bay, Luanda, Lagos and

Tema) and Hutchison (for Dar es Salaam). Bolloré is involved at some level in the management of all the major port developments in West Africa.

13 DPW claims to operate more than sixty terminals on six continents. It has taken the Djibouti government to court over this issue.

14 See www.maersk.com/en/the-maersk-group/about-us/publications/group-annual-magazine/2015/west-africas-next-generation-ports, accessed 28 December 2017.

15 Interview with a representative of international organization (name withheld), Accra, 28 August 2017.

16 I am grateful to Hugh Lamarque for pointing me towards press coverage of this affair.

17 These observations are based on fieldwork in Ghana in August 2017 and Uganda (with Isabella Soi) in October 2017.

18 See www.portdedjibouti.com/statistics/, accessed 28 December 2017.

19 See www.kpa.co.ke/InforCenter/Performance%20Reports/KPA%20Annual%20Report%202015%20(without%20photos).pdf, accessed 28 December 2017.

20 See www.wbcg.com.na/news-info/news/detail//developing-the-walvis-bay-ndola-lubumbashi-development-corridor/home-page.html, accessed 28 December 2017.

References

African Development Bank. 2010. *African Development Report 2010: Ports, Logistics and Trade in Africa*. Oxford: AfDB.

African Development Bank. 2013. *The New Port of Walvis Bay Container Terminal Project: Project Appraisal Report*. Abidjan: AfDB.

ALCO. 2016. *Abidjan–Lagos Corridor Organization*. Cotonou: ALCO.

Bach, D. 2016. *Regionalism in Africa: Genealogies, Institutions and Trans-state Networks*. Abingdon: Routledge.

Cantens, T., G. Raballand and S. Bilangna. 2010. 'Reforming Customs by Measuring Performance: A Cameroon Case-Study', *World Customs Journal* 4(2), 55–74.

Chalfin, B. 2010. *Neoliberal Frontiers: An Ethnography of Sovereignty in West Africa*. Chicago: University of Chicago Press.

Curtis, B. 2009. *The Chirundu Border Post: Detailed Monitoring of Transit Times*. Washington, DC: World Bank/Subsaharan Africa Transport Policy Program.

Deen-Swarray, M., B. Adekunle and G. Odularu. 2014. Policy Recipe for Fostering Regional Integration through Infrastructure Development and Co-ordination in West Africa. In D. Seck, ed., *Regional Economic Integration in West Africa*. Heidelberg: Springer.

Deloitte. 2015. *A 360° View: Africa Construction Trends Report 2015*. Johannesburg: Deloitte.

Engel, U. and P. Nugent, eds. 2010. *Respacing Africa*. Leiden and Boston, MA: Brill.

Fau, N. 2014. Maritime Corridors, Port System and Spatial Organization in the Malacca Straits. In N. Fau, S. Khonthapane and C. Taillard, eds, *Transnational Dynamics in Southeast Asia: The Greater Mekong Subregion and Malacca Straits Economic Corridors*. Singapore: Institute of Southeast Asian Studies.

Ferguson, J. 2006. *Global Shadows: Africa in the Neoliberal World Order*. Durham NC: Duke University Press.

Fjeldstadt, O.H. and M. Moore 2009. 'Revenue Authorities and Public Authority in Sub-Saharan Africa', *Journal of Modern African Studies* 47(1), 1–18.

Guttman, J., A. Sy and S. Chattopadhyay. 2015. *Financing Africa's Infrastructure: Can the World Deliver?* Washington, DC: Brookings Institution.

Hoyle, B.S. and D. Hilling, eds. 1970. *Seaports and Development in Tropical Africa*. London: Macmillan.

Infrastructure Consortium for Africa. 2014. *Infrastructure Financing Trends in Africa – 2013*. Tunis: ICA.

Infrastructure Consortium for Africa. 2016. *Infrastructure Financing Trends in Africa – 2015*. Tunis: ICA.

Killick, T. 1978. *Development Economics in Action: A Study of Economic Policies in Ghana*. London: Heinemann.

Nugent, P. 2016. 'The Future of States in Africa: Prospects for the Ordering of Space and the Remaking of Bureaucracies', *Comparativ* 26(2), 75–91.

OECD/SWAC. 2017. *Cross-border Co-operation and Policy Networks in West Africa*. Paris: OECD.

OECD/WTO. 2011. *Aid for Trade Case Story on Chirundu One-stop Border Post*. Paris: OECD/WTO.

Raballand, G. and A. Whitworth. 2014. Transport Policy. In C. Adam, P. Collier and M. Gondwe, eds, *Zambia: Building Prosperity from Resource Wealth*. Oxford: Oxford University Press.

Siva, R. 2011. Developing a National Single Window: Implementation Issues and Considerations. In G. McLinen, E. Fanta, D. Widdowson and T. Doyle, eds, *Border Management Modernization*. Washington, DC: World Bank.

Söderbaum, F. and I. Taylor, eds. 2008. *Afro-regions: The Dynamics of Cross-border Micro-regionalism in Africa*. Uppsala: Nordiska Afrikainstitutet.

Soi, I. and P. Nugent. 2017. 'Peripheral Urbanism in Africa: Border Towns and Twin Towns in Africa', *Journal of Borderlands Studies* 32(4), 535–556.

Trujillo, L. and G. Nombela. 1999. *Privatization and Regulation of the Seaport Industry*. Policy Research Working Paper No. 2181. Washington, DC: World Bank.

World Bank. 1981. *Accelerated Development in Sub-Saharan Africa: An Agenda for Action* [Berg Report]. Washington, DC: World Bank.

World Bank. 2009. *World Development Report 2009: Reshaping Economic Geography*. Washington, DC: World Bank.

World Bank. 2014. *Building Integrated Markets within the East African Community: EAC Opportunities in Private–Public Partnership Approaches to the Region's Infrastructure Needs*. Washington, DC: World Bank.

2 Port geographies

Africa's infrastructure boom and the reconfiguration of power and authority

Jana Hönke[1]

Introduction

While African states have often been portrayed as peripheral to major global economic flows, many parts of Africa are neatly integrated into networks of global extraction, production and trade. Copper and gold mines in the Democratic Republic of the Congo (DRC) as much as the key ports of the continent are at the heart of Africa's integration into the global economy (and into global politics). Large transport infrastructure as gateways to the African continent are once again high on the international agenda (Ford 2006; Hönke and Cuesta-Fernandez 2017; Chapter 1, this volume). Prominent among them are the ports as major chokepoints through which African goods and resources are accessible and fed into the global market. In Tanzania alone, the World Bank pledged $565 million to 'Open ... the Gates' (World Bank 2014) via refurbishment of Dar es Salaam port. But new funding opportunities have also given rise to a proliferation of new *entrepôts* along the Tanzanian coast, with several major projects under way to varying degrees. Among them is an expansion of the port of Mtwara in anticipation of offshore gas exploitation by BG Resources Ltd., Statoil and Ophir, as well as Tanga port, to the north, as a hub for the oil to come through the new Uganda pipeline. The most spectacular project, however, is not directly linked to resource extraction. It is a new, 800-hectare, $10-billion megaport at Bagamoyo, about 60 kilometres north of Dar es Salaam, funded by Chinese and Omani investors.[2]

Debates about the political economy of the African state have long stressed how much control over the sites that connect '*l'Afrique utile*' with the outside world has been a major source of revenue for colonial and postcolonial states (Boone 1998; Cooper 2002, 2014). While much of the literature focuses on domestic elites, political settlements and patronage-based politics within African states (e.g. Kelsall 2013; Gray 2015; Beresford 2015), other studies usefully stress the reconfiguration (not decline) of the state through the internationalization, privatization and indirect discharge of state functions to commercial actors (Hibou 1999; Hönke 2010; Schlichte 2008). Postcolonial governments, together with a plethora of international and transnational actors, have continued to reproduce such structures. It is indeed important to look beyond false dichotomies of African states or elites versus the global economy, or market versus state.

The following analysis of reconfigurations of power and authority around large-scale infrastructure projects will thus include – but significantly go beyond – state dynamics. 'Gateway' metaphors are used ubiquitously by donors and investors of large-scale infrastructure projects on the continent, thus stressing the transnational character of these structures.[3] Furthermore, an ever more diverse set of external actors is involved in large-scale infrastructure projects, funded by traditional donors as well as 'new' actors from the Global South. The guiding question this chapter addresses is thus what geographies of power and authority the new gateways reveal.

To answer this question, a focus on domestic elite coalitions and the state as gatekeeper of resource rents would ignore configurations of governing beyond the state, as well as the crucial role of travelling ideas and technologies in making certain practices of governing legitimate and feasible, and others not. I thus argue that new large-scale investments – beyond the frequent study of extractive industries – provide windows onto the reconfiguration of power and authority in Africa in new ways. They might affect reconfigurations of how 'states' are performed, as much as give rise to new transnational political geographies. While thus exploring some of the 'state effects' (Mitchell 1991) of new port projects, the chapter is also an exploration of their complex transboundary topologies, which comprise a multiplicity of actors, standards and technologies (Barry 2013; Hönke and Cuesta-Fernandez 2017). This should help to illustrate that current infrastructure politics should not be reduced to resource politics – the notion that new roads and ports are solely about a new scramble for Africa's mineral resources.

The argument is developed through analysis of the existing port of Dar es Salaam and the planned port of Bagamoyo, both in Tanzania. Fieldwork was conducted in spring 2015 and consisted of interviews within the port of Dar es Salaam as well as with key port stakeholders, including the Tanzanian Port Authority. In addition, reports published by the port authority and international funders over the past seven years were consulted, and complemented with an analysis of relevant articles in Tanzanian newspapers. After a discussion of perspectives on infrastructure hubs and the African state, the chapter turns to the port of Dar es Salaam and state politics relating to the gateway in Tanzania. This is followed by an exploration of the port as a transnational project before a final section on the powerful imaginaries of development and modernity – from a Dubai to a Shenzen 'model' – that drive new gateway projects.

Infrastructure hubs and the African state

Cooper (2002, 2014) and others have traced the emergence of fragmented territoriality organized around selected economic hubs back to the colonial past. These studies have shown how 'gatekeeper states' emerged during this process and have been sustained by postcolonial governments as well as international and transnational actors. African states, so the argument goes, were characterized by their reliance on controlling access to revenue derived from movement and processes between the inside of the state and the outside world.[4] These arguments draw on a long tradition of thought, such as the rentier state literature (Beblawi and Luciani 1987; Ross 1999; Kühn 2008). In return for rents (from resources, aid, strategic military location), host governments deploy their coercive capacities to protect oil and mining installations or outsource these services to transnational actors.

An important limitation of such depictions of the African state is their tendency to remain overly broad-brushed and to limit politics to contestation over access to rents. As Beresford (2015, 4) argues, exoticizing African politics as synonymous with corruption or neopatrimonialism is also misleading. Instead of being a pathology of African states and societies, corrupt and clientelist practices are part of a broader spectrum of capitalist practice, especially in little-diversified and resource-dependent economies (for critiques of the concept of neopatrimonialism, see Erdmann and Engel 2007 and Pitcher *et al.* 2009.) 'Harvesting' revenue from key gateways between the internal and external worlds, based on the symbolic capital of the state mediating between the two, is a more widespread and indeed legal practice of governments across the globe.

A second limitation in the literature is the focus on elite coalitions within states, and on government revenues and rent-seeking behaviour. In most studies of the political economy of infrastructure in Tanzania, there is a tendency to prioritize the 'who' question, and thus to echo a protracted research agenda intent on explaining policy outcomes as a result of elite bargains and factional struggles (e.g. Cooksey and Kelsall 2011; Kelsall 2013; Gray 2015). This literature only tangentially touches upon issues of *how* forms of authority fluctuate over time. When it comes to infrastructure, the literature remains even more silent on the 'how' question. Matteo Rizzo's exploration of the delays in the Bus Rapid Transit System project in Dar es Salaam is concerned with 'what different Tanzanian actors stood to lose from its implementation, and the way in which they were able to resist and influence the project' (Rizzo 2015, 251). Others focus on whether and how state elites retain control over revenues and side-payments from large-scale investment.

While important, this approach pays insufficient attention to the role of perceptions and ideas in making old and new actors and practices of governance legitimate and possible. It also accepts the state as a given and the most relevant political entity, which sidesteps questions about configurations of governance beyond the state. In many parts of Africa, the limited territorial reach of the central state is nothing new, and it has always operated in combination with a multiplicity of parallel, overlapping and sometimes competing spatial orders and sovereignties (see Hansen and Stepputat 2006; Mbembe 2002). This fits well with the processual view of the state that

Schubert, Engel and Macamo suggest in the Introduction, where they build on Migdal and Schlichte (2005) as well as Hagmann and Péclard (2010).

In addition, as Deborah Cowen (2014) has argued recently, different governmental logics – that of a global space of logistics and that of nation-state territoriality – clash at nodes of global transport. 'Global territories' (Opitz and Tellmann 2012) proliferate as transnational zones and are a core feature of neoliberal capitalism (see Barry 2006; Easterling 2012; Hönke and Cuesta-Fernandez 2017). African ports are 'frontier zones' (Sassen 2006) of these reconfigurations, making visible how 'emergent global assemblages coexist with vast stretches of older historical formations constitutive of the modern nation state' (ibid., 403).

In addition to focusing on the state, it is important to shed light on ports as bubbles of transnational governance characterized by a proliferation of transnational standards, technologies and professionals (see Hönke and Cuesta-Fernandez 2017). As Sidaway (2007) and Ong (2006) suggest, African ports are prototypical sites in which sovereignty is graduated.

The port of Dar es Salaam and (state) politics of the gateway

Over at least the past thirty years, the growth and integration of the shipping and logistics industry have increased, while economic financialization and deregulation have eased transoceanic trade. In Tanzania, these transformations have manifested in a shift from the port of Dar es Salaam owned and run by the state-owned Tanzania Port Authority to the private management of parts of the port. In the early 2000s, cargo and container operations were split into two terminals, with the container terminal handed over to a private operator, Tanzania International Container Terminal Services Ltd. (TICTS). This is a joint venture between world-leading port operator Hutchison Port Holdings of Hong Kong and a Tanzanian business group. TICTS exclusively started to handle the containerized cargo mooring in Berths 8 to 11, and also utilized the largest section of the container yard for temporary storage.

This privatization of part of the port should not be misunderstood as a loss of state control over the gateway per se (see Sassen 2006; Hibou 1999). Rather, here 'Gatekeepers have a capacity to grant or deny access to resources and opportunities' (Beresford 2015, 4). The monopoly to grant licences to private actors to run key infrastructure, such as the licence to TICTS to run the container terminal, as with mineral concessions, is a classic privilege and source of rent for governments across the world. The Dar es Salaam landlord model is a widespread model of contemporary port management and considered the most efficient in Africa (Adolf and Ducruet 2014; Trujillo *et al.* 2013).

Furthermore, specific positions in the state administration offer privileged opportunities to control further access to revenues from the gateway in the form of corruption. Importantly, gatekeeper politics are not synonymous with corruption, but corruption is a symptom of it, as are battles over who controls the various rents accrued from the gateway. In the case of the port of Dar es Salaam, eyebrows were raised over opaque and collusive politics. First, the local shareholders of TICTS have not been disclosed by Hutchison Port Holdings. Second, the Tanzanian government ignored negative parliamentary votes in 2008 and 2010 and extended TICTS's concession by fifteen years.[5] In addition, widespread corruption and mismanagement have continued to plague the hierarchy of the Tanzania Ports Authority (TPA), with a succession of scandals coming to light. For instance, in 2012, the Director-General, the Port Manager and the Oil Jetty Manager were all suspended amid allegations of cargo theft. The following year, the new head of the TPA was dismissed after further accusations of cargo and oil theft and criticism over the awarding of a contract to build new berths to a Chinese company. Finally, in February 2015, the TPA's acting Director-General, Madeni Kipande, was dismissed, pending an investigation into alleged mismanagement.[6] In the words of one interviewee:

> I think the TRA [Tanzania Revenue Authority] and the Port Authority were losing a lot of containers earlier … the containers disappeared. People think it was theft … We don't know whether it was theft or an inside job … It's not only always corruption; it's also part of the failure to oversee things.[7]

Such large-scale theft is scarcely possible without insider information and collusion from core positions within the port.

The issue of massive container theft made it into the headlines of national newspapers again immediately after the election of President John Magufuli in late 2015, when it was alleged that 349 containers had disappeared from the port. In response, the President, Prime Minister and Minister of Transport launched a concerted disciplinary campaign against corruption and pilfering at the port. This entailed an impromptu visit to the port by Prime Minister Kassim Majaliwa and the subsequent dismissal of a number of top officials. The Prime Minister made a second visit on 3 December 2015, when he ordered Port Manager Hebel Mhanga to elaborate on reports about the disappearance of 2,400 containers without due payment of taxes.[8] Subsequently, the President sacked the Permanent Secretary at the Ministry of Works, the TPA's latest Director-General and three senior and eight mid-ranking managers. He also dissolved the TPA's board.[9]

As Tanzanians learned of the sheer scale of embezzlement, the government, the TPA and low-ranking port officials such as clearing agents all sought to lay the blame on each other. Magufuli had campaigned against corruption during the presidential election and presented himself as a determined fighter against immorality in public office. It is important to remember, however, that there have been regular reshuffles of administrators in state-owned enterprises (SOEs) and bureaucracies in Tanzania for many years (see Gray 2015). It remains to be seen whether those initiated by the new President will change practices of gatekeeping in the port of Dar es Salaam. They may prove to be little more than yet another expression of the ongoing tension between different factions within the ruling party, Chama Cha Mapinduzi (CCM; or the Party of the Revolution), with the anti-corruption discourse used to justify reallocation of the same old rents from the gateway (Jacob 2017, 351–352).

In addition to high-level corruption, the port of Dar es Salaam has been plagued by petty corruption at various levels. The centralization of petty rents from gateways is limited in Tanzania (see Cooksey and Kelsall 2011; Gray 2015). With the digitalization of the port, information has become less accessible and container theft has declined as a consequence. However, such activity has merely been pushed outside the port. In the eyes of some consignees, inland container depots (ICDs) brought about collusive business relations between private owners and top officials in the TPA, who secured protection and more activity for certain ICDs.[10] Whilst the ICDs have helped to ease port congestion, they have only displaced – if not exacerbated – harassment from public agents, due to the alleged collusion between the TPA authorities and ICD owners that creates a perverse incentive towards further delays and, hence, storage charges.[11] Higher-ranking port officials roam around the port or the ICDs in search of opportunities for harassment.[12] There is also a profusion of controls, with different offices and agencies performing similar functions. Again, this becomes understandable once the political economy of corruption is brought into the equation.[13] Port and customs authorities mobilize the seven-day grace storage period – which attracts port charges if exceeded – to their advantage, pushing back inspections, signatures and the issuing of release orders. Overall, petty corruption is accepted, and 'decentralized rentscrapping', Cooksey and Kelsall (2011, 29) argue, is 'part of what it takes to do business or merely go about one's daily life in Tanzania'.

Thus, from large-scale corruption among high-level bureaucrats in the TPA and TRA to petty corruption in the lower echelons of state administration and the business sector, the Tanzanian government at best loosely centralizes rent management (ibid., 85). High-level corruption is more centralized by key figures of the ruling party, but not necessarily controlled by the President (Gray 2015). Thus, it is crucial to unpack the 'state' in order to look at different practices of controlling revenues from the gateway.

Extending, multiplying and transforming gateways: Dar es Salaam port as transnational project

Of course, it is not only African governments that are concerned with gateways. Seaports, much like airports and undersea cable landing points, are 'gateways, nodes that function as a region's entry or exit point, house a range of technologies, and comply with standards that knit together heterogeneous communities of practice' (Starosielski 2015, 97). Such gateways are strategic geopolitical locations, where items that circulate can be controlled, censored or intercepted. But they are also sites for potential disruption – and thus sites for the application of insulation strategies to protect (and retain) the gateway – by various actors. Narrow questions about the nature and survival of the state (elites) overlook such dynamics.

Indeed, the metaphor of 'gatekeeping' is as much about preventing others from accessing revenues as it is about allowing items to keep flowing through the existing gateways, and establishing new ones. For that, ports are managed by a heterogeneous set of actors with distinct, graduated (Ong 2006) claims to authority over particular issue areas and spaces. Beyond traditional elite politics, a broader 'respacing' of Africa (Engel and Nugent 2010) is under way. Ports are global 'zones' (Barry 2006) through which extraction and trade are organized and secured by a multiplicity of standards and technologies (Barry 2006; Hönke 2013; Hönke and Cuesta-Fernandez 2017). Thus, different governmental strategies implemented by a multiplicity of actors are at work in the port of Dar es Salaam.

As mentioned above, the port transitioned from a state-centred arrangement to a public–private landlord model in the early 2000s, when the container terminal was handed over to TICTS. It is also in the process of being refurbished and substantially extended. This is an international project. Donors such as the European Commission, the World Bank and the British Department for International Development (DfID) apportion the funding required to push forward the global agenda of trade facilitation. The World Bank and the DfID – through its subsidiary TradeMark East Africa – are footing the $565-million bill for the port's refurbishment (World Bank 2014) with a view to doubling throughput. This follows earlier grants from the World Bank to the TPA to train security officers, install CCTV and purchase patrol boats and vehicles. International donors also provide the intellectual impetus for this agenda within the Big Results Now framework (see Chapter 3, this volume). This initiative, inspired by the 'Malaysian development model', has been implemented since 2013 to deliver quantifiable policy outcomes in six priority areas. Predicated upon the trinity of trade, investment and poverty reduction, this 'theory of change' anticipates increased physical access to markets, an enhanced trade environment and improved business competitiveness.[14]

The internationalization inherent in these port reform projects has ambivalent effects. On the one hand, ideas about how the port should be governed have shifted and market logic has been integrated into efforts to build a 'governance state' (Harrison 2004). For instance, one Tanzanian government minister demanded that the TPA must 'stop being so buerau-cratic'[15] and should focus on facilitating throughput and the global flow of goods. The Maritime Gateway project to reform the port of Dar es Salaam also aims to improve 'good governance' and anti-corruption. On the other hand, the reform agenda keeps the government in the privileged position of controlling the allocation of new licence agreements and contracts for refurbishment, and interpellates the state as sovereign and legitimate authority to regulate and control what passes through the port. Thereby, the (gatekeeper) state is enacted and reinforced in practice (see Migdal 2001; Schlichte 2005).

The TPA saw its role diminish with privatization of the container terminal in the sense that it no longer runs it. However, it continues to operate the remaining berths, and it has regulatory authority over the privatized 'global zone' of the container port. Meanwhile, the TRA has retained jurisdiction over the taxation of trade activities. In particular, it alone authorizes the displacement of containers, or bulk cargo, inside and outside the port. State agencies – ranging from the Tanzanian Revenue Authority to the Weights and Measures Agency and various other ministries and sector-specific agencies – have been assigned controls that alter container flows. Thus, the transformations have not resulted in a diminution of state power, contrary to what prominent critics of privatization have argued. Rather, ideas and practices relating to how ports should be run have been rearticulated through transnational 'modes of government', including companies, transnational experts and other intermediaries (Ferguson and Gupta 2002: 989–990; Ong 2006).

A further indicator of the port as 'frontier zone' and transnational project is the Fair Competition Commission (FCC), which was installed as a new mediator between multinational corporations and the port authority. Attempts on the part of the FCC to enforce anti-counterfeit regulations supplemented the efforts of multinationals such as Samsung, Philips and Unilever to protect their high-value trade across transnational routes and marketplaces. As a result, engineers and representatives from such multinational companies now need to visit Tanzania only once every three months, as they feel they can rely on the FCC to oversee their interests in the Tanzanian market. '[T]transnational apparatuses of governmentality … overlay … and coexist … with older, nation-state based modes of governance' (Ferguson and Gupta 2002, 994).

As Sidaway (2007, 334) suggests, while the Tanzanian goverment remains the main gatekeeper by issuing licences and collecting other revenue by granting access to the port, such hubs can also 'be read as spaces of sovereign graduation'. Infrastructural developments and state authority may coevolve but lead to much more diverse results in terms of power and authority than a simple re-enforcement of the gatekeeper state. In the course of her research in the Ghanaian port of Tema, Brenda Chalfin established that the government's strategic partnership with prvate logistical operators granted the port operator the ability to enact 'modalities' of governance that the state could never fully pursue on its own (Chalfin 2010b, 586). At the same time, however, international standardization, such as the International Shipping and Port Security Code (ISPS), as well as transnational technological devices, such as cargo scanners and other electronic equipment, have transformed how power is exercised and have created a form of 'derivative sovereignty' (ibid.) through highly technocratic political arrangements that are neither state nor non-state.

One such global technology in Dar es Salaam is the e-customs programme TANCIS (Tanzania Customs Integrated System). The TRA launched TANCIS in 2014, 'built on hi-tech principles with a view to increasing effectiveness, efficiency, transparency, and reliability in the Customs administration'.[16] It follows similar systems introduced in Hong Kong (1986), Singapore (1989–1991), Malaysia (1996–2004), Ghana (2001) and Nigeria (2009). Crucially, TANCIS has replaced tax officials and clearing agents with electronic procedures and has thus transformed who controls, and therefore who is able to interfere with, flows of cargo. It is not all-powerful, though, as some handling is still carried out on paper. An unintended effect of this is that tax agents can now switch from the virtual to the physical environment at their convenience and thus retain a margin for manoeuvre in governing port activities.[17] Nevertheless, the electronic system and the standards it enforces illustrate that gateways are now parts of a global zone that is bounded by universal standards and harmonized technology, not physical borders (Barry 2006). Supply-chain governance can decouple exceptional zones and 'secure areas' from domestic politics and integrate them within contemporary logistical landscapes (Cowen 2014).

Gate-making: imaginaries of development from Dubai to Shenzen

This final section turns to the new gateways that are being constructed across Africa and along African coasts. This booming gateway economy is based on new sources of investment, accompanied by alternative imaginaries of development. These are not restricted to resource extraction but encompass broader futures. Imaginaries about infrastructure as a sign of modernity have always been crucial drivers of large infrastructure projects and they continue to be so today (Larkin 2013), yet these imaginaries have evolved and significantly diversified, and they are no longer limited to versions of Western modernity.

Lobo-Guerrero (2012, 314) illustrates a shift from the port imaginaries of the early twentieth century to contemporary narratives about ports. While the port was once viewed as a place of exchange and a 'clearing-house for international commerce', it is now understood as a 'future-oriented, market-seeking, successful economic venture' (ibid.). Much of this shift in discourse is also apparent in Dar es Salaam. Traffic jams are a new cause for concern in the Tanzanian port as well as in Hamburg, where the port authority has called for 'no jams in front of the gateway to the world' (Hamburg Port Authority cited in Lobo-Guerrero 2012, 314). This illustrates the changing ideas and practices of states as facilitators of global trade.

Infrastructure is back on the agenda not only of African governments but also international development more broadly. In addition to working with the World Bank, the Western-led Infrastructure Consortium Africa and the

New Partnership for Africa's Development-led Programme for Infrastructural Development, many African governments and the African Union have concluded deals with the governments of China, Brazil and the Gulf monarchies to develop ports and other infrastructure. These new investors, with the models and imaginaries of modern futures they evoke, merit further attention.

The most spectacular new project in Tanzania is an 800-hectare megaport at Bagamoyo, about sixty kilometres south of Dar es Salaam, with funding as well as inspiration in the form of visions of development and modernity coming from the Gulf and China (see below). President Kikwete proposed a new port in his hometown of Bagamoyo as early as 2007, but planning did not begin in earnest until October 2014, when Tanzania signed a memorandum of understanding with China and Oman. Thereafter, progress seemed to stall until a major breakthrough occurred in October 2015: two months before his mandate expired, Kikwete laid the foundation stone for the new port as well as an adjacent 1,700-hectare export processing zone (EPZ). The government insisted that the new facility would be able to handle even the largest Panamax container vessels, and that it would have a maximum capacity of twenty million containers a year (Dar es Salaam can handle fewer than one million).[18] Three months later, the new Magufuli administration announced its intention to shelve the project,[19] but work subsequently resumed, with the Deputy Minister of Trade, Industry and Investment announcing in October 2017 that the port would be operational from 2020/2021.[20]

The Kikwete government characterized Bagamoyo as a 'gateway' to modernity for the Tanzanian state. While this echoed the World Bank's language in relation to the Maritime Gateway Project, which is focused on the port of Dar es Salaam, Western donors were against the proposal and advocated exhausting the existing port's full potential before investing in new infrastructure (Hönke and Cuesta-Fernandez 2018). Yet, the envisioned modernity, and the funding to realize it, no longer depend on Western models. Instead, imaginaries of how to be(come) modern are taking new and more diverse routes. This has been argued more broadly by Sidaway (2007); and references to it are notable along the East African coast. For instance, Djibouti, aside from hosting US, French, Japanese and Chinese military bases, has commissioned DP Dubai World to construct a large, multi-purpose port at Dolareh. Similarly, Rwanda and Kenya are both attempting to establish new commercial hubs on the basis of South–South investment and vision.

In the case of Bagamoyo, the port and the planned adjacent special economic zone (SEZ) have been modelled on two major archetypes of new zones of development: Dubai and Shenzen. In 2014, Kikwete stated: 'If we invest in logistic centres, improve on infrastructure and create a facilitative environment, we can easily turn Dar es Salaam into another Dubai.'[21] The new Bagamoyo project adheres to this principle, and indeed taps into a more general narrative about Dubai as a model for commercial success.[22] As

I have argued elsewhere, this Dubai model (Chorin 2010; Hönke and Cuesta-Fernandez 2018) has come to embody the idea of an enactment of seamless 'topological compression' but also distinct 'economies of anticipation' (Cross 2015). However, as Wippel *et al.* (2016, part 4) and Chorin (2010) have shown, the precise nature of the Dubai model is often rather vague. For Bagamoyo, it boils down to anticipating that the megaport may emulate Dubai's exceptional development as global shopping mall and logistics hub, notwithstanding the Gulf state's unique circumstances, which are unlikely to be replicable elsewhere (Hönke and Cuesta-Fernandez 2018).

Of course, Dubai is not the only imaginary – or source of funding – for new gateways. The Chinese ambassador to Tanzania recently announced that the Bagamoyo project would turn the town into a new Shenzhen.[23] As Brautigam and Xiaoyang (2011, 30) explain, Shenzhen was part of an early experiment with foreign direct investment and market liberalization in China, and one of the first four SEZs on the mainland, created in 1979. It is seen as particularly successful, having transformed the community 'from fishing village to an industrialised metropolis within a generation' (ibid.). The China Merchants Group had a key role to play in Shenzen's development and China Merchants Holding International is now chiefly involved in building and running the new Bagamoyo megaport.

Both narratives resonate with the argument that infrastructures do not merely perform technical functions but also generate vision and evoke desire (Larkin 2013), although this is rarely mentioned in the political economy and rentier state literature discussed at the beginning of this chapter. There is a long tradition of using large-scale infrastructure projects to represent state power to citizens (Chalfin 2010b; Swyngedouw 2007). While they are also about establishing new gateways and garnering revenue from them, the anthropology of the state has shown that new roads, dams and ports all enact 'the state' and generate symbolic capital to legitimise it (Larkin 2013). In the case of Bagamoyo, even newspapers such as *The Citizen* and *The East African*, which are generally critical of the Tanzanian authorities, have praised the project.[24] Such support is not always linked to functionality as infrastructure comes to represent 'the possibility of being modern, of having a future, or the foreclosing of that possibility' (Larkin 2013, 333).

Conclusions

Against the expectation that much of Africa's infrastructure boom, especially when linked to Chinese investment, is driven by resource extraction, this chapter has looked at the reconfiguration of power and authority around major African ports along the Tanzanian coast. While, for extractive industries, it has been shown that 'indirect discharge' is an important technology by which seemingly weak states (re)gain centralized control over revenue through transnational actors (Hibou 1999; Hönke 2010), the infrastructure boom and investment in East African ports reveal more complex dynamics.

Ports are gateways from which governments derive rents and revenue, but more attention needs to be paid to the broader transformations of power and authority that are visible through them. New, large-scale investments in infrastructure – beyond the frequently studied extractive industries – bring governance practices among various branches of government and state administration, corporations, competing groups of port professionals and security services and devices into view. They are veritable frontier zones where transnational political geographies emerge and are then contested and transformed (see Hönke and Cuesta-Fernandez 2018 on 'infrastructure controversies'). In particular, the new (but also quite old) imaginaries of development that 'new' investors such as China and the Gulf monarchies evoke are striking. These inform how 'states' are performed alongside transnational political geographies, and point to other 'travelling models' (Behrends *et al.* 2014) rather than the familiar liberal-capitalist ones.

Notes

1 I would like to thank the editors of this volume and the other participants at the authors' workshop for their comments and suggestions. Thanks also to the Stellenbosch Institute for Advanced Study (STIAS) for providing an excellent space in which to develop this chapter. Some of the early ideas were discussed at the BISA pre-conference workshop 'Beyond the Gatekeeper State: IR Perspectives on African States in the Twenty-first Century'. The research was supported by a University of Edinburgh CHSS Challenge Investment Grant for 'New Political Topographies'. Special thanks to Iván Cuesta-Fernandez for excellent research assistance. Thanks to *Third World Thematics* for permission to reuse some material from Hönke forthcoming.
2 'Bagamoyo Port Set to Start Operations by 2020', *Tanzania Daily News*, 29 October 2017.
3 See www.icafrica.org/en/ (accessed 13 March 2017) and World Bank 2014.
4 See also, for instance, Hilboom 2011 and Poole 2013.
5 'Tanzania: Landmark Decision', *The Citizen*, 25 April 2008 (http://allafrica.com/stories/200804250650.html, accessed 3 April 2016) and www.ippmedia.com/frontend/index.php?l=13713, 21 February 2010 (accessed 3 April 2016).
6 'Tanzania: Stakeholders Now Demand Stability at TPA', 15 March 2015 (www.bunkerportsnews.com/News.aspx?ElementId=8584d503-d868–476d-92bb-759bd5b8e56b, accessed 9 January 2017).
7 Interview with anonymous clearing agent, 2015, Dar es Salaam.
8 'Meticulous Study on Port Containers Scam Underway', *Daily News* (www.dailynews.co.tz/index.php/home-news/44832-meticulous-study-on-port-containers-scam-underway, accessed 9 January 2017).
9 'Magufuli Axes TPA Board over Port Scandal', *Daily News* (www.dailynews.co.tz/index.php/home-news/44876-magufuli-axes-ps-dissolves-tpa-board-over-port-scandals, accessed 9 January 2017).
10 Interview with anonymous consignee, 2015, Dar es Salaam.
11 'Many of these TPA authorities, they joined hands with some entrepreneurs and put an ICD where some of these guys are partners' (interview with anonymous consignee, 2015, Dar es Salaam; 'ICDs … make anything which might create an obstacle to clearance of the goods' (interview with anonymous freight forwarder, 2015, Dar es Salaam).

12 Interview with anonymous clearing agent, 2015. The One-Stop Centre was inaugurated in April 2012 and hosts all eleven agencies involved in the clearing of cargo under a single roof (http://tanzania.usembassy.gov/pr_07262012.html, accessed 24 November 2016).
13 'There is so much money here. They don't want to lose that grip. All those people, all the decision-makers or whatever, those guys … they make it so easily' (interview with anonymous consignee, 2015, Dar es Salaam).
14 According to TradeMark East Africa's website (www.trademarkea.com, accessed 27 May 2016). See also the Big Results Now website (www.pmoralg.go.tz/quick-menu/brn/, accessed 30 March 2016).
15 www.youtube.com/watch?v=6-LEgv2l5-A&app=desktop (accessed 10 May 2015).
16 'What is TANCIS?' (www.tra.go.tz/index.php/faqs/405-what-is-tancis, accessed 26 May 2016).
17 Interview with anonymous freight forwarder, 2015, Dar es Salaam; and interview with marketing manager at TICTS, 2015, Dar es Salaam.
18 http://allafrica.com/stories/201401280647.html (accessed 28 January 2014); http://allafrica.com/stories/201401280647.html (accessed 15 March 2015); http://country.eiu.com/article.aspx?articleid=1572286741&Country=Tanzania&topic=Economy&subtopic=Forecast&subsubtopic=Policy+trends&u=1&pid=323098416&oid=323098416&uid=1 (accessed 17 September 2014).
19 Announced by the Minister of Works: 'Govt Halts Building of Bagamoyo Port', *The Citizen*, 8 January 2016.
20 'Bagamoyo Port Set to Start Operations by 2020', *Tanzania Daily News*, 29 October 2017.
21 E. Blair and F. Ng'wanakilala, 'Tanzania President Maps out Plan for Transport Hub', Reuters, 11 April 2014 (www.reuters.com/article/2014/04/11/us-africa-summit-tanzania-transportation-idUSBREA3A1JN20140411, accessed 27 May 2016).
22 'Zanzibar is endowed with potential resources that can transform the Islands into a business centre like Dubai' (Iddy Mwema, 'Zanzibar Economic Prospects Promising', *Daily News*, 10 May 2017; http://dailynews.co.tz/index.php/home-news/50484-zanzibar-economic-prospects-promising, accessed 23 October 2017); 'Dubai experience offers vital lessons for Tanzania' (Samuel Kamndaya, 'Tanzania Needs Visionary Leader', *The Citizen*, 17 October 2013; www.thecitizen.co.tz/oped/Tanzania-needs-visionary-leader/1840568-2036484-view-printVersion-j77xh2z/index.html, accessed 23 October 2017).
23 Katare Mbashiru, 'Bagamoyo Port Set to Start Operations by 2020', *Tanzania Daily News*, 29 October 2017.
24 'Tanzania Plan for 11bn Port Threat to Mombasa', *The East African*, 11 May 2013 (www.theeastafrican.co.ke/news/Tanzania-plan-for–11bn-port-threat-to-Mombasa/-/2558/1849536/-/14pu3bd/-/index.html, accessed 11 May 2013).

References

Adolf, K.Y. and C. Ducruet. 2014. The changing tides of port geography (1950–2012). *Progress in Human Geography* 38(6), 785–823.

Barry, A. 2006. Technological zones. *European Journal of Social Theory* 9(2), 239–253.

Barry, A. 2013. *Material politics: Disputes along the pipeline*. Hoboken, NJ: Wiley.

Beblawi, H. and G. Luciani, eds. 1987. *The rentier state*. London: Croom Helm.

Behrends, A., S.-J. Park and R. Rottenburg. 2014. *Travelling models in African conflict resolution: Translating technologies of social ordering*. Leiden and Boston, MA: Brill.

Beresford, A. (2015) Power, patronage, and gatekeeper politics in South Africa. *African Affairs* 114(455), 226–248.

Boone, C. 1998. 'Empirical statehood' and reconfiguration of political order. In L.A. Villalón and P.A. Huxtable, eds, *The African state at a critical juncture*. Boulder, CO: Lynne Rienner, 29–141.

Brautigam, D. and T. Xiaoyang. 2011. African Shenzhen: China's special economic zones in Africa. *Journal of Modern African Studies* 49(1), 27–54.

Calderón, C. 2009. *Infrastructure and growth in Africa*. Washington, DC: World Bank.

Chalfin, B. 2010a. *Neoliberal frontiers: An ethnography of sovereignty in West Africa*. Chicago: University of Chicago Press.

Chalfin, B. 2010b. Recasting maritime governance in Ghana: The neo-developmental state and the port of Tema. *Journal of Modern African Studies* 48(4), 573–598.

Chorin, E. 2010. *Articulating a 'Dubai model' of development: The case of Djibouti*. Dubai: Dubai School of Government.

Cooksey, T.and T. Kelsall. 2011. *The political economy of the investment climate in Tanzania*. London: Africa Power Project, ODI.

Cooper, F. 2002. *Africa since 1940: The past of the present*. Cambridge: Cambridge University Press.

Cooper, F. 2014. *Africa in the world: Capitalism, empire, nation-state*. Cambridge, MA: Harvard University Press.

Cowen, D. 2014. *The deadly life of logistics: Mapping violence in global trade*. Minneapolis: University of Minnesota Press.

Cross, J. 2015. The economy of anticipation: Hope, infrastructure, and economic zones in South India. *Comparative Studies of South Asia, Africa and the Middle East* 35(3), 424–437.

Easterling, K. 2012. Zone: The spatial softwares of extrastatecraft. *Places*, https://placesjournal.org/article/zone-the-spatial-softwares-of-extrastatecraft/ (accessed 27 February 2018).

Engel, U. and P. Nugent, eds. 2010. *Respacing Africa*. Leiden and Boston, MA: Brill.

Erdmann, G. and U. Engel. 2007. Neopatrimonialism reconsidered: Critical review and elaboration of an elusive concept. *Commonwealth & Comparative Politics* 45(1), 95–119.

Ferguson, J. and A. Gupta. (2002) Spatializing states: Toward an ethnography of neoliberal governmentality. *American Ethnologist* 29(4), 981–1002.

Ford, N. 2006. African ports and harbours: Africa's gateway to world trade. *African Business* 321, 14–15.

Gray, H.S. 2015. The political economy of grand corruption in Tanzania. *African Affairs* 114(456), 382–403.

Hagmann, T. and D. Péclard. 2010. Negotiating statehood: Dynamics of power and domination in Africa. *Development and Change* 41(4), 539–562.

Hansen, T.B. and F. Stepputat. 2006. Sovereignty revisited. *Annual Review of Anthropology* 35, 295–315.

Harrison, G. 2004. *The World Bank and Africa: The construction of governance states*. Abingdon and New York: Routledge.

Hibou, B. 1999. La 'décharge', nouvel interventionnisme. *Politique Africaine* 73, 6–15.

Hillbom, E. 2011. Botswana: A development-oriented gatekeeper state. *African Affairs* 111(442), 69–89.

Hönke, J. 2010. New political topographies: Mining companies and indirect discharge in Southern Katanga (DRC). *Politique Africaine* 120, 105–127.

Hönke, J. 2013. *Transnational companies and security governance: Hybrid practices in a postcolonial world*. London: Routledge.

Hönke, J. Forthcoming. Beyond the gatekeeper state: African infrastructure hubs as sites of experimentation. *Third World Thematics.*

Hönke, J. and I. Cuesta-Fernandez. 2017. A topolographical approach to infrastructure: Political topography, topology and the port of Dar es Salaam. *Environment and Planning D: Society and Space* 35(6), 1076–1095.

Hönke, J. and I. Cuesta-Fernandez. 2018. Mobilising security and logistics through an African port: A controversies approach to infrastructure. *Mobilities* 18(2), 246–260.

Jacob, T. 2017. Competing energy narratives in Tanzania: Towards the political economy of coal. *African Affairs* 116(463), 341–353.

Kelsall, T. 2013. *Business, politics and the state in Africa: Challenging the orthodoxies on growth and transformation*. London: Zed Books.

Kühn, F. P. 2008. Aid, opium, and the state of rents in Afghanistan: Competition, cooperation, or cohabitation? *Journal of Intervention and State-building* 2(3), 309–327.

Larkin, B. 2013. The politics and poetics of infrastructure. *Annual Review of Anthropology* 42, 327–343.

Lobo-Guerrero, L. 2012. Connectivity as the strategization of space: The case of the port of Hamburg. *Distinktion* 13(3), 310–321.

Mbembe, A. 2001. *On the postcolony*. Berkeley: University of California Press.

Mbembe, A. 2002. At the edge of the world: Boundaries, territoriality, and sovereignty in Africa. In M.R. Beissinger and C. Young, eds, *Beyond state crisis? Postcolonial Africa and post-Soviet Eurasia in comparative perspective*. Washington, DC: Woodrow Wilson Center Press, 53–80.

Migdal, J.S. 2001. *State in society: Studying how states and societies transform and constitute one another*. Cambridge and New York: Cambridge University Press.

Migdal, J.S. and K. Schlichte. 2005. Rethinking the state. In K. Schlichte, ed., *The dynamics of the state: The formation and crisis of state domination*. Aldershot: Ashgate, 1–40.

Mitchell, T. 1991. The limits of the state: Beyond statist approaches and their critics. *American Political Science Review* 85(1), 77–96.

Ong, A. 2006. *Neoliberalism as exception: Mutations in citizenship and sovereignty*. Durham, NC: Duke University Press.

Opitz, S. and U. Tellmann. 2012. Global territories: Zones of economic and legal dis/connectivity. *Distinktion: Scandinavian Journal of Social Theory* 13(3), 261–282.

Pitcher, A., M.H. Moran and M. Johnston. 2009. Rethinking patrimonialism and neopatrimonialism in Africa. *African Studies Review* 52, 125–156.

Poole, A. 2013. Ransoms, remittances, and refugees: The gatekeeper state in Eritrea. *Africa Today* 60(2), 66–82.

Reno, W. 2001. How sovereignty matters: International markets and the political economy of local politics in weak states. In T.M. Callaghy, R. Kassimir and R. Latham, eds, *Intervention and transnationalism in Africa: Global–local networks of power*. Cambridge: Cambridge University Press, 197–215.

Rizzo, M. 2015. The political economy of an urban megaproject: The Bus Rapid Transit Project in Tanzania. *African Affairs* 114(455), 249–270.

Ross, M. 1999. The political economy of the resource curse. *World Politics* 51(2), 297–322.

Sassen, S. 2006. *Territory, authority, rights: From medieval to global assemblages*. Princeton, NJ: Princeton University Press.

Schlichte, K. 2005. *Der Staat in der Weltgesellschaft. Politische Herrschaft in Asien, Afrika und Lateinamerika*. Frankfurt am Main: Campus Verlag.

Schlichte, K. 2008. Uganda, or: The internationalisation of rule. *Civil Wars* 10(4), 369–383. Sidaway, J.D. 2007. Enclave space: A new metageography of development? *Area* 39(3), 331–339.

Starosielski, N. 2015. *The undersea network*. Durham, NC: Duke University Press.

Swyngedouw, E. 2007. Technonatural revolutions: The scalar politics of Franco's hydro-social dream for Spain, 1939–1975. *Transactions of the Institute of British Geographers* 32(1), 9–28. Trujillo, L., M.M. González and J.L. Jiménez. 2013. An overview on the reform process of African ports. *Utilities Policy* 25, 12–22.

Wippel, S., K. Bromber, C. Steiner and B. Krawietz, eds. 2016. *Under construction: Logics of urbanism in the Gulf region*. London: Ashgate.

World Bank. 2014. *Dar es Salaam Maritime Gateway Project*, www.worldbank.org/projects/P150496?lang=en (accessed 20 August 2017).

3 The 'blue economy' and Operation Phakisa

Prospects for an emerging developmental state in South Africa?

Ulf Engel

Introduction

This chapter looks at the recent hype about Africa's 'blue economy' – that is, the exploration and exploitation of the continent's waters for the purpose of economic prosperity and 'development' – and South Africa's own version of the 'blue economy' – that is, Operation Phakisa. In the context of a tradition of corporatism between state, labour and capital, and a debate about the developmental nature of the post-apartheid state (on the country's macro-economics, see Marais 2001; Freund 2010; Gelb 2010), insights from Operation Phakisa will be used to discuss the changing nature of the South African state.

The African Union and the UN Economic Commission for Africa (UNECA) have served as continental norm entrepreneurs to canvass for the strategic development of African waters, both inland and offshore, and in particular the Combined Exclusive Maritime Zone of Africa (CEMZA). The 'blue economy' is Africa's latest frontier of resource development and governance (for more traditional forms, see Börzel and Thauer 2013; Campbell 2013; Grant *et al.* 2015). In January 2014 the African Union endorsed the '2050 Africa Integrated Maritime Strategy' (2050 AIM Strategy), which sketches a continental security, economic and environmental vision for the next three and a half decades (African Union 2012). Two years later, and based on earlier 'green economy' approaches, UNECA published a 'policy handbook' to stimulate discussion around best practice on 'Africa's Blue Economy', or what it also termed the 'New Frontier of African Renaissance' (UNECA 2016, x; see also UNECA 2012). In this line of thinking, developing the 'blue economy' is seen as a major factor in Africa's 'structural transformation' (UNECA 2016, xi).

Operation Phakisa was launched in South Africa in 2014. It represents both a method for planning developmental state interventions *and* a set of concrete activities to boost the country's economy. Currently this is done with an emphasis on the ocean economy that has already been labelled, rather euphemistically, South Africa's 'tenth province'.[1] Developing the country's coastal economy is said to have the potential to increase South

Africa's GDP by 4 per cent per annum, or something like R129–177 billion by 2033, and create between 800,000 and a million direct new employment opportunities (SA Government 2015).[2] Operation Phakisa is moderated within a governance framework of 'clustered' public–private sector relations that may set South Africa on the path of becoming a developmental state. Because of the country's specific trajectory of colonialism and apartheid, the case differs from most other African countries discussed in this edited volume.

This chapter will proceed as follows: in the next section, I will provide the context of Operation Phakisa by looking at the corporatist nature of South Africa, ongoing debates about the developmental state and current dynamics of 'state capture'. Then I will explore Operation Phakisa in greater detail, highlighting the introduction of 'cluster' governance around state institutions and state-owned enterprises (SOEs) or parastatals, on the one hand, and research and private sector actors, on the other. Finally, conclusions will be offered with regard to what the government's handling of the 'blue economy' reveals about the changing strategies of the post-apartheid state vis-à-vis the business sector, and the nature of the South African state constantly in-the-making.

South Africa between corporatism, developmental state and state capture

Politically and academically, the ANC government's macro-economic policy is discussed against the background of more fundamental debates about the changing nature of the South African economy and its specific variant of capitalism since the end of apartheid (Adam *et al.* 1997; Padayachee 2008), sometimes echoing the old state/economy debate during the apartheid era (see, for instance, Lipton 1985; Stadler 1987; Sarakinsky 1995). In order to provide context for Operation Phakisa, three interrelated aspects of South Africa's macro-economic politics and the country's political economy will be introduced briefly here. (Unfortunately, limitations of space preclude more detailed discussion.)

First, the corporatist governance arrangement between government, the private sector and labour that has emerged during the transition from apartheid to democracy (see Pretorius 1996; Habib 1997; Adam 1998; Hönke *et al.* 2013; Kim and van der Westhuizen 2015). This arrangement has been described as 'transitionary' (Venter *et al.* 2012, 575), and it is said to be slowly dissolving – a dynamic that is somewhat similar to developments Sinwell (2011) noticed at the level of township governance and the way civic participation is mediated. The open question, then, is: what will replace this arrangement?

Second, there is an ongoing debate about the nature, existence and perspectives of South Africa as a 'developmental state' (Lodge 2009). In principle, South Africa under President Jacob Zuma could be considered as another example of the developmental turn in Africa that has been advocated so strongly since 2011 by UNECA. Despite substantial differences in terms of governance and the quality of democracy, conceptually South Africa is not so different from, for example, Ethiopia or Rwanda, in that 'the market [is used] as an instrument rather than a sole mechanism for fostering long-term investment, rapid and sustained economic growth, equity and social development (UNECA 2011, xiii). The developmental state, as conceived by UNECA, 'must play a central role in resource allocation and in efficient coordination of crucial economic activities' (ibid., 7). And, although the notion of 'developmental state' as discussed by the government and the ruling African National Congress (ANC) may have shifted over the years, rhetorically South Africa claims to follow a particular policy that is propagated by some South-East Asian countries, such as Japan, Malaysia, Singapore and South Korea (see, for instance, Bischoff 1998; Johnson 1999; Kalinowski 2008; Shelton 2009; Lee 2015). However, academic observers have either questioned the possibility of South Africa ever becoming a 'proper' developmental state (Lawrence 2013) or at least expressed scepticism as to whether it will become a 'functioning' developmental state (Fine 2011, 113–120; Satgar 2014).

Third, Operation Phakisa has to be understood in the context of current policies of 'state capture' that emerged gradually after Zuma become the country's president in May 2009. Increasingly, the state has become a vehicle for self-enrichment of competing ANC factions (so-called 'tenderpreneurs'). In the academic literature, South Africa is described as a 'dominant-party' state – that is, a liberal democracy in which just one party (the ANC) has dominated electoral politics since 1994 (Giliomee 1998). Over the years, the quality of the country's democracy and the ANC's governance performance have both declined. Many observers have argued that South Africa suffered political and moral demise under the Zuma administration (see Booysen 2015; Boraine 2014; Calland 2013; Johnson 2015). This analysis is framed in terms of 'clientelistic gate keeper politics' (Beresford 2015) or 'ANC politics "eats the state"' (Matthee 2015, 28). Following the revelations in 2014 on the 'upgrading' of Zuma's private homestead in Nkandla, kwaZulu-Natal, with taxpayers' money (Public Protector 2014), notions of 'decline' (Booysen 2015), 'corruption' (Feinstein 2010), 'neopatrimonialism' (Lodge 2014), illegal enrichment (Southall 1998, 2008) or 'party machine' politics (Southall 2014) have been invoked. The jury is still out on whether this will change substantially with the accession of Cyril Ramaphosa to the presidency in February 2018.

This line of reasoning was reinforced when the 'state capture' debate on the influence of the Gupta family over Zuma, his family and his administration started to have a significant impact on South Africa's international financial reputation in 2016 (see Public Protector 2016). In South Africa, 'state capture' has become a synonym for ANC-induced cronyism, corruption and clientelism. Conceptually, the term refers to a situation where

> Political parties often perceive state capture for the control of the resources and personnel of the state as a source of elite enrichment;

> therefore politics itself becomes a means to an end, devoid of any idea of protecting public interests vis-à-vis private gains.
>
> (IDEA 2007, 21)

The combination of developmental state-planning and interventionist projects, on the one hand, and increasing signs of clientelism and corruption, on the other, has led to alienation between capital and the ANC state: 'state–business relations in South Africa are characterised by high levels of mistrust and ad hoc engagements' (Makokera 2015, 1). In addition, in the crucial mining sector, a dual crisis of production and legitimacy has arisen: the former relates to dramatic falls in commodity prices, with many mines no longer making any profit, while the latter relates to the handling of the Lonmin Marikana massacre of August 2012, when police killed a total of forty-one striking miners near Rustenberg during a stand-off between competing trade unions (see Frankel 2013; Farlam *et al.* 2015). At the same time, relations between the ANC and the Congress of South African Trade Unions (COSATU) have been strained since the expulsion of the National Union of Metalworkers of South Africa (NUMSA) from the latter on 8 November 2014 and COSATU Secretary-General Zwelinzima Vavi's open declaration of opposition to the Zuma government on 30 March 2015 (see Buhlungu and Tshoaedi 2012; Beresford 2016).

Developing a South African 'blue economy': Operation Phakisa

The origin of Operation Phakisa is a classic case of cultural transfer. According to the Department of Environmental Affairs (DEA), on a state visit to Malaysia on 25–27 August 2013, President Jacob Zuma was introduced

> to the Big Fast Results Methodology through which the Malaysian government achieved significant government and economic transformation within a very short time. Using this approach, they addressed national key priority areas such as poverty, crime and unemployment.
>
> (DEA 2017b)[3]

In Malaysia, the BFR Methodology has been developed in response to the Thatcherist new public management (NPM) approach, which was developed in the United Kingdom and other Commonwealth countries in the 1980s. Based on public choice theory, governments wanted to become more businesslike in their problem-solving approaches. The Malaysian government emphasised results-based performance management within a developmental conception of the state (see Siddiquee 2006; Khalid and Nabiha 2008; Haque 2011). On the African continent, Tanzania was the first country to embrace the BFR approach in 2011, followed by Rwanda and Nigeria.

When applied to South Africa, and initially only the 'blue economy', the Department of Environmental Affairs boldly claims:

> Operation Phakisa represents that new spirit of moving faster in meeting government's targets. South African Government's starting point was that South Africa is surrounded by a vast ocean … [and] has not fully taken advantage of the immense potential of this untapped resource. The oceans have the potential to contribute up to 177 billion rand to the gross domestic product (GDP) and create just over one million jobs by 2033.
>
> (DEA 2017b)

Operation Phakisa – Sesotho for 'hurry up' (as well as 'rapid', 'fast' or 'move faster') – was officially launched on 19 July 2014 (see *Ujuh* 2014; *Engineering News* 2014). It is packaged by the government as an initiative that is addressing some of the key goals of the National Development Plan (NDP) 2030, 'such as poverty, unemployment and inequality' (ibid.). It represents both a method for the planning and implementation of state interventions to foster 'development' and a series of concrete activities in various prioritised fields – currently oceans and health (DEA 2017a).[4] In his 2015 State of the Nation Address, President Zuma announced the extension of Operation Phakisa to the mining industry (SA Government News Agency 2015). Methodologically speaking, a key step in the Operation Phakisa approach is a management tool called 'delivery laboratories' or 'intensive work sessions': 'Multiple stakeholders work full-time in one location for about five weeks. At the end of this period, they deliver complete and signed-off action plans for presentation to the Cabinet' (ibid.).

On oceans, Operation Phakisa is addressing four 'work streams': aquaculture; offshore oil and gas exploration; marine protection services and ocean governance; and marine transport and manufacturing. Thus far, the aquaculture work stream has contributed less than 1 per cent of South Africa's fish supply, and it is thought to have huge potential 'for rural development, especially for marginalised coastal communities' (DEA 2017b). According to the DEA's website, so far eight initiatives and twenty-four projects have been identified for implementation by 2019. The expected increase in the sector's revenue is an additional R900 million in 2019. In order to create 'an enabling regulatory environment', an Inter-Departmental Authorisations Committee has been established to coordinate aquaculture applications and approvals with the aim of reducing processing periods from about 890 days to 240 days. In addition, a R500-million Aquaculture Development Fund has been established. And, with a view to state–private sector relations, the founding of a 'South African industry body' has been suggested 'that will establish seventy to eighty buyer relationships such as local retailers and food service companies' (ibid.).

Activities with regard to the offshore oil and gas exploration work stream are based on the DEA's estimate that

> South Africa's coast and adjoining waters have possible resources of approximately nine billion barrels of oil. This is equivalent to 40 years of South African oil consumption. We also have eleven billion barrels oil equivalent of natural gas, which is equal to three hundred and seventy five years of South African gas consumption.
>
> (Ibid.)

Thirty exploration wells are to be drilled within the next ten years:

> Over the next 20 years, this work could lead to the production of three hundred thousand (370 000) barrels of oil and gas per day. This is approximately eighty % of current oil and gas imports. The result would be one hundred and thirty thousand jobs and a contribution of two point two billion US dollars (US $2.2 billion) to GDP.
>
> (DEA 2017b; see also Carnie 2014)

Again, in order to create an enabling environment for South African companies to invest in this sector, the government is planning to provide a legislative framework, build a 'one-stop shop' within the Department of Mineral Resources (DMR) 'to streamline and regulate the licensing process for offshore oil and gas exploration and production', conduct emergency response drills, operationalise the International Oil Pollution and Compensation Fund, and invest in research that 'will unlock data ecosystems, marine resources, and ocean related renewable energy' (DEA 2017b).

The third work stream – marine protection services and ocean governance – is addressing jurisdiction over South Africa's exclusive economic zone, which covers an estimated 1.5 million square kilometres. An overarching governance plan to harmonise legislation in this area was to be finalised by March 2015, though no final document has yet been released. Earlier drafts referred, among others, to a National Marine Spatial Planning Framework and a draft Oceans Bill for marine spatial planning. Monitoring of this work stream comes under the auspices of the Department of Planning, Monitoring and Evaluation in the presidency. The Mineral Resources and Petroleum Development Amendment Bill (B15–2013) of 6 April 2013 (Parliamentary Monitoring Group 2013) passed the National Assembly on 12 March 2014 but remains under consideration by the National Council of Provinces. In August 2015, Zuma stated that the draft Oceans Management Bill had been finalised, and the Marine Spatial Planning Bill (X-2016) was gazetted on 28 March 2017. *Inter alia*, the latter foresees the creation of an Ocean Economy Ministerial Management Committee (Parliamentary Monitoring Group 2016).

Finally, planning in the area of marine transport and manufacturing is based on the observation that the country has not yet fully exploited its 'strategic location, infrastructure and skills base to accelerate growth of this sector' (DEA 2017b). South Africa currently has no registered ships, but every year its eight ports handle 300 million tons of imports and exports. Operation Phakisa aims to develop marine manufacturing, including ship and rig repair, refurbishment and boatbuilding, in the hope of creating 4,000 jobs. To this end, eighteen initiatives have been developed across three categories – infrastructure and operations; skills and capacity-building; and market growth – to accelerate sector growth.[5]

Nominally, Operation Phakisa is run by the DEA's Oceans Economy Secretariat, but the DMR and the Petroleum Oil and Gas Corporation of South Africa (SOC) Limited (PetroSA) are heavily involved, too.[6] The latter two organisations grant licences for mining and oil and gas prospecting and exploitation. PetroSA is a state-owned enterprise that was established in 2002 as a subsidiary of the Central Energy Fund (CEF). It reports to the Department of Energy.[7] Other stakeholders are the Department of Trade and Industry (DTI); more SOEs, such as the Transnet National Ports Authority (TNPA), which is managing the country's ports, and the Port Elizabeth-based Coega Industrial Development Corporation (IDZ), which is operating 11,500 hectares of industrial land in the Nelson Mandela Bay Metropolitan Municipality; research institutions, such as the South African International Maritime Institute (SAIMI) at Nelson Mandela Metropolitan University (NMMU) in Port Elizabeth; and the South African Maritime Safety Authority (SAMSA), which falls under the Department of Transport. In addition, some private sector companies are involved, such as the Durban-based Southern African Shipyards (established 1960), the country's biggest naval shipbuilder and ship repair company. Thus far, two 'clusters' have been formed to bring together these state bodies and private sector entities in various forms of public–private partnership (PPP): the KZN (kwaZulu-Natal) Maritime Cluster[8] and the Nelson Mandela Bay Maritime Cluster (NMBMC). While the former was established by a top-down public sector approach, the latter was supposedly founded by a bottom-up private sector approach (DEA 2016b).

Meanwhile, the implementation of Operation Phakisa has gathered pace. In a progress report presented on 13 August 2015, President Zuma highlighted that the government had already committed a total of R9.2 billion to develop Saldanha Bay, north-west of Cape Town, as an oil and gas hub. Geographically defined ('phased') gas pipeline routes have also been defined. In addition, environmental authorisation was approved for the building of the R600-million Burgan fuel storage facility in the port of Cape Town, with construction commencing in August 2015 (DEA 2015; see also SA Government 2016). In his final progress update, delivered on 9 October 2017, Zuma claimed that Operation Phakisa had already garnered investments worth R24.6 billion (of which R15 billion had come from the government) and had created 6,500 job opportunities (*Business Report* 2017).

On the research side, the Departments of Environmental Affairs and Science and Technology (through the National Research Foundation; NRF) have commenced a research programme on marine protected areas and marine spatial planning. The Council for Scientific and Industrial Research's Meraka Institute has been appointed to establish a national oceans and coastal information system. In the area of oil and gas exploration, and with a view to fostering more PPPs, the South African Marine Research and Exploration Forum was launched on 29 January 2016.

On 6–7 June 2016, the DEA's Oceans Economy Secretariat, SAIMI and SA Shipyards organised a two-day seminar titled 'Operation Phakisa: Oceans Economy – Exploring Opportunities: Towards a National Maritime Cluster' to push forward maritime industrial clustering and 'create synergies characterized by greater co-operation with shared benefits along values chains' (SAMSA 2016). The seminar was run in collaboration with the Norwegian Embassy in Pretoria, which is understandable as Norway serves as a role model in the ocean oil and gas industry because it has designed its own 'cluster programme' (DEA 2016a). It was attended by 'leaders from diverse maritime industry sub-sectors, such as marine manufacturing, shipping, cargo owners, finance institutions, academia, government and potential investors', while its ultimate aim was to develop 'a roadmap towards the creation of a South African Maritime Industries Cluster' (ibid.).

The notion of cluster governance has become more pronounced over recent years. A cluster, according to the NMBMC, is a constructed 'population of geographically concentrated and mutually related business units, associations and public (private) organizations centred around a distinctive economic specialization'. Hence, clusters are populations, not entities. Second, they are geographically concentrated, which makes them different from networks. Third, the cluster population consists of business units, associations, public–private organisations and public organisations. Fourth, each cluster is 'centred around' a particular economic specialisation that may be regarded as the 'core' of that cluster. Finally, 'clusters consist of business units and associations that are a part of, or relatively strongly related to, the core of the cluster' – that is, 'leader firms' (DEA 2016b). Therefore, one could summarise, conceptually 'clusters' go beyond PPPs (see Fombad 2015) because they may be organised inclusively and involve all actors (who are often referred to as 'stakeholders'), not just the state and the private sector. Currently, open questions around the Nelson Mandela Bay Cluster are discussed with regard to its structure – a single Eastern Cape Maritime Cluster or two maritime clusters (i.e. the Nelson Mandela Bay Maritime Cluster (West) and the East London Maritime Cluster (East)), the precise structure in terms of relevant sub-sectors and leader firms, and the nature of the economic specialisation or core of the Eastern Cape maritime clusters.

The language of Operation Phakisa is technical, developmental and innocent. It also implies legitimacy and inclusive stakeholder participation. During his presentation at the 2016 seminar, the head of the DEA's Oceans

Economy Secretariat, André Share, referred to the 'exploitation of opportunities', 'supportive funding', 'unlocking investment in new and existing port facilities', 'implementing strategic prioritised projects', 'providing legislative clarity and stability' and 'enhancing the environmental governance capacity of the oil and gas regulator', among other buzzwords and -phrases (see DEA 2016b). Earlier, at the launch of Operation Phakisa, the myth of the Big Fast Results approach was reinvoked by President Zuma to claim that 'Delivery Labs create transparency and help to remove bottlenecks and resolve the most critical challenges facing a sector' (*Engineering News* 2014).

However, while the government has consistently linked Operation Phakisa to a wealth of development opportunities, a number of voices have urged caution. For instance, in a briefing to the Land and Mineral Resources Committee of the National Council of Provinces on 4 August 2015, the DMR admitted that oil and gas drilling 'is a costly, long-term, and dangerous project with historically low success rates' (Parliamentary Monitoring Group 2015). Members of the committee also aired concerns about the extent to which jobs would be created in South Africa rather than somewhere else.

Moreover, Operation Phakisa has not been embraced by all sectors of society. The country's mining industry has been particularly sceptical, and environmentalists highly critical. Relations between the ANC government and the mining sector have been strained for a some time anyway. Reportedly, the mining industry's primary concern is that Operation Phakisa will be just another 'talk-shop', similar to other encounters between unions and the private sector, such as the Mining Lekgotla, the mining industry's annual fair, which was finally cancelled in 2016 (see McKay 2016). In addition, the industry is still awaiting agreement on a Mining Charter,[9] and it has repeatedly called for more 'honest' conversations between the private sector and the ANC government.

Furthermore, environmentalists and fishing communities have criticised the Minerals Department for putting food security at risk by 'rushing prospecting rights for untested technology into place'. After conducting research into the 'blue economy', the non-governmental Centre for Environmental Rights declared, 'Alarm bells should be sounding.' It claimed that the government was endangering livelihoods by planning to exploit 'critically endangered ecosystems' for the sake of commercial development in the oceans. PetroSA's licences for exploration off the coast are said to cover 99 per cent of the country's exclusive economic zone, which has been steadily increased over the past few years, especially by making the southern Antarctic – the Prince Edward Island Group (Marion and Prince Edward islands) – part of the zone and thereby extending it from 370 to 650 kilometres off the mainland (Kings 2015).

Although the DEA has addressed some of these concerns in a green paper on environmental ocean governance (DEA 2012), environmental and social activists remain sceptical and insist that Operation Phakisa will fail. For instance, on 15 October 2014, the NGO Earthlife Africa (ELA) Durban argued that the operation 'has very little to do with poverty alleviation and everything to do with profits for corporates, most likely with the familiar kickbacks for well-connected tenderpreneurs and their political allies' (Earthlife Africa 2014).[10] Closer to home, ELA Durban and the South Durban Community Environment Alliance (SDCEA) were 'concerned about the speed with which public participation for projects like oil exploration and shipping expansion take place, the general lack of advertising and the failure of government to address concerns of communities, labour and environmentalists' (ibid.).

However, it is also obvious that, depending on the policy arena and geographical location, there are different levels of inclusiveness in governance, as demonstrated by Chevallier in a paper on a recent shift in South Africa's approach 'from coastal management focused on ecological sustainability to one that primarily supports its broader socio-economic agenda through inclusive management and sustainable livelihoods strategies' (Chevallier 2015, 5; for the shale gas sector, see Chapman *et al.* 2016).

Evidently, Operation Phakisa also has energy and climate change dimensions, although these are mainly sidelined in the current public South African debate (but see Mytleka *et al.* 2015; Worthington 2015). Hence, the jury is still out on the precise implications of developing the 'blue economy' from an environmentalist perspective (see *Daily Maverick* 2017). Needless to say, however, the country must broaden its sources of energy, move away from carbon dependency yet increase its energy production. In this respect, Operation Phakisa offers opportunities as well as environmental challenges. In spite of the innocent language used throughout, the real question is how Operation Phakisa will relate to the clientelistic logic of parts of government and the ruling party. Can implementation be carried out in pockets of accountability and bureaucratic ethos, or will the current logic of 'state capture' encroach on Operation Phakisa? Either way, what will be the end result?

Conclusions: developmental accommodation 2.0?

During the last decade, South Africa has experienced a change in relations between state, ruling party, capital and labour. The emphasis on a corporatist organisation of the economy around a triangle of government, private sector and trade unions, which dominated the 1990s, has been partly replaced in a transitionary process by an approach that evolves around problem-solving clusters.[11] In some fields, the emerging mode of governance is a state-centric form of reinvented, no longer corporatist, developmentalism; in others, it is clearly neoliberal (Ansari 2017). In reality, it is less bottom-up and inclusive than the government wants it to appear. Governance is evolving around defined economic cores and geographically concentrated spatialities. While the ANC's notion of 'development' started changing from redistribution to different versions of growth as early as the mid-1990s, now the focus is on making planning and implementation more efficient. Apparently, the Africanized version of the Malaysian approach to New Public Management will soon be extended to other key economic sectors, such as mining and education, and ultimately to agriculture and land reform (DIRCO 2016). Operation Phakisa has become a core central state management tool for the National Development Plan (NPC 2011), with weekly briefings to the President. But is it the central tool?

Although South Africa is a member of the BRICS group of states, it does not seem to draw its main inspiration from the macro-economic models practised by India or China (which are, of course, rather different in themselves). Rather, to some extent at least, it follows the examples of developmental democracies, such as Malaysia, and countries like Norway, which has tried to develop a sustainable 'blue economy' around North Sea oil and gas exploitation clusters.[12] Given that maritime clusters of various kinds exist all over the world, from Canada to Japan, Latvia to the Netherlands, this is indeed a deliberate and crucial choice.

The extent to which South Africa's 'blue economy' policy and Operation Phakisa approach are different from the other case-studies presented in this volume remains to be seen. The general language of '(neo)liberalism' may be similar, but it is still far too early to say with respect to policy outcomes. In the case of South Africa and the 'blue economy', these outcomes are mediated and negotiated in clusters, and so far they have avoided some of the illiberal outcomes described in other chapters. In this respect, crucial questions relate to the inclusivity of development around the 'blue economy' and the likelihood of benefits being distributed throughout society. Many dynamics have just begun. And it remains to be seen how they play out in terms of efficiency, accountability and inclusive consultation in a policy and business environment that is still dominated by the ANC. Nevertheless, within a short space of time, Operation Phakisa has become a very dynamic example of how the state–corporate nexus can change, in this case around the 'blue economy'.

Finally, it must be said that South Africa and the other case-studies presented in this volume have much in common with respect to the socio-spatial effects of new forms of resource exploitation. The country's 'blue economy' and its related marine spatial planning have already led to tangible large-scale respatialisations of socio-economic relations (see Engel and Nugent 2009). This is true for harbour development and expansion work, value-chain development, dwelling, offshore exploration rights, clustered rather than networked governance and so on, and it affects aquaculture, mining and shipping as much as fisheries and conservation.

Notes

1 See the South Africa Maritime Safety Authority's website at https://blog.samsa.org.za.

2 With the inclusion of the Prince Edward and Marion islands in the Southern Ocean, South Africa's coastline is said to be 3,924 kilometres in length (as opposed to 2,500 kilometres-plus for the continental coastline).
3 See also the BFR Institute's website at http://bfrinstitute.com.
4 The operation's website refers to three 'labs' – on the ocean economy, health and education – but provides no information on the latter two. 'Operation Phakisa Ideal Clinic Realisation and Maintenance' was launched on 18 November 2014.
5 Later, two more fields, or 'work streams', where introduced: small harbours development (led by the Department of Public Works) and coastal and marine tourism (led by the Department of Tourism).
6 For an analysis of the shale gas sector's governance, see Chapman *et al.* (2016); and for traditional natural resource governance (mining and fishery), see Masters and Kisiangani (2010).
7 See PetroSA's website at www.petrosa.co.za/discover_petroSA/Pages/Our-Company.aspx.
8 Later referred to as the eThekwini Maritime Cluster (EMC), based in Durban. For one of the few studies on governance in South African PPPs, see Fombad (2015), who uses the term 'PPP governance' very closely to NPM approaches with a view to policy, service delivery, infrastructure, capacity-building and economic development (ibid.: 1202).
9 A draft 'Reviewed Broad Based Black Economic Empowerment (BBBEE) Charter for the South African Mining and Minerals Industry, 2016' (Draft Mining Charter) was published by the DMR for comment on 15 April 2016. It aims to reconcile the provisions of its predecessor to the DTI codes of good practice ('BBBEE Codes'). The 'Broad Based Socio-Economic Empowerment Charter for the South African Mining and Minerals Industry' (Mining Charter) 'was first issued in 2004 under the Mineral and Petroleum Resources Development Act, 2002 in order to advance the participation of historically disadvantaged South Africans in the mining industry' (Campbell *et al.* 2016).
10 Earthlife Africa also draws attention to differences in programme focus and social orientation between Malaysia and South Africa.
11 Partly this is attributed to the declining role of COSATU, which is a member of the 'tripartite alliance' alongside the ANC and the South African Communist Party (SACP). See also Bond (2011) and Nattrass and Seekings (2016).
12 See the website of the European Network of Maritime Clusters at www.enmc.eu.

References

Adam, H. 1998. 'Corporatism as ethnic compromise: Labour relations in post-apartheid South Africa', *Nations and Nationalism*, 4(3), 347–362.

Adam, H., F. Zyl Slabbert and M. Moodley. 1997. *Comrades in Business: Post-liberation Politics in South Africa*. Cape Town: Tafelberg Press.

African Development Bank. 2014. 'Africa's blue economies vital for development' (www.afdb.org/en/news-and-events/article/africas-blue-economies-vital-for-development-13105/). Accessed: 10 September 2016 (but no longer available).

African Union. 2012. *2050 Africa's Integrated Maritime Strategy (2050 AIM Strategy)*. Addis Ababa: African Union.

Ansari, S. 2017. 'The neo-liberal incentive structure and the absence of the developmental state in post-apartheid South Africa', *African Affairs*, 116(463), 206–232.

Benkenstein, A. and R. Chevallier. 2015. *Effective Governance Central to Unlocking the Potential of the Blue Economy*, South African Institute of International Affairs,

Johannesburg (www.saiia.org.za/opinion-analysis/effective-governance-central-to-unlocking-the-potential-of-the-blue-economy). Accessed: 1 November 2017.

Beresford, A. 2015. 'Power, patronage, and gatekeeper politics in South Africa', *African Affairs*, 114(455), 226–248.

Beresford, P. 2016. *South Africa's Political Crisis: Unfinished Liberation and Fractured Class Struggles*. Basingstoke: Palgrave Macmillan.

Bischoff, P.H. 1998. 'Democratic South Africa and the Asian paragon: Issues of foreign policy orientation', *Africa Spectrum*, 33(2), 189–210.

Bond, P. 2011. 'South African splinters: From "elite transition" to "small-a alliances"', *Review of African Political Economy*, 38(127), 113–121.

Booysen, S. 2015. *Dominance and Decline: The ANC in the Time of Zuma*. Johannesburg: Wits University Press.

Boraine, A. 2014. *What's Gone Wrong? On the Brink of a Failed State*. Johannesburg andCape Town: Jonathan Ball Publishers.

Börzel, T.A. and C. Thauer, eds. 2013. *Business and Governance in South Africa: Racing to the Top?*Basingstoke: Palgrave Macmillan.

Buhlungu, S. and M. Tshoaedi, eds. 2012. *COSATU's Contested Legacy: South African Trade Unions in the Second Decade of Democracy*. Leiden and Boston, MA: Brill.

Business Report. 2017. 'President Zuma gives us all the details on Operation Phakisa', 9 October (www.iol.co.za/business-report/watch-president-zuma-gives-us-all-the-details-on-operation-phakisa-11508369). Accessed: 1 November 2017.

Calland, R. 2013. *The Zuma Years: South Africa's Changing Face of Power*. Cape Town: Zebra Press.

Campbell, B.K., ed. 2013. *Modes of Governance and Revenue Flows in African Mining*. Basingstoke: Palgrave Macmillan.

Campbell, R.et al. 2016. 'Draft Mining Charter would restructure BBBEE transactions in the South African mining industry', 6 May (www.whitecase.com/publications/alert/draft-mining-charter-would-restructure-bbbee-transactions-south-african-mining). Accessed: 1 November 2017.

Carnie, T. 2014. 'SA to drill for offshore oil – Zuma', *The Mercury*, 16 October (www.iol.co.za/news/politics/sa-to-drill-for-offshore-oil-zuma-1.1765872#.VLawmk0cSM8). Accessed: 1 March 2017.

Chapman, G.P., R. Wait and E. Kleynhans. 2016. 'The governance of shale gas production in South Africa', *South African Journal of International Affairs*, 23(1), 69–88.

Chevallier, R. 2015. *Promoting the Integrated Governance of South Africa's Coastal Zone*. Johannesburg: South Africa Institute for International Affairs.

Daily Maverick. 2017. 'GroundUp: Plan to drill for fossil fuels off KZN coast', 10 November (www.dailymaverick.co.za/article/2017-11-09-groundup-plan-to-drill-for-fossil-fuels-off-kzn-coast/). Accessed: 10 November 2017.

DEA. 2012. *Green Paper on the National Environmental Management of the Ocean for General Comment*. Government Gazette, General Notice 828 of 2012, 568(35783), 30 October.

DEA. 2015. 'Report by President Jacob Zuma to media and stakeholders on Operation Phakisa implementation', 13 August (www.environment.gov.za/speech/presidentzuma_operationphakisa). Accessed: 1 November 2017.

DEA. 2016a. 'Operation Phakisa: Oceans Economy Seminar – Exploring Opportunities: Towards a National Maritime Cluster', 6 June (www.environment.gov.za/events/department_activities/operationphakisa_nationalmarine_cluster_seminar). Accessed: 1 November 2017.

DEA. 2016b. 'Presentation of the Nelson Mandela Bay Maritime Cluster', 6 June (www.environment.gov.za/sites/default/files/docs/B6_mrmyles_constructingamaritimecluster.pdf). Accessed: 1 November 2017.

DEA. 2017a. 'Operation Phakisa' (www.operationphakisa.gov.za). Accessed: 1 November 2017.

DEA. 2017b. 'Operation Phakisa – Oceans Economy' (www.environment.gov.za/projectsprogrammes/operationphakisa/oceanseconomy). Accessed: 1 November 2017.

DIRCO. 2016. 'Statement on the Cabinet meeting of 28 September 2016', 29 September (www.dirco.gov.za/docs/2016/cabinet0928.htm). Accessed: 1 November 2017.

Earthlife Africa. 2014. 'Press eelease: Environmentalists protest against Zuma's plans for our coast', 15 October (http://earthlife.org.za/2014/10/press-release-environmentalists-protest-against-zumas-plans-for-our-coast/). Accessed: 1 November 2017.

Engel, U. and P. Nugent, eds. 2009. *Respacing Africa*. Leiden and Boston, MA: Brill.

Engineering News. 2014. 'Jacob Zuma: Address by the President of South Africa, at the launch of Operation Phakisa Big Fast Results Implementation Methodology, Inkosi Albert Luthuli International Convention Centre, Durban (19/07/2014)', 19 July (http://engineeringnews.co.za/print-version/sa-jacob-zuma-address-by-the-president-of-south-africa-at-the-launch-of-operation-phakisa-big-fast-results-implementation-methodology-inkosi-albert-luthuli-international-convention-centre-durban-19072014-2014-07-19). Accessed: 1 November 2017.

Farlam, I.G.et al. 2015. *Marikana Commission of Inquiry: Report on Matters of Public, National and International Concern Arising out of the Tragic Incidents at the Lonmin Mine in Marikana in the North West Province*. South African Human Rights Commission, Pretoria (www.sahrc.org.za/home/21/files/marikana-report-1.pdf). Accessed: 1 November 2017.

Feinstein, A. 2010. *After the Party: Corruption, the ANC and South Africa's Uncertain Future*. London: Verso.

Fine, B. 2011. 'The developmental state?' In B. Maharaj, A. Desai and P. Bond, eds, *Zuma's Own Goal: Losing South Africa's 'War on Poverty'*. Trenton, NJ: Africa World Press, 101–124.

Fombad, M.C. 2015. 'Governance in public–private partnerships in South Africa: Some lessons from the Gautrain', *Journal of Southern African Studies*, 41(6), 1199–1217.

Frankel, P.H. 2013. *Between the Rainbows and the Rain: Marikana, Migration, Mining and the Crisis of Modern South Africa*. Bryanston: Agency for Social Reconstruction.

Freund, B. 2010. 'Development dilemmas in post-apartheid South Africa'. In B. Freund and H. Witt, eds, *Development Dilemmas in Post-Apartheid South Africa*. Scottsville: University of KwaZulu-Natal Press, 1–31.

Gelb, S. 2010. 'Macroeconomic policy and development: From crisis to crisis'. In B. Freund and H. Witt, eds, *Development Dilemmas in Post-Apartheid South Africa*. Scottsville: University of KwaZulu-Natal Press, 32–61.

Giliomee, H. 1998. 'South Africa's emerging dominant-party regime', *Journal of Democracy*, 9(4), 128–142.

Grant, J.A., W.R.N. Compaoré and M.I. Mitchell, eds. 2015. *New Approaches to the Governance of Natural Resources: Insights from Africa*. Houndmills: Palgrave Macmillan.

Habib, A. 1997. 'From pluralism to corporatism: South Africa's labour relations in transition', *Politikon*, 24(1), 57–75.

Haque, M.S. 2011. 'Structures of New Public Management in Malaysia and Singapore: Alternative views', *Journal of Comparative Asian Development*, 1(1) , 71–86.

Hönke, J.et al. 2013. 'Business, governance and government in South Africa: The legacy of apartheid'. In T. Börzel and C. Thauer, eds, *Business and Governance in South Africa: Racing to the Top?* Basingstoke: Palgrave Macmillan, 18–38.

IDEA. 2007. *Political Parties in Africa: Challenges for Sustained Multiparty Democracy*. Stockholm: International Institute for Democracy and Electoral Assistance.

Johnson, C. 1999. 'The developmental state: Odyssey of a concept'. In M. Woo-Cumings ed., *The Developmental State*. Ithaca, NY: Cornell University Press, 32–60.

Johnson, R.W. 2015. *How Long Will South Africa Survive? The Looming Crisis*. London: Hurst.

Kalinowski, T. 2008. 'Korea's recovery since the 1997/98 financial crisis: The last stage of the developmental state', *New Political Economy*, 13(4), 447–462.

Karwowski, E. 2015. 'The finance-mining nexus in South Africa: How mining companies use the South African equity market to speculate', *Journal of Southern African Studies*, 41(1), 9–28.

Khalid, A. and S. Nabiha. 2008. 'New public management in Malaysia: In search of an efficient and effective service delivery', *International Journal of Management Studies*, 15, 69–90.

Kim, Y. and J. van der Westhuizen. 2015. 'Why corporatism collapsed in South Africa: The significance of NEDLAC', *Africa Spectrum*, 50(2), 87–100.

Kings, S. 2015. 'SA gung ho about mining oceans', *Mail & Guardian*, 3 July.

Lawrence, A. 2013. 'Neoliberalism, mineral resource governance and developmental states: South Africa in comparative perspective'. In J.N. Singh and F. Bourgouin, eds, *Resource Governance in Developmental States in the Global South: Critical International Political Economy Perspectives*. Basingstoke: Palgrave Macmillan, 40–60.

Lee, H. 2015. 'Affirming action in Malaysia and South Africa: Contrasting structures, continuing pursuits', *Journal of Asian and African Studies*, 50(5) , 615–634.

Lipton, M. 1985. *Capitalism and Apartheid: South Africa, 1910–84*. Aldershot: Gower.

Lodge, T. 2009. 'The South African developmental state?', *Journal of Southern African Studies*, 35(1), 253–261.

Lodge, T. 2014. 'Neo-patrimonial politics in the ANC', *African Affairs*, 113(450), 1–23.

Makokera, C.G. 2015. *South African Economic Diplomacy: Engaging the Private Sector and Parastatals*. Pretoria: Institute for Security Studies.

Malikane, C. 2016. 'Who is in charge of the economy of the developmental state? The state, economic power and the National Development Plan'. In D. Plaatjieset al., eds, *State of the Nation: South Africa 2016: Who Is in Charge? Mandates, Accountability and Contestations in the South African State*. Cape Town: HSRC Press, 159–180.

Marais, H. 2001. *South Africa: Limits to Change: The Political Economy of Transition*. 2nd ed. London andNew York: Zed Books; Cape Town: UCT Press.

Marais, H. 2011. *South Africa Pushed to the Limit: The Political Economy of Change*. London andNew York: Zed Books.

Masters, L. and E. Kisiangani, eds. 2010. *Natural Resources Governance in Southern Africa*. Pretoria: Africa Institute of South Africa.

Matthee, H. 2015. *Zuma's Hybrid Regime and the Rise of a New Political Order: The Implications for Business and NGOs*. Durban: South African Monitor.

McKay, D. 2016. 'Mining leaders worry Phakisa is just talk', *Miningmx*, 3 November (www.miningmx.com/news/markets/14256-mining-leaders-worry-phakisa-is-just-talk/). Accessed: 1 November 2017.

Mytleka, L.K., V. Msimang and R. Perrot, eds. 2015. *Earth, Wind and Fire: Unpacking the Political, Economic and Security Implications of Discourse on the Green Economy: An Integrated Policy to a Green Economy*. Johannesburg: Mapungubwe Institute for Strategic Reflection.

Nattrass, N. and J. Seekings. 2016. 'Trade unions, the state and "casino capitalism" in South Africa's clothing industry', *Review of African Political Economy*, 43(147), 89–106.

NPC. 2011. *National Development Plan: Vision 2030*. Pretoria: National Planning Commission.

Padayachee, V. 2008. 'Capitalism of a special type? South African capitalism before and after 1994', *Journal für Entwicklungspolitik*, 24(4), 50–77.

Parliamentary Monitoring Group. 2013. 'Mineral and Petroleum Resources Development Amendment Bill (B15–2013)' (https://pmg.org.za/bill/551/). Accessed: 1 November 2017.

Parliamentary Monitoring Group. 2015. 'Operation Phakisas offshore oil and gas exploration: Department of Mineral Resources briefing', 4 August (https://pmg.org.za/committee-meeting/21235/). Accessed: 1 November 2017.

Parliamentary Monitoring Group. 2016. 'Marine Spatial Planning Bill (X-2016)' (https://pmg.org.za/bill/631/). Accessed: 1 November 2017.

Parsons, R. ed. 2009. *Zumanomics: Which Way to Shared Prosperity in South Africa? Challenges for a New Government*. Auckland Park: Jacana.

Pretorius, L. 1996. 'Relations between state, capital and labour in South Africa: Toward corporatism?', *Journal of Theoretical Politics*, 8(2), 255–281.

Public Protector. 2014. *Secure in Comfort: Report on an Investigation into Allegations of Impropriety and Unethical Conduct Relating to the Installation and Implementation of Security Measures by the Department of Public Works at and in Respect of the Private Residence of President Jacob Zuma at Nkandla in the KwaZulu-Natal Province*. Report No. 25 of 2013/2014 (www.publicprotector.org/library%5Cinvestigation_report%5C2013-14%5CFinal%20Report%2019%20March%202014%20.pdf). Accessed: 16 February 2016.

Public Protector. 2016. *State of Capture: Report on an Investigation into Alleged Improper and Unethical Conduct by the President and Other State Functionaries Relating to Alleged Improper Relationship and Involvement of the Gupta Family in the Removal and Appointment of Ministers and Directors of State-owned Enterprises Resulting in Improper and Possibly Corrupt Award of State Contracts and Benefits to the Gupta Family's Businesses*. Report No. 6 of 2016/2017 (www.news24.com/SouthAfrica/News/download-the-full-state-of-capture-pdf-20161102). Accessed: 18 December 2016.

Royeppen, A. and F.A. Kornegay, Jr. 2015. *South(ern) Africa and the Indian Ocean–South Atlantic Nexus: Blue Economy and Prospects for Regional Cooperation*. Johannesburg: Institute for Global Dialogue.

SA Government. 2015. 'President Jacob Zuma provides progress report on Operation Phakisa', 12 August (www.gov.za/speeches/president-zuma-provide-progress-report-operation-phakisa-12-aug-2015-0000). Accessed: 1 November 2017.

SA Government. 2016. 'President Jacob Zuma: Address on Operation Phakisa: Oceans Economy initiatives', 8 April (www.gov.za/speeches/president-jacob-zuma-address-operation-phakisa-oceans-economy-initiatives-8-apr-2016-0000). Accessed: 1 November 2017.

SA Government News Agency. 2015. 'State of the Nation Address 2015', 12 February (www.gov.za/president-jacob-zuma-state-nation-address-2015). Accessed: 1 November 2017.

SAMSA. 2016. 'Maritime sector industry clustering: from competition to synergy', 7 June (https://blog.samsa.org.za/2016/06/07/maritime-sector-industry-clustering-from-competition-to-synergy/). Accessed: 1 March 2017.

Sarakinsky, I. 1995. 'Review essay: Rethinking the economy/state debate in South Africa, 1948–1961', *Politikon*, 22(1), 79–92.

Satgar, V. 2014. 'South Africa's emergent "green developmental state"?', in M. Williams, ed., *The End of the Development State?*New York and Abingdon: Routledge, 126–153.

Shelton, G. 2009. *Korea and South Africa: Building a Strategic Partnership*. Braamfontein: Institute for Global Dialogue.

Siddiquee, N.A. 2006. 'Public management reform in Malaysia: Recent initiatives and experiences', *International Journal of Public Sector Management*, 19(4), 339–358.

Sinwell, L. 2011. 'Rethinking South Africa's transition: From transformative to mainstream approaches to participatory development', *Journal of African Studies*, 70(3), 359–375.

Southall, R. 1998. 'The centralization and fragmentation of South Africa's dominant party system', *African Affairs*, 97(389), 443–469.

Southall, R. 2008. 'The ANC for sale? Money, morality & business in South Africa', *Review of African Political Economy*, 35(116), 281–299.

Southall, R. 2014. 'From liberation movement to party machine? The ANC in South Africa', *Journal of Contemporary African Studies*, 32(3), 331–348.

Spamer, J. 2015. 'Riding the African blue economy wave: A South African perspective'. Mimeo, 4th IEEE International Conference on Advanced Logistics and Transport (ICALT).

Stadler, A. 1987. *The Political Economy of Modern South Africa*. London: Croom Helm.

Ujuh. 2014. 'Zuma: On adaptation of Malaysian "Big Fast Results"', 24 July (www.ujuh.co.za/zuma-on-adaptation-of-malaysian-big-fast-results/). Accessed: 1 November 2017.

UNECA. 2011. *Economic Report on Africa 2011: Governing Development in Africa – the Role of the State in Economic Transformation*. Addis Ababa: African Union/UN Economic Commission for Africa.

UNECA. 2012. *Unlocking Full Potentials of the Blue Economy: Are African SIDS Ready to Embrace the Opportunities?* Addis Ababa: UN Economic Commission for Africa.

UNECA. 2016. *Africa's Blue Economy: A Policy Handbook*. Addis Ababa: UN Economic Commission for Africa.

Van Wyk, J. 2014. 'Defining the blue economy as a South African strategic priority: Toward a sustainable 10th province'. Paper presented at The Blue Economy and the Challenge of Maritime Security for South and Southern Africa: A Symposium on South Africa's Leadership Dilemmas in Promoting a Global South Dialogue on Governance in the Indian and South Atlantic Oceans, organised by DIRCO, IGD, Open Society and FES, Pretoria, 17–19 November (www.academia.edu/9407838/Defining_the_Blue_Economy_as_a_South_African_Strategic_Priority_Toward_a_Sustainable_10th_Province). Accessed: 1 November 2017.

Venter, R. et al., eds. 2012. *Labour Relations in South Africa*. 4th ed. Cape Town: Oxford University Press.

Walker, T. 2014. 'Avoiding the siren's song: Will Operation Phakisa deliver prosperity? South Africa is implementing a plan that, if successful, could shape African maritime development', Institute for Security Studies, Pretoria, 28 November (www.issafrica.org/iss-today/avoiding-the-sirens-song-will-operation-phakisa-deliver-prosperity). Accessed: 1 November 2017.

Worthington, R. 2015. 'A brief analysis of climate change and energy politics in South Africa leading up to Paris COP 21', 12 October (www.boell.de/sites/default/files/uploads/2015/11/analysis_of_cop_21_south-africa_positioning.pdf). Accessed: 1 November 2017.

4 The dynamics and processes involved in the emergence of participatory mining codes in Cameroon

Erika Tchatchouang

Introduction

The paradox of population poverty alongside a rich subsoil remains a reality. According to the World Bank (2016), nearly 3.5 billion people live in countries rich in hydrocarbons or mineral resources and 30 per cent of the world's reserves are concentrated in Africa, with 10 per cent of oil reserves and 8 per cent of natural gas reserves. Unfortunately, in most of these countries, this wealth is accompanied by conflict, misery, violation of human rights, destruction of the environment, corruption and so on. Furthermore, the digging and development of mines has negative and often irreversible consequences on the environment and society, including the destruction of ecosystems as a result of toxic waste, land expropriation leading to forced displacement of populations, influx of foreign workers to areas of mining activity, abandonment of farming, public health problems and so on. Nevertheless, the extractive sector is the base on which many countries, particularly African countries, have resolved to build their economic development, given the economic constraints many of these countries have faced and the promise of rapid income generation through mining. It has always been linked to the challenges and stakes of socio-economic development of these countries, thereby constituting an important element of their policies and strategies to fight poverty that are implemented by local, regional and international institutions.

Boosted by the development of its natural resources, Africa has known sustained economic growth for more than a decade, which should help lift it out of the condition of 'underdevelopment'. Giants such as Nigeria and South Africa, as well as small states like Equatorial Guinea and Botswana, have all enjoyed significant growth (IMF 2015). The extraction of oil, diamonds, gold, bauxite, coltan and so on has contributed significantly to this growth, or represents the bulk of state revenues. This is certainly the case in Congo, where oil represents more than 75 per cent of the state budget and more than 80 per cent of the country's exports.[1] Mining companies can also contribute to the development of basic social services in mining communities (water supply, electricity supply, transport, school buildings, health and sports facilities, etc.) through public–private partnerships. The establishment and development of mines provides opportunities to strengthen local planning and territorial management capacities. However, in order to seize such opportunities and prevent or at least mitigate the negative effects of extractive resource development, an appropriate legal framework for the sector is needed.

Industrial mining during the colonial period in Africa led to legislation to regulate this very lucrative sector. From the 1960s, African nationalists' demands for independence emphasized, among other issues, a return of natural resources to the state as a manifestation of national sovereignty. This also led to the development of new legal frameworks for the extractive sector to help it adapt to the needs of the newly independent states. In Cameroon, this meant moving from a rather fragmentary regulation (Law 64/LF/3/1964) to effective and complex mining codes that are more inclusive with respect to the domains managed by the law.

Considering the evolution of postcolonial mining law in sub-Saharan Africa, three main stages can be distinguished: the genesis of mining codes followed by their adaptation to structural adjustment plans (SAPs) and then to poverty reduction strategies (PRSs). These steps can be traced to three generations of extractive codes. With the mining boom in Africa, the sector's legal framework is scalable and has resulted in recent years in increasingly participatory mining codes. This participatory character reflects the strong will of African governments – under pressure from monitoring bodies and international institutions that demand more transparency and accountability in the extractive sector – to increase the state's benefits while also increasing the sector's attractiveness vis-à-vis investors, mainly foreigners. A procedure that is ordinarily governed by the sovereign power of the state is thus open to stakeholders who are normally subject to the law – civil society, the media and mining companies themselves – which through their inclusion become co-legislators. Therefore, the state appears to concede some of its sovereignty.

What is the significance of this process of developing participatory mining codes? In this chapter I seek to analyse the dynamics that have redefined the process of gestation or modification of mining codes for the extractive sector by the association of other actors such as civil society and companies, making them new legislators.

The gestation and/or revision of the legislation governing extractive activity are of major interest for optimizing the availability of state revenues in this sector so that they support the development of the country. First, government revenues originate from standard taxes (taxes and duties), but also come from sector-specific mechanisms that pay for the use of resources for commercial purposes and the good performance of the market (royalties, payments in kind, premiums, government participation, rents). Taking into account the competitive environment and the weakness of its capacity to develop its own extractive resources, the state creates an attractive tax environment for investors by introducing tax incentives and tax exemptions that can greatly diminish its income. Beyond pecuniary considerations, the legal texts governing mining activities are the prime means of guaranteeing and protecting the environment and the fundamental rights of populations affected by the development of mining resources.

Given the significance and unique challenges of the extractive sector, a new wave of reform of mining codes has emerged, with the aim of generating more income for the state and improving the governance of the sector as a whole (see MEADD and MEF 2015, i).

Here, I analyse – on the basis of interviews with the actors involved and documentary research – the dynamics and processes involved in the emergence of participatory codes, specifically the Cameroonian Mining Code, by highlighting the advantages and limitations with respect to the clearly stated objective of capitalization of foreign direct investment. I begin with a historical overview of the political and economic environments in which African mining codes have been designed since independence, before focusing on the case of Cameroon.

Conventional gestation of the three generations of extractive codes: the search for foreign direct investment

As early as the 1980s, embedded in the remodelling and reorientation of national economic policies, a wave of renovations of the legal and regulatory frameworks governing the extractive sector in sub-Saharan Africa – particularly in countries where mining had been truly significant up to that point – was prompted and facilitated mainly by the World Bank.

The first mining codes were introduced in mineral-rich African countries in the 1980s, consecrating the first generation of mining codes (Campbell 2008). Corollaries to the structural adjustment programmes imposed by the World Bank, this first generation of mining codes enshrined in law the planned and almost complete withdrawal of the state from the management of the sector. Ghana, where the exploration of gold began long before colonization, perfectly illustrates the effects of this approach. At the time, the government sought to improve the country's declining financial situation and reduced Ghana's budget deficit through the reform of (mainly gold) mining with two decisive steps:

- Restructuring collieries in operation by allowing means of rehabilitation through loans granted by multi- and bilateral donors, as well as facilities and guarantees granted by the government.
- Massive privatization of public mining enterprises, manifested, on the one hand, by systematic disengagement of the state through the sale of its shares in the private sector[2] and, on the other hand, by the state's withdrawal from mines over which it had full control, with retention

of only a 10 per cent share (free equity) in each enterprise, as required by law.

Although this first-generation code allowed Ghana to expand its mining sector with some positive economic consequences (the development of different sectors of activity, such as food supply, transport, production of explosives, titration laboratories, etc.), the non-extractive economy did not benefit (Eberhardt and Teal 2010, 44). The extractive revenues of the state have suffered considerable limitations due to excessive exemptions and incentives; above all, mining has only 'served to shake the rights of most vulnerable groups (rural populations, women and children)' (Diallo 2014, 207). Indeed, the development of extractive resources has paved the way for the expropriation of populations who have been dispossessed of their ancestral lands without any (or at best with insufficient) compensation. Usually from deeply rural areas, these people tend to have little education and therefore do not know their rights and cannot claim them. Beyond their economic rights (to land, property, access to water, etc.), their right to a healthy environment has been violated by substantial and almost permanent environmental damage. As extractive resources were exploited, environmental concerns were virtually ignored.

To readjust the mining sector, a second generation of mining codes was once again pushed through by international donors. For example, in the late 1980s and early 1990s, the World Bank encouraged Guinea to adopt environmental protection policies through implementation of a National Environmental Action Plan (NEAP) to complement the country's Mining Code (World Bank 2010, 34–35). The basis for this incentive was the need to address environmental damage caused by mining sector.

The first NEAP, enacted in 1993, was a somewhat confused attempt to draw attention to the negative effects of mining on the environment. The second, which was promulgated in 1994, backtracked on the assumption that much of the damage to the environment was due to mining, suggesting instead that it was due to population growth. In fact, the international financial institutions (IFIs) that guided Guinea through this process emphasized the need to establish a legal framework that was favourable to foreign direct investment (FDI). For the IFIs, environmental problems had to be subject to the will of mining companies that were capable of reducing them, with allocation of facilities that would enable the development of their activities, rather than restricting them through the introduction of coercive and binding measures (World Bank 2010). In other words, environmental issues come under the auspices of purely voluntary corporate social responsibility (CSR), as do the fundamental rights of local populations, which are still not explicitly taken into account in the regulation of mining sector.

Due to the disappointing results of this second generation of codes – which once again did not provide the state with the anticipated returns, did not satisfy investors, and were decried by civil society and criticized by advocacy groups – a third generation of mining codes arose, as illustrated by the case of Mali. As the country's SAPs came to an end, Mali started to specialize in the development of its extractive industry (first gold, then bauxite and manganese), which became its first sector of activity for economic development in the 1990s. However, despite all the measures that have been introduced, the mining sector still contributes little to the development of the country; worse, the Malian state has gone from being the sole owner to a minority shareholder in the exploitation of its own subsoil, sometimes receiving minimal income from resource extraction. The Malian Mining Code of 1999 is entirely consistent with the PRSs deployed in many heavily indebted poor countries (HIPCs; see Idrissa et al. 2002, 292).

PRSs have been realized through the establishment of a governance framework that favours partnerships approach between the state, donors, investors and civil society actors. The Malian Mining Code has broadly increased fiscal incentives mainly with the aim of stimulating FDI and has increased the state's share of profits by introducing the notion of priority dividends which require the granting of 10 per cent of profits to the state, but has still failed to guarantee consistent income for the state. Nevertheless, it is more explicit in the constraints it places on the companies, in transparency and, to some extent, in the distribution of benefits and protection of environment. For instance, Article 80 stipulates that requests for authorization/permits must be submitted to an environmental and social impact assessment. However, there have been no corresponding, significant developments regarding human rights.

> In fact, the introduction of mining code in 1999 served only to encourage private investment from abroad, through tax breaks granted to mining companies. While there has been a rush of foreign investors into the gold sector and a significant increase in gold production and export volumes as well as growth in exploration spending, the valuation of domestic gold potential has benefited neither local communities, which are often excluded from their natural environment, nor the national economy as a whole. In reality, the only directly perceptible effects of the development of Malian mining sector are limited to harmful social and environmental impacts and the growing impoverishment of communities at the national level.
>
> (Diallo 2014, 207)

Cameroon's first Petroleum Code (Law No. 99/013 of 24 December 1999) and first Mining Code (Law No. 001 of 16 April 2001, initiated by the Ministry of Mines, Water and Energy but written by a private firm, IMC (International Mining Consultants Ltd), and implemented with World Bank funding) both fall within the third generation of extractive codes. These two pieces of legislation repealed the provisions that had hitherto governed the extractive sector in Cameroon, and they remained focused on the industrial exploitation of oil and mines. The earlier provisions were: Act No. 64/LF/3 of 6 April 1964, relating to mineral substances of the Federal Republic of Cameroon, and Act No. 78/24 of 29 December 1978, which had established the base, rates and method of collecting fixed duties, royalties and mining taxes.

The new regulations, in addition to being richer and more detailed in quantitative terms than the old ones, addressed contemporary issues that were becoming increasingly important to civil society with respect to sustainable development (protection of the environment and recognition of the status of mining artisans). But they still hoped to attract FDI by outlining several new total and partial exemptions, freedom of capital transfer and greater income for foreign investors. This was highly detrimental to the state, because it could no longer hold more than a 10 per cent share in any mining company established in Cameroon. Therefore, the state was deprived of consistent income and civil society was left dissatisfied, too.

The three types of codes detailed above were all initiated in the 'classic' manner by political legislators in their respective states: the drafting was done by the supervisory ministry or by a specialized cabinet under its purview, then submitted for parliamentary approval. No entity other than the government was involved in their elaboration because legislation falls under the exclusive prerogative of parliament and the public administration understood in its broad sense, as provided for in Cameroon's constitutional law No. 96/06 of 18 January 1996, which revised the Constitution of 2 June 1972, in Article 25: 'The initiative of the laws belongs concurrently to the President of the Republic and the members of the Parliament.'

The relationship between the state and the private sector is highly dependent on the economic objectives and strategies of the former. After independence, Cameroon prioritized investment in the agricultural sector, but following a number of economic crises and their negative consequences, economic diversification was pursued to aid recovery and guarantee against shocks generated by falls in the prices of cocoa and coffee, the country's main export products at the time. The Cameroonian subsoil therefore represents an alternative resource from which the state hopes to prosper.

In the first generation of codes, in general terms, the relationship between the state and the private sector was akin to offering incentives by removing all possible barriers that could hinder the arrival of private investors. The failure of SAPs and the persistent decline of cash crops reinforced the idea that states had to develop the mining sector, despite the environmental damage it causes. The second generation of codes formed part of a strategy of strengthening the position of the mining sector in the economy as a whole while also paying some attention to environmental concerns. The principal aim remained to attract as many investors as possible, but with the hope that they would pay more attention to the environment. Finally, the third generation of codes still pursued the strategy of strengthening the country's economy through the generation of revenues from extractives, while learning from the mixed successes of the first two generations of codes.

All these three categories of reforms resulted in legislation that constitutes the backbone of the mining sector today. Given that they were initiated and implemented by the state, the three generations of extractive codes were purely the result of the state's sovereign action. As Bonnie Campbell emphasizes: 'These reforms have to a certain extent helped to stimulate and revitalize Foreign Direct Investment [...] but paradoxically have led in many countries to lower norms and standards in areas critical to economic and social development and for the protection of the environment' (Campbell 2004, 7).

After three decades of reform, the mining codes of most of the countries of sub-Saharan Africa still fall well short of the promises and prospects formulated by donors in the early 1980s for sustainable development in the region as they largely neglect protection of the environment and especially protection of human rights. Nevertheless, the mining sector has gained a prominent position in the economy of every country that has chosen to develop it.

Derogatory gestation of the fourth generation of extractive codes: quest for a consensus among the various stakeholders in the sector

The extractive sector has indeed supported increasing economic growth over the last fifteen to twenty years in Africa. Yet, the continent's population is stagnating in poverty, as is indicated by the relatively low positions on the human development index (HDI) of African countries that are rich in extractive resources. In 2015, out of a total of 188 countries, Botswana ranked 106th, Cameroon 153rd, DRC 176th, Equatorial Guinea 138th, Gabon 110th, Guinea 182nd, Mali 179th, Nigeria 152nd, Niger 188th and so on (UNDP 2015). The HDI aggregates the performance of each state in various social fields, including health, education, nutrition and so on. In general, countries that are rich in natural resources tend to rank lower than those that are not (UNDP 2015, 30).

Ongoing poverty even in periods of rapid economic growth implies fragile development, rendered ephemeral by the non-renewable nature of extractive resources and the permanence of extremely harmful environmental damage caused by their development. What Africa is seeking is *sustainable* development (AfDB *et al.* 2015, 2–4): that is to say, economic development that is associated with the well-being of populations and the preservation of an optimum living environment for them. In other words, sustainable development implies reconciling economic growth with effective environmental protection and people's perpetual enjoyment of their fundamental rights, as they are the recipients and ultimate objects of development. In the opinion of attentive observers from civil society and various IFIs (World Bank, AfDB, etc.), mining contracts – which comprise specific legal provisions that supplement the general mechanisms of the mining codes – continue to be poorly negotiated. For the most part, while these contracts have attracted foreign investment via substantial incentives and tax exemptions, they have failed to optimize profits for the state, and, even worse, have threatened people's fundamental rights and the environment. As Dembélé (2000) writes, 'Environmental problems have been taken into account when negotiating contracts with operating companies, by implementing environmental restoration projects, but one should recognize that the implementation of genuine restoration and environmental programs remains rather timid.'

While many African nations offer lucrative tax breaks in their efforts to attract FDI for extractive projects, mining companies look beyond these tax breaks and benefits to assess the viability and profitability of each project; they are also influenced by factors such as business environment, a country's security situation, the presence of a reliable workforce and so on. Well-structured and clear legislation, a healthy business environment that is relatively free from corruption, a stable country where the safety of foreign workers and company facilities are not threatened, adequate transport infrastructure and reliable, affordable energy and water supplies all come into play when companies consider investing in a country. Hence, although an attractive tax environment can be important, it is not imperative. There is no need for African states to deprive themselves of valuable revenue by offering over-generous tax concessions to foreign firms, as the Africa Progress Panel (2013, 64–65) has highlighted. This practice was especially prevalent in the 1990s because of the unfavourable economic environment for African countries, but it continued even when the economic situation improved and the projects became highly profitable, resulting in substantial losses of revenue for the nations concerned.

There are three main actors in the development of extractive resources, and they have very different but complementary visions. The extractive companies seek to maximize profits and always hope to operate under the lowest regulatory burden. The state tries to maximize income to support the country's economic and social development. And civil society, which claims to represent the interests of the population, insists that the sector should make a contribution to the citizens' well-being without endangering their way of life or the environment. In an ideal world, reconciling these three contrasting priorities would lead to the sustainable development of the country: the optimization of profits from extractive activity at the lowest possible cost for both private investors and the state; the preservation of the environment and the rights of the people; and the judicious distribution of income, ideally to strengthen other sectors (economic, social, political and cultural). Unfortunately, however, preserving the environment and safeguarding people's fundamental rights is sometimes seen as incompatible with the realization of the visions of the state and the private sector.

A fundamental element in the decision-making chain of the extractive sector – the Environmental and Social Assessment – insists that the success of any extractive project, according to the visions of the state and the private sector, rests on their internalization and mitigation of the social and environmental impact of that project. Therefore, they must take the perspective of civil society into consideration. However, the inclusive balancing of these three visions is not yet sufficiently integrated within the discourse and political strategy of the state, which means that private companies are not obliged to address the concerns of civil society. Hence, there are still tensions among the three actors. Nevertheless, the increasing number of spaces for multi-stakeholder dialogue, the determination of many multinationals to present themselves as 'responsible' companies, and the growing capacity of civil society to educate the population about their rights and the importance of protecting the environment have all helped to decrease these tensions and, incidentally, have improved the governance of the extractive sector.

Beyond pecuniary considerations, the legislation governing mining activities is the most important means of guaranteeing and protecting the environment and the fundamental rights of populations, although other legislation may be taken into account or more specialized. Moreover, shortcomings in state apparatus – difficulties in negotiating extractive contracts that are favourable to the state, corruption, poor knowledge of the sector among state agents in charge of calculating and collecting extractive industry revenue – highlight the inadequacy of regulation in relation to development objectives. Civil society, aided by the media, has worked tirelessly in Cameroon and throughout Africa with the aim of reformulating legislation so that it complies with international, regional, national and local requirements for the sector (Africa Progress Panel 2013, 71). In consequence, there was a new wave of reform, starting with the Malian Mining Code of 2012, which subsequently also informed the conceptual logic underlying the Cameroonian Code in 2016.

The Malian Mining Code was introduced with the aim of generating more income for the state and improving governance of the sector (MEADD and MEF 2015, i). It grants more financial advantages to the state and imposes more obligations on mining companies with regards to preservation of the environment. Similarly, Guinea (Articles 107ff. of the Mining Code), Cameroon (Articles 63ff. of the Gas Code), Côte d'Ivoire (Articles 53ff. of the Petroleum Code), the Congo (Articles 15ff. of the Petroleum Code), Benin (Article 103 of the Mining Code) and Gabon (Article 198 of the Mining Code) have made room for local content, in particular with regards to contributions to development and compensation for local populations, as well as the employment and training of local staff. This fourth generation of mining codes is characterized by its 'participatory' nature, in the sense that the revision (or elaboration) of codes has been made at the instigation of civil society or at least integrates other stakeholders' proposals, including those of civil society and extractive companies.

Civil society has been determined to make its voice heard alongside those of other stakeholders in the extractive sector. Its participation in various forums has been linked to the notion of resource nationalization, with many civil society organizations insisting that natural resources belong to the people, so the people should play a significant role in the sector's management and should benefit from its development. Obviously, the local populations who happen to live where the resources are located are of primary concern here; however, in the spirit of resource nationalization, there is also an argument that every citizen of a country with natural resources should profit from the private sector's exploitation of those resources. Civil society organizations have argued that CSR is an inadequate means of ensuring this, as it is too dependent on the will of the companies involved, so they have demanded the inclusion of local content in legislation. This local content consecrates the idea of resource nationalization by promoting the development of infrastructure for local communities, subcontracts with local businesses for services and supplies, and the preferential training and employment of locals and nationals. Privileging local supply chains accentuates resource nationalism at the local level, leading to a kind of 'regionalism' of the resource.

The promotion of local content, as well as the education and supervision of local populations by a number of civil society organizations, which themselves have received training from the German development agency GIZ (Gesellschaft für Internationale Zusammenarbeit) and other institutions, has allowed civil society to increase its control over the governance of the sector. Its intervention strategies have enabled local communities to analyse the sector's impact on their well-being and to participate in the defence and promotion of their own interests. This is the case, for example, within those communities who live in the vicinity of the Logbaba gas site in Cameroon, who have formed themselves into committees supervised by the Action Centre for Life and Earth (CAVT) and are developing their own advocacy strategies. CAVT then transmits their concerns to the relevant institutions. Hence, local content does not deprive civil society of its roles as a monitoring body in the governance of extractives, a whistleblower, and an educator and voice of the people. On the contrary, it reinforces and confirms all of those roles.

In Cameroon, after five years of pressure from civil society, the government organized a participatory workshop in Limbe from 7 to 14 March 2015 to review a preliminary draft law revising the 2001 Mining Code. Present at this workshop were civil society actors, representatives from the Prime Minister's office and various sectoral ministries (Mines, Finance, Planning, Environment, etc.), delegates from private companies via the Federation of Mining Enterprises in Cameroon and CamIron, an academic researcher and a number of traditional leaders. Prior to this workshop, some of these participants had attended an earlier workshop that had invited suggestions on the content and wording of the draft law. These proposals were then collated in the document that was discussed at the second workshop, leading to a draft law that was presented to parliament for consideration and eventual adoption. All of the parties involved, aside from the government representatives, were termed 'Consultative Parties to the Draft Mining Code'.

Initially, however, only two of Cameroon's leading civil society organizations – RELUFA (Hunger Control Network) and CED (Centre for Environment and Development) – had been designated 'consultative parties', and then only at the insistence of the World Bank. These two organizations were chosen on the basis of the quality and influence of their work with respect to improving the governance of the extractive sector in Cameroon. RECTRAD (the Network of Traditional Leaders) was involved because of its increasing interest in using some of the wealth generated by the extractive sector to improve living conditions for local populations and as a representative of the state at the local level. It supported its argument for an overhaul of the sector's tax regime with a number of studies, including one undertaken by the Columbia Centre on Sustainable Investment (CCSI), which was published by the Publish What You Pay (PWYP) Coalition. This study highlighted the low impact of tax exemptions on the quality of implementation of the Mbalam iron-ore development project and called for more transparency, accountability, local content, CSR, environmental protection and respect for people's rights. Meanwhile, the Federation of Mining Enterprises insisted that the tax and customs exemptions should be maintained or even increased, and that the procedures for granting mining titles should be simplified.

The civil society organizations also raised cultural and religious issues and demanded compensation, allowances or reparations in this regard. In particular, they asked for due consideration of worship and cultural rights as well as compensation for affected populations over rights of use. These issues were not explicitly addressed in the promulgated code, although traditional authorities and civil society organizations demanded their inclusion, even in a subtle way, in the decree that implemented the code. For example, they highlighted local communities' ritual use of sacred forests and cemeteries. In the context of the operationalization of an exploration licence, the population may accept relocation from the area that is covered by the permit, but will categorically oppose any attack on its sacred spaces. In such spaces, even if it does not 'own' the land, the local population enjoys an ancestral moral right, because sacred land cannot be possessed by anyone, and its destruction or alienation could have adverse consequences for the community.

Public administration both motivated and retained control over the elaboration of these participative codes. Simply put, and taking into account the obvious shortcomings of previous legislation, the expertise and relevance of civil society proposals, and its need to mobilize and appease investors, public administration preferred to make these other parties provisional co-legislators. These co-legislators only intervened for the extractive sector, and the public administration reserved the right to ignore any unwelcome proposals. Here, the state does not lose any sovereignty or its prerogative; it is simply assisted in the implementation by the co-legislators.

Although the initiative to invite other stakeholders to participate in the drafting of the new Cameroonian Mining Code is commendable, there was no formal process of measuring the degree to which contributions by non-state stakeholders were taken into account. It is therefore incumbent on the parties involved to undertake (or invite the government to undertake) an assessment of the level of consideration given to third-party proposals in the code that was promulgated in December 2016. Such an evaluation would help to establish the effectiveness of the participatory character of the new Mining Code and its degree of consensuality. In addition, codes often have general provisions that must be specified in implementing decrees. However, these implementing decrees sometimes take too long to come into force (allowing illegal situations to continue), may contain contradictory provisions, or may fail to respect the spirit of a proposed provision. To remedy this, third parties who contribute to the drafting of the revised code should also participate in the drafting of the implementing decree; or, better still, the two documents should be drafted at the same time.

Changes in the legal framework of the extractive sector are the result of joint action by government, civil society, IFIs, analysts and researchers, all of whom were dismayed by the shortcomings of earlier legislation and the sector's reluctance to contribute to sustainable development. In consequence, governments amended their economic policies and strategies, either independently or when encouraged to do so by IFIs. Later, monitoring bodies throughout civil society and especially the media ensured that the measures introduced by the state and the companies' activities were commensurate with sustainable development. Finally, local populations gained more confidence to assert their rights and demand a fair share of the wealth generated by the extractive sector. And certain companies were more willing to listen to them because of their desire to project an image of corporate social responsibility by presenting themselves as more accessible and stressing their credentials as protectors of both the environment and the rights of local populations.

In Cameroon, it may be said that other actors participated fully in the development of the fourth-generation codes, as many of their proposals were incorporated within the final texts. At the end of the first stage (drafting the code), all of the stakeholders were given an opportunity to assess whether their proposals had been given fair consideration. At the end of the second stage (rereading the draft code), they could verify whether the promulgation of the code had taken those proposals into account. During interviews, the organizations that participated in the review process insisted that their proposals had indeed been integrated into the legislation. A comparative reading of the code and a document that contains the civil society proposals reveals that all of the major points raised by civil society appear in the code, albeit with a few specific details missing. For instance:

- Significant progress in improving governance and transparency in the mining sector, through the requirement to respect the principles of the Extractive Industries Transparency Initiative (EITI) and the Kimberly Process (KP) that is required from mining companies (Sections 141–145).
- The right to information of riparian populations of extractive sites prior to the allocation of land to the company (Article 106).

- Local content, with the creation of a special local capacity development account that is based on the desire for fair redistribution of income from mining (Articles 164–169).
- Compensation, allowances and reparations (Articles 116–125) that significantly widen the right to compensation for populations affected by mining projects.

However, rather than giving clear, specific guidelines, the code frequently advises the reader to consult other regulations for further details. Moreover, the code cannot be applied until an application decree has been issued. Such a decree may well provide the necessary details, but it has not yet been drafted. This has left some civil society organizations dissatisfied, and they have proposed a number of provisions for inclusion in the application decree to fill the gaps in the existing code.[3]

Conclusion

As this chapter has demonstrated, the reform of regulatory frameworks in the mining sector in sub-Saharan Africa has had major implications for the design, legitimacy and implementation of mining operations, in particular because it has been accompanied by increasing violation of human rights, destruction of the environment and, above all, scarcely any of the expected benefits for society. Thus, mining codes have been constantly changed, as evidenced by the revisions carried out every decade over the past forty years, during the evolution of the mining sector. These revisions have still not addressed every outstanding issue, but they are finally moving in the right direction.

The first three generations of extractive codes, initiated and realized by the usual legislators, had the primary objective of attracting more foreign direct investment with the ultimate aim of stimulating development, without much success. However, as the case of Cameroon shows, the participation of other stakeholders, such as civil society (people's voices) and extractive companies (investors' voices), has facilitated significant improvement in the codes towards a desired consensual outcome: implementation of a legal framework in the mining sector that is sufficiently attractive for local and foreign investors, guarantees effective and adequate protection of people's fundamental rights and the environment, and ensures optimum income for the state, whose redistribution of revenue and good management will promote truly sustainable development. The next decade will determine whether this more inclusive objective has been achieved.

Notes

1 See www.portail242.info/2016-une-annee-qui-s-annonce-difficile-pour-l-economie-et-les-finances-au-Congo_a1056.html, accessed 13.10.2016.

2 The government's share of Ashanti Goldfields decreased from 55 per cent to 19 per cent between 1993 and 1998, and its stake in Ghana Bauxite declined from 55 per cent to 20 per cent over the same period.
3 Interview with three members of civil society organizations involved in the drafting of the code, Yaounde, 10.11.2017.

References

AFDB, AU and ECA. 2015. *Africa Regional Report on the MDGs*. Addis Ababa: AU.

Africa Progress Panel. 2013. *Equity and Extractive Industries in Africa, for Management at the Service of All*. Geneva: APP.

Campbell, B. 2004. Issues of new mining regulations in Africa, the second generation of mining codes Guinea: Deregulation and its consequences for the protection of the environment. In B. Campbell, ed., *Enjeux des nouvelles réglementations minières en Afrique*. Uppsala: Nordiska Afrika Institutet, 34–35.

Campbell, B. 2008. Mining as a driver of development in Africa: Some issues raised by the review of mining regulatory frameworks. Presentation at the Conference on Mining and Sustainable Development in Africa, Conakry, 9–13 June.

Dembélé, S. 2000. Environment in Mali: NGOs: partners or service providers? CCA-*Info* (newsletter of the Coordination Committee of NGOs Action).

Diallo, L. 2014. Mining of industry: Challenges and prospects for sustainable development in sub-Saharan Africa, case of the Republic of Guinea. Ph.D. thesis, Laboratoire de Recherche sur les Énergies Renouvelables, la Compétitivité et la Géopolitique (LARERCO-G), Settat: Université Hassan Ier.

Eberhardt, M. and F. Teal. 2010. Ghana and Côte d'Ivoire: Changing places. *Revue Internationale de Politique de Développement*, 1, 37–54.

Idrissa, D., J.-F. Gautier, M. Marouani and M. Raffinot. 2002. Le DRSP au Mali: 'Gagner l'argent' ou formuler une politique de développement? In J.-P. Clinget al., eds, *Les Nouvelles Stratégies internationales de lutte contre la pauvreté*. Paris: Economica, 229–248.

IMF. 2015. *Regional Economic Outlook: Sub-Saharan Africa, Facing a Degrading Environment*. Washington, DC: IMF.

MEADD and MEF. 2015*Analyse Economique du développement du secteur minier et des défis de la préservation de l'environnement et des ressources naturelles, projet initiative pauvreté-environnement du Mali*. Bamako: Gouvernment du Mali.

UNDP. 2015. *Human Development Report*. New York: UNDP.

World Bank. 2010. *Issues of New Mining Regulations in Africa*. Washington, DC: World Bank.

World Bank. 2016. *Extractive Industries Overview*. Washington, DC: World Bank. www.worldbank.org/en/topic/extractiveindustries/overview, accessed 10.12.2016.

5 The politics of LNG

Local state power and contested demands for land acquisitions in Palma, Mozambique

Padil Salimo[1]

Introduction

The early years of the 2010s confirmed Mozambique as an emerging player in the global energy sector. It was already known that the country had important reserves of hydrocarbons and several other ores, but confirmation of the existence of huge natural gas reserves in the Rovuma Basin in Cabo Delgado, Mozambique's northernmost province, amounting to 124 trillion cubic feet (tcf) (Maugeri 2014),[2] has reconfigured the political and economic landscape as ruling elites scramble for land and concessions there. Mozambique and Tanzania are the two countries in East Africa where the largest reserves of offshore natural gas have been discovered, possibly contributing to the transformation of the region into a new liquefied natural gas (LNG) supply frontier (IGU 2016; Maugeri 2014). In both countries, there are plans to build LNG plants and other related infrastructure to meet the market demand for this commodity, which is still growing despite a recent drop in price. Mozambique expects to produce about 44 million tons per year (mtpa) against Tanzania's 20 mtpa (IGU 2016, 19). Currently, there are two leading consortium companies operating in two natural gas blocks where large reserves have been found: the US company Anadarko Petroleum Corporation[3] operates in Area 1 and Italy's Eni East Africa (EEA) in Area 4. The first phase of development of LNG plants in onshore Rovuma Basin consists of two trains with capacity to produce up to 12 mtpa. The LNG developments in the Rovuma Basin will include both onshore and offshore projects. The latter will entail floating LNG trains with capacity for 2.5 mtpa (Maugeri 2014), implemented by the consortium in Area 4, with prospective investments of US $8 billion.[4]

The onshore LNG plants will be built in the Afungi Peninsula, in the district of Palma, operated by both Anadarko and Eni, with Anadarko being the key company in the project. An investment of about US$15–30 billion for construction of the first LNG trains is planned for 2022/3.[5] These investments have influenced a massive demand for land acquisition in recent years in the region of Palma, as well as steady pressure on the neighbouring district of Mocimboa da Praia, where some other facilities will be implanted to serve the natural gas logistics. The LNG project in Afungi was projected to occupy an area of 7,000 hectares, directly affecting more than 2,500 people living in the area who will have to be resettled, as well as other families from the neighbourhoods of Maganja, Senga, Palma Sede and Monjane, who should be compensated for economic losses.

Several studies on large investments in the extractive industry that are related to foreign direct investment (FDI) show two distinct effects. On the one hand, FDI creates elevated expectations relating to possible contributions to social and economic development (Melina and Xiong 2013; Deininger 2011); on the other hand, they create suspicion and fear about security of land tenure and access to resources that are indispensable for the survival of local communities (Cotula *et al.* 2009; Borras *et al.* 2011; Schoneveld 2014; Jayne *et al.* 2014). Borras *et al.* (2011), for example, argue that investments resulting in large-scale land acquisition deals are ambiguous and often produce land dispossession, livelihood loss, environmental degradation and loss of access to land and natural resources upon which local populations depend. Such a confusing mix of perceptions is exacerbated in societies where the local government authorities have limited decision-making capacity vis-à-vis national authorities (Weimer and Carrilho 2017) and therefore weak commitment to defending local interests in the face of large investments. This is a significant issue when large investments in extractives are related to large-scale land acquisition, due to their displacements of local populations and the resultant fractured access to basic livelihoods they cause, as argued by the land-grabbing literature (Cotula *et al.* 2009). This being the case, the questions are: what kind of local state emerges with large-scale investment in LNG and how does it deal with the rights and interests of local populations?

In Mozambique, recent examples of marginalization of local populations affected by coal-mining projects in Tete Province – where there have been serious violations of fundamental rights (Mosca and Selemane 2011; HRW 2013), including loss of land and other sources of livelihood – serve as a warning to local communities in the Afungi Peninsula, as well as the surrounding areas, where populations are living in uncertainty with regard to both land tenure and their livelihoods as the LNG developments loom. The economic opportunities associated with onshore LNG investments and other natural-gas-related facilities have strongly influenced an extraordinary demand for land in Palma and other locations that are strategically connected to the projects in the Rovuma Basin, such as Mocimboa da Praia and Pemba. Multinational oil companies, private sector actors and ruling elite groups have been exerting pressure on the local government officials who formally manage local land acquisitions, while, from the other side, the processes by which they are acquiring the land are contested by local communities and civil society organizations.

Hence, there is a fear that the land to be allocated in compensation may not be appropriate for agriculture and that other opportunities emerging from the large-scale investments will not benefit the local populations. This view has been influenced by a common debate around the implications of large investment in natural resources which emphasizes the negative impact on the affected communities, and therefore neglects the potential of those investments to effect positive transformation of traditional economic and social practices, as well as the way in which communities are exploring the land use.

This chapter analyses the relations between international oil companies and local populations[6] with regard to negotiation processes for compensation for lost land related to the LNG infrastructural investments. Key to the analysis is an examination of the role played by local government officials in these negotiations. The study concludes that the weakness of their bargaining position and their inability to manage the competing pressures of multinationals and ruling elites leave them unable to defend the interests of local communities, either by protecting their tenure or by securing 'a good deal' for them in terms of compensation for land.

This research is based primarily on a review of the existing literature on large-scale land acquisitions and investments in natural resources in Africa. Several interviews were also conducted in various places and institutions in Maputo and Cabo Delgado provinces. The interviews in Maputo focused on actors in the petroleum sector, both government and private; civil society organizations (CSOs); and academics. In Cabo Delgado, particularly in Pemba, Palma and Mocimboa da Praia, interviews were conducted with government officials, private sector actors, members of CSOs, local communities and others.[7] The analytical framework informing the research process is described below.

Analytical framework

The chapter utilizes political economy analysis and an analytical tool – the 'triangle of exchange relations' (Buur *et al.* 2017) – to explore the relations that occur between ruling elites, investors and local populations in the event of large investments in natural resources and land acquisition. Figure 5.1 shows all three types of relations in the framework, between: (i) ruling elites and investors; (ii) ruling elites and local communities; and (iii) investors and local communities.

As pointed out earlier, this research focuses chiefly on relations between investors and local communities.[8] These relations are based on a 'reciprocal exchange deal'. The starting point is that investors and local communities have their own expectations. An investor's wishes to obtain guarantees of stable development for the investment project; communities seek inclusion in the decision-making process leading to the establishment of projects as well as direct and indirect material benefits from their implementation. Inevitably, despite my focus on these relations, the other two types of relations will be mentioned. For example, any process involving negotiation and

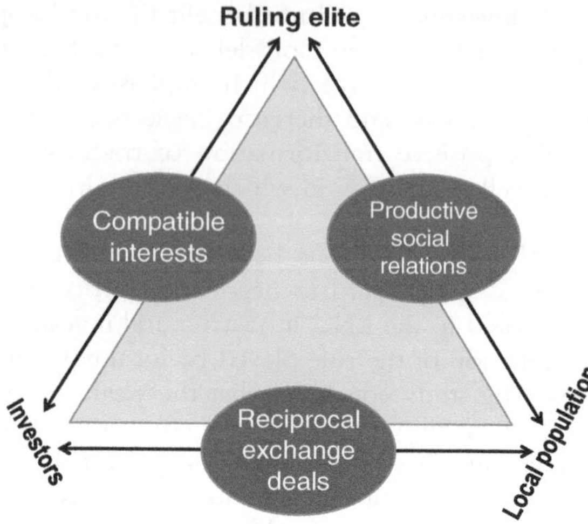

Figure 5.1 Triangle of exchange relations
Source: Adapted from Buur *et al.* (2017, 6); reprinted courtesy of the Danish Institute of International Studies

compensation will require local and/or national government involvement in specific issues, as the government plays a key role in the process. Investments in natural resources involving large-scale land acquisitions are inherently conflictual and unequal, and local populations may undermine the sustainability of investments if they are inadequately compensated (Buur *et al.* 2017, 7).

An effective relationship between investors and local populations, then, is an important factor in stable investment implementation. This relationship is established on the basis of an exchange of deals in which investors aim to gain the trust and confidence of the local population to secure the stability of their investments, and the local population demands consideration of and respect for their rights, involvement and a voice in decision-making, and, ultimately, direct and indirect benefits from the project's implementation. In order to establish an appropriate model for a productive and effective relationship, United Nations (UN) agencies, financial institutions such as the International Finance Corporation (IFC), the African Development Bank (AfDB) and other actors, including multinational companies, have adopted various guiding principles and models as frameworks for relations between investors and local populations.[9] One of these, the IFC's Performance Standard 5 (PS-5), is a key guiding principle that has been adopted by multinational oil companies.

These guiding principles for what is termed 'responsible investment' emphasize respecting tenure right-holders and protecting tenure rights against threats. They also call for consultation, participation, transparency and accountability (Zoomers 2013). Such instruments tend to refine the model of relations between investors and local populations, regardless of a call they also make on the state's responsibility within that relationship. However, and notwithstanding some changes to the general thinking that they bring into the field, in practice the implementation of these guiding instruments remains a problem, because the politics characterizing the context in which investments take place are more influential and the implementation is essentially voluntary and based on moral principles.

This chapter seeks to make a contribution to understanding some of the dynamics related to large-scale investments in LNG in Palma and the implications they may have for the quality of compensation to local communities when the interests of international oil companies and those of the ruling elite are intertwined and how this impacts on the nature of the local state.

The following section analyses the role of local government in land management under petroleum investment. Next, I explore the narrative of land acquisition in Palma and how this relates to current debates on land tenure and fair compensation for involuntary loss of land and livelihood. This discussion focuses on the relationship between LNG investors and local populations as the compensation negotiations unfolded. The chapter then analyses how the potential LNG investment is reconfiguring local state power and authority and the implications of this with respect to local communities' ability to secure fair compensation. The key argument here is that the negotiations over compensation relating to land and economic losses are intertwined with the contested nature of local government politics.

Local government and land management under petroleum investment

Mechanisms of governing land in Mozambique are entrenched between the formal and institutionalized processes embedded in the land legislation framework, petroleum legislation and other legislation relating to specific sectors, such as mining and tourism. A number of different institutions play roles (Cabral and Norfolk 2016) – a common phenomenon in African countries (Kjœr 2017; Jayne *et al.* 2014; Lund and Boone 2013) – given the wide range of issues that relate to rights of access to and use of land. In many African countries land management and land governance lie primarily in the hands of the government (Kjœr 2017; Lund and Boone 2013; Cotula *et al.* 2009). Toulmin (2005: 38–39) provides a clear explanation of the nature of ownership and rights to land in a number of African countries. In Tanzania, for example, the president holds the rights to land in the name of all Tanzanians, presupposing that he secures for all of them their rights to land. The governments of Senegal, Burkina Faso and Mali claim ownership of the land and insist that it belongs to the state domain, even though customary rights to land are recognized. In Ghana, the state owns only a small amount of land, with about 80 per cent in private hands and managed by customary chiefs, although the government has been known to confiscate customary land and control access to it and allocation of it because of potential large-scale investments (ibid.).

The legal framework in Mozambique clearly locates management and administration of land within the government at both central and local levels, including municipalities. This chapter focuses on those local government authorities that represent extensions of the central government at the local level, where they answer to the central state rather than the municipality. Primarily, administration and management of land are the responsibility of the Ministry of Land, Environment and Rural Development (MITADER), created in 2015 after the previous year's general election, which was won by Frelimo and its presidential candidate, Filipe Nyusi. Previously, for many years, responsibility had lain with the Ministry of Agriculture. At the local level, land is administrated and managed by Provincial Directorates of Land, Environment and Rural Development through the Provincial Services of Geography and Cadastre. At the district level, currently there are confusing overlaps between the roles of two institutions: the District Services of Planning and Infrastructure (SDPI) and the District Services of Economic Activities (SDAE).

The level of government responsibility in land management varies according to the system established. Land management can be centralized at the highest levels of government, or more decentralized at varying levels of local government. In some countries, traditional authorities are charged with controlling and managing land properties (Lund and Boone 2013), while in others, including Mozambique, they merely participate in the governance of land issues (Cabral and Norfolk 2016; Norfolk and Hanlon 2012; Salimo forthcoming). In Mozambique, where the land belongs to the state, the government is responsible for regulating, controlling, managing and allocating land, despite its recognition of customary land and the roles local communities and local authorities play in this regard.

In general, the customary chiefs – or traditional and/or community authorities in African countries –participate in the management of land and/or, in some cases, 'decision-making' processes because of the existing formal recognition of customary land rights (Kjær 2017; Cabral and Norfolk 2016; Lund and Boone 2013). As Weimer and Carrilho (2017) point out, the community authorities in Mozambique have little influence in this realm. Nevertheless, in some specific contexts they have played an important role in negotiating land deals with investors and other actors, including members of the ruling elite. This happened in Palma, where community land areas were allocated to private interests in deals facilitated by community authorities, or through an articulated combination with the local state authorities who, in general, seek to manipulate their support and consent to legitimize acquisitions by investors and other actors. During the fieldwork for this chapter in 2015, 2016 and 2017, some particular dynamics were apparent: while traditional chiefs' decision-making powers are relatively fragmented between the interests of local government and those of the ruling elite at the central level, local government authorities used them to persuade local communities and to secure land allocations to multinational oil companies and other investors, including members of the ruling elite.

Decisions on land allocation are organized on the basis of the amount of land involved. For areas up to 1,000 hectares, the decision is made by the provincial governor; between 1,000 and 10,000 hectares, it is made by the minister who oversees land issues; and the Council of Ministers is responsible for the allocation of any parcel of land that exceeds 10,000 hectares. This model of distribution of authority indicates local government's limited role when it comes to large-scale land acquisition, although it does play a role in procedural issues, such as administration and management, and in negotiations with local populations. A brief survey of cases from a number of African countries, including Mozambique, suggests that institutions with the power to decide on the allocation of land are significantly influenced by powerful 'clientelist' groups (Lund and Boone 2013). The fact that some groups hold considerable power due to their position of authority, or their financial, political or social influence, within an environment of weak incentives for effective management and performance supported by formal institutions (Kjœr 2017) is key to understanding how local government performs its role of managing land issues, and the incentives that drive the way in which land is allocated, negotiated and compensated.

Exploring the incentives to govern within formal, conventional institutions may not be helpful when attempting to understand the dynamics and practices of state management and governance of land. As Kjœr (2017) and Lund and Boone (2013) suggest, although institutions are important even in the context of African countries, in general the informal relationships between various groups seem to be much more significant. These characterize the processes involving land management in Mozambique, where decisions relating to the allocation of land are usually taken out of the formal procedures that are influenced by the interests of powerful groups within the ruling elite. The engagement of those powerful groups in land management varies significantly according to their interest in the likely usage of the land in question. For example, the massive investment in onshore LNG in Palma, which requires huge tracts of land and has tremendous potential for economic transformation of the area, represents a significant incentive for members of the ruling elite to position themselves above the formal institutions that govern the land, with consequent significant impact on the authority of local government land management.

In 2014/15, amidst massive demand for land in Palma, members of the ruling elite were able to secure significant tracts for themselves despite the provincial governor's prohibition on the allocation of any land in both Palma and the neighbouring district of Mocimboa da Praia (see below). The district government's official objection to the allocation of land to high-ranking members of Frelimo and their relatives was dismissed in the context of the 'paternalistic' relations that pervade state politics. District government officials also exploited the opportunity to sell land, enabled by weak enforcement institutions, the nature of politics at both the central and the local level, and the lucrative rewards for corrupt practices.[10]

LNG investments and the rush for land acquisition in Palma

On 20 December 2006, the government of Mozambique signed an exploration and production concession contract (EPCC) with the two existing concessionaires in the Rovuma Basin – Anadarko and Eni – following an announcement in July 2005 of the results of the second round of bidding for petroleum licences. The National Oil Company, ENH, the sole representative of the state in each of the petroleum exploration blocks where the companies had stakes, was also a signatory of each concession contract.[11] The massive volume of proven natural gas reserves discovered by Anadarko and Eni led to an agreement between the concessionaires and the government to develop an onshore liquefied natural gas (LNG) facility, to be utilized by both concessionaires of Areas 1 and 4. For this purpose, Anadarko and Eni, the offshore operators of Areas 1 and 4 in the Rovuma Basin, signed an agreement in December 2012 that allows both companies to work jointly in the development of LNG plants and other related infrastructure (Gqada 2013).

The LNG project's aim is to respond to the challenge for development and monetization of the gas reserves discovered in these two blocks. The location of the gas fields and their distance from the main market, in Asia, pose significant financial and technological challenges, since the conventional model of supplying natural gas via a pipeline is unfeasible. LNG technology is considered to be the best option, although it is relatively new in the industry. There were at least seven options of sites[12] for the onshore LNG infrastructure, but the Afungi Peninsula was eventually selected.[13] The government of Mozambique has indicated that it does not want the operators in Areas 1 and 4 to develop their own separate logistical infrastructures to serve the gas gathering system. Instead, it has insisted that these massive investments in natural gas production need to be used in a way that promotes the country's industrial development by investing in the private sector and facilitating job creation.[14]

Before 2010, Palma District was a remote rural region with minimal economic infrastructure. When news of the unprecedented investment in LNG in Afungi broke, the local government was completely unprepared for the enormous pressure on land acquisition. The land administration capacity was and remains inadequate, and the government has shown no sign of making the necessary investment to develop the technical and human resources capacity to deal with the phenomenon. In February 2012, the governor of Cabo Delgado Province, Eliseu Machava (who later became secretary-general of the ruling party from 2014 to October 2017), issued an official order which instructed the district governments of Palma and neighbouring Mocimboa da Praia not to grant any DUAT (Direito de Uso e

Aproveitamento da Terra; i.e. land use and exploitation rights).[15] Some actors – including several within the government – initially viewed this decision to suspend allocations of DUATs as an opportunity for the local government to strengthen its organizational and technical capacity to manage land issues, although others were concerned that the moratorium might undermine development.[16] However, it seems that some members of the ruling elite were able to exploit the situation because, while allocations of DUATs were restricted for ordinary people, the process of allocating land continued for the ruling elite and other powerful actors in the business realm. Thus, one administrative decision ensured that key members of the ruling elite maintained control of the allocation of land, particularly in Palma.

The absence of a territorial plan directing future development of the district was part of the narrative used to justify the provincial government's allocation freeze. Then, in 2016, the district government of Palma elaborated two detailed land planning documents. The first presented the area as an industrial zone, while the second focused on tourism. The provincial governor of Cabo Delgado approved both. Another three plans were drafted and approved in April 2016, detailing housing expansion plans for the villages of Nkumbi, Nkalanga and Manguna, which comprise a total area of 994 hectares.[17] Those instruments of territorial planning are key for an informed and relatively well-organized process of land management and allocation, although not necessarily sufficient to guarantee that the processes related to land acquisition will play out within the formal mechanisms and desired standards of territorial development, as many other contextual and informal practices also have roles to play. For one thing, the question of weak administrative capacity and inefficiency in land management and land governance is not limited to local government. Several studies have shown that the problem is found at every level of land administration, and the relevant bodies are seldom able to perform their statutory functions efficiently (Weimer and Carrilho 2017; Cabral and Norfolk 2016; USAID 2007; Salimo forthcoming). The political economy of land management in Mozambique is complex. To some extent, poor capacity favours both members of the ruling elite with interests in land and bureaucrats who can exploit the inefficient enforcement of the institutional framework to manipulate the allocation of land to their advantage. The contextual reality says much about the nature of the state that exists in Mozambique, as discussed earlier.

The pressure on land acquisition in Palma is related to multinational oil companies' need to secure large tracts of land for their natural gas operations. As part of the ruling elite's efforts to maintain control over land access and use amid the onshore LNG investments, in 2012 the National Oil Company (ENH) requested a parcel of land either to secure a certain amount of leverage with the international oil companies in negotiations over natural gas operations and/or to protect specific state interests that are inherently associated with land and sovereignty.[18] The requested area amounted to 25,731.14 hectares in Palma,[19] but the government guaranteed only 7,000 hectares, issuing the DUAT on 12 December 2012 to Rovuma Basin LNG Land (RBLL), a shell company created the previous month by ENH and Anadarko Mozambique Area 1 (AMA1). The remaining 18,000 hectares were not officially allocated as no DUAT for them was issued. However, local government officials and key informants within central government institutions assert that ENH does indeed hold the land.[20] In 2016, the district government of Palma made a presentation to a number of stakeholders interested in investing in Palma.[21] The slideshow suggested that the 18,000 hectares in Afungi have been reserved for ENH to use in forthcoming industrial and urban projects.

RBLL was created specifically to acquire the DUAT. Although the 7,000 hectares were allocated to RBLL for the development of onshore LNG infrastructure by operators in Areas 1 and 4 of the Rovuma Basin, RBLL is not a concessionary company of natural gas. As such, RBLL could not operationalize the aims for which it nominally acquired the land, and thus had to transfer the DUAT to an operator. This arrangement was adopted to avoid dispersal of natural gas projects along the coast of Palma, something that would have led to a loss of ENH control and therefore a reduction in the government's leverage over companies. However, because RBLL is not a concessionaire of petroleum exploration and production, it had to ask the government to transfer its assignment of DUAT to AMA1. This was done via an 'Assignment of Exploration Agreement', signed a day after the DUAT was issued to RBLL.[22] With that agreement, RBLL ceded its exploration rights to AMA1 for the implementation of the LNG project. The aim of this was twofold. First, it formalized AMA1's right to implement the project, including design, construction, operation and maintenance of all equipment related to the LNG infrastructure; and, second, it cleared the way for AMA1, as the lead company in the LNG project, to conduct an Environmental Impact Assessment, a key instrument for approval of a Resettlement Plan – on which, in turn, implementation of the entire LNG project would depend.

The idea of ENH controlling acquisition of and access to land is of considerable importance for the government, even though it has never been addressed openly. Eni has requested land in Quionga, a coastal village located close to Afungi, as a complementary site for future natural gas infrastructure, arguing that the massive volume of natural gas in the Rovuma Basin will generate demand for more land, but its request has not been approved.

Land lost to oil companies and the dynamics of compensation deals

Land acquisition by investors in Mozambique is formally defined. Any investor, including those in the oil and gas sector, must comply with the formal institutions that oversee land acquisition. The land and petroleum legal frameworks (Law 68/1997 and Law 21/2014, respectively), as well as legislation relating to resettlement resulting from economic activities (Decree 31/2012), are the key instruments that inform domestic practices related to land acquisition by investors in the oil and gas sector. Additionally, the companies are committed to abide by international standards regarding best practice, with significant emphasis on the IFC's PS-5.[23]

The LNG project in onshore Afungi Peninsula will physically and economically affect close to 6,000 families whose livelihoods depend on their use of the land and sea. The project will reduce access to both land and sea. On the land, there will be a number of total exclusion zones and a noise buffer zone, so the population that currently resides in and uses those areas will be substantially affected. Meanwhile, fishermen will have no access to the security exclusion zone around the jetties and materials offloading facility (MOF), and the pipeline corridor will be sealed during the construction phase and possibly permanently. In general, the dominant livelihood activities of the population of Afungi and the villages of Maganja, Senga, Palma Sede and Monjane revolve around agriculture and fishing.[24] The Resettlement Plan indicates that at least 1,508 households will be directly affected by implementation of the project, with 556 affected both physically and economically.[25] A further 952 households will need to be compensated economically. In addition, 3,285 fishermen, most of whom live in Afungi, will no longer have access to the open sea via the area covered by the maritime infrastructure, such as the MOF and the marine terminal services.[26]

The acquisition of the 7,000 hectares in Afungi was conducted without community consultation. The remaining 18,000 hectares requested by ENH are not currently a matter of debate as this tract of land is not directly integrated in the LNG project. Yet, it is considered an 'area reserved to the state', represented in this instance by ENH, and the people who currently occupy the land will surely be affected by future projects. Therefore, despite the absence of discussion on this particular area, it has the potential to generate considerable conflict over land rights. Returning to the acquisition of the 7,000 hectares, the local communities and civil society organizations have exerted pressure on the government to review the allocation of the DUAT, given that there was no community consultation. For instance, in 2015, Centro Terra Viva (CTV) – a civil society organization working in advocacy and research on land issues in Mozambique – commissioned an independent study to analyse the allocation of land to RBLL. This study, which was conducted by Trindade *et al.* (2015), reinforced the claims of local communities and civil society organizations relating to the lack of community consultation and labelled the process 'illegal'.

The government acknowledged that certain procedures had not been adequately followed, but that did not lead to a decision to nullify the DUAT that was awarded to RBLL and then transferred to AMA1. The multinational oil companies with stakes in RBLL continue to deny any responsibility regarding the claims, insisting that due process relating to the acquisition and transfer of the DUAT was followed according to the legislation. This being the case, the main concern moved from the acquisition of the land to performance standard procedures that were directly related to implementation of the LNG project. This time, the company, AMA1, expressed an interest in conducting a community consultation process, focusing on compensation and resettlement. Over the next two years, AMA1 held four community consultations as well as informal meetings with various community groups.

In 2015, the third community consultation was organized amid significant criticism from civil society organizations. Moreover, the committees created to represent community interests in the consultation process started to fragment as conflicting perspectives regarding the resettlement process and compensation emerged. A report by the Provincial Peasant Union of Cabo Delgado (UPC) stated that these disagreements among the committee members could be attributed to the salaries that some of them had started to receive from the companies (UPC 2016). Additionally, there has been criticism of a lack of transparency and failure to involve keys actors within the local communities and civil society organizations in the consultation process. Although the stated intention of the oil companies was to involve local communities in discussions over fair compensation, the process has resulted in a contested proposal for compensation. Community members argue that their contributions have not been given due consideration, and that the companies are dragging their heels over both compensation and resettlement packages. Land restoration and some activities relating to compensation have not been finalized, which is impacting negatively on the local residents' social and economic life, as they are not allowed to develop certain durable activities within the project site.[27] AMA1 commissioned the Centre of Agriculture and Natural Resource Studies (CEAGRE) at the University of Eduardo Mondlane in Maputo[28] to research whether the proposed compensation for agricultural crops accorded with PS-5 principles. The study recommended inclusion of a number of crops that were not mentioned in the proposed scheme, as well as an upward revision of prices of those crops that were mentioned. Although the oil companies included the local communities in some of the discussions over compensation, the proposed packages failed to meet community expectations. The villagers feel that they were sidelined in the main negotiations over compensation for their land, crops and other assets, and argue that the compensation framework represents a deal between investors and the government.

Although civil society organizations are working with the local populations in the hope of promoting their rights and strengthening their capacity to negotiate better deals with the oil companies and the government, these efforts have proved largely ineffective.[29] Despite the key role the community has been assigned in theory and needs to play in negotiating compensation, in practice its capacity to hold fair dialogue with powerful groups, such as the oil companies, is poor.[30] This is because: the local residents lack knowledge of their rights with regard to land governance and possess an insufficient understanding of the petroleum industry; the divide-and-conquer tactics described above have resulted in certain community members receiving salaries from the oil companies while others have been promised rewards by local government officials; the local government itself has generally backed the investors over questions relating to implementation of the project, with little consideration of the local communities' demands; and there was an absence of information sharing prior to the community consultations. However, the most significant factor has been the politics behind the relations between the companies and the local communities in a context where the companies are often connected with the ruling elite at the central level, with both parties far less concerned with meeting the local communities' demands than pursuing their own interests. As a consequence of these dynamics, the negotiations for compensation between the companies and the local populations are generally undermined. In practice, the key process and issues relating to the negotiations are controlled and directed mainly by the central-level ruling elite due to the magnitude of the revenues expected from the investments. Members of that elite have maintained a certain level of control over the benefits from the current project, and have done all they can to ensure that the compensation scheme will not jeopardize the implementation of future projects.

Local government's power and authority to secure fair compensation

The LNG investments have the potential to effect a reconfiguration of local government power and authority. A key question is how influential this power might be, bearing in mind the centralized nature of politics in Mozambique (Weimer and Carrilho 2017). There are many examples of large-scale investments in natural resources throughout Africa that raise serious concerns in relation to inadequate compensation and negative impacts on living standards for the affected populations (Jayne *et al.* 2014; Borras *et al.* 2011). These experiences have prompted the emergence of civil society organizations that engage with the local populations to combat poor deals and violations of their rights (Lund and Boone 2013).

The activities of these civil society organizations in the context of profound struggles over rights to the land may also challenge the existing power and authority of the local government, as Lund and Boone (2013) argue. The main question behind the power and authority of the local government in relation to land use is: who has the political power to impose one interpretation at the expense of others (Lund and Boone 2013: 2–3)? Lund and Boone suggest that prevailing interpretations of disputes over land will have implications not only for the actors involved, but also for the existing institutional arrangements that guarantee land tenure relations. Then, as these authors observe, the politics that generate any changes in the interpretations could shape authority relations in how control over land is distributed.

As discussed earlier, the process of acquiring land in Palma violated both formal institutional procedures and the basic governance mechanisms outlined in Mozambique's land legislation, and it has been strongly contested as a result. The potential delay in following the formal mechanisms for accessing the land was considered too risky for the central-level ruling elite who wanted the land, and for this sleight of hand to be accomplished, it was crucial to secure state participation and to control the mechanisms for determining land allocation. The authority to decide on the allocation of such a large area of land rests with the central government (while the administration and management processes rest with local government), *de jure*; however, *de facto*, decisions made by the powerful Frelimo ruling elite trump any formal mechanisms. For example, RBLL, the shell company to which the 7,000 hectares in Afungi were assigned, was designed to be able to integrate future concessionaires operating in the Rovuma Basin as shareholders, but the mechanisms involving land allocation bypassed the legal procedures.

Eni joined RBLL in 2014, at which point shares in the company were divided equally between Eni, ENH and AMA1.[31] This arrangement gave the government leverage in its negotiations with the multinationals via ENH's control of access to the land. The debate among the key government institutions in the petroleum sector revolved around concerns that allocating land to multinational oil companies might threaten Mozambique's sovereignty: if infrastructure for other projects was constructed along the coast to serve the natural gas operation in Rovuma Basin, ENH would have less control in a context of weak financial and technological capabilities for significant participation in these projects. In 2013, when the government refused Eni's application for a DUAT in Quionga village,[32] on the coast south of Palma, it justified its decision by saying that its preferred policy was for unification of the gas project's infrastructure in Rovuma Basin; in other words, geographical dispersal was to be avoided. In order to secure control of access to the land, the Instituto Nacional de Petroléo (INP) recommended transforming the area requested by Eni into a 'state reserve' (*reserva do estado*) and then giving ENH the role of managing it.

Clearly, against this backdrop, local government has little power to take decisions that conflict with those of the central-level ruling elite, even in the face of clear violations of formal institutional procedures. The violations occurred because certain institutional mechanisms were weak enough to be bypassed, distorting the triadic relations of Buur *et al.*'s (2017) model. Such practices, when confronted by increasing demands for fair compensation from civil society organizations and the ruling elite's responses to those demands, have contributed to a reconfiguration of local government in order to address the emerging challenges of securing deals between investors and local communities. Simultaneously, the dynamics of the relationship between these two parties are profoundly influenced by the ruling elite's interests in natural-gas-related business. One possible consequence of the civil society organizations' criticism of the way in which the land was allocated and the dissatisfaction with the mechanisms of community consultation in

Palma may have been the appointment of two new district administrators within the space of just three years. It is important to take into consideration the fact that investment in LNG represents an opportunity for the central-level ruling elite – and indeed local government – to reinvigorate the country's economy, but it also represents an important source of revenue which could be used to secure the elite's grip on power. As such, there is a danger that members of the elite will hamper local government's efforts to protect community rights and secure fair compensation for the local population.

The politics of LGN investment and the implications for local state-making

The context in which economic transformation is proceeding in Mozambique – specifically with respect to mineral and hydrocarbon discoveries – means that it is imperative to consider the promotion of foreign investment through land allocation (Cabral and Norfolk 2016; Fairbairn 2013) and the security of land tenure for local communities. Of course, the state plays the principal role in both guaranteeing local communities' security of land tenure and granting land use rights to investors. At the most basic level, it does this by enforcing the implementation of existing formal mechanisms. However, members of the ruling elite may reshape or bypass these mechanisms to serve their own interests (Khan 2010; Whitfield and Buur 2014).

As argued above, the ruling elite and other powerful groups are able to exert significant influence over land governance and land management. In this regard, Lund and Boone (2013) argue that the balance of power among those who hold various forms of institutional authority over land issues governs who is most likely to succeed in achieving their aims. This view correlates with that of Pedersen and Kweka (2017), who conclude that any research into petroleum investments and land acquisition in Africa would benefit by widening the focus to encompass the broader political economy of land and petroleum investments, rather than concentrating solely on the behaviour of oil companies, as they are unlikely to be the only – or the most important – actors with respect to how land is acquired. Such research is driven by the issue of the type of local state that is constituted as a consequence of large-scale investment in LNG and its related ability to protect local community rights within the context of that investment.

Key to understanding what drives changes at the heart of state power is recognizing the potential influence of a variety of societal forces. This being the case, the dynamics involving the multiple actors who interact with and outside the state may have a significant impact on the nature of the state that emerges in the event of large-scale natural resource investment. These multiple actors – members of the ruling elite, multinational oil companies, civil society organizations, donors and other international agencies, and local populations –all have their own interests to defend. Therefore, due to the high economic value of large-scale investments, their relations are usually conflictual, as they may need to engage in tense negotiations in relation to specific issues, such as compensation deals, future business opportunities and protecting the interests of particular groups. Decisions made by the ruling elite may serve to exacerbate this tension and generate further contestation, while the competing demands of right-holders and other important actors may constrain the state and therefore influence new paths of state-making.

For example, the oil companies must consider the interests of the central-level ruling elite in order to secure the successful implementation of their projects. Likewise, members of the ruling elite must take the oil companies' interests into account because they need to secure revenue and other benefits from the multinationals' investment in the LNG project. By contrast, both sides have largely ignored local government, which has left the latter ill-equipped to perform its principal role: protecting the local community's rights and interests during negotiations for compensation. As a result, the local population has been largely sidelined during these negotiations, weakening its already fragile bargaining position. One consequence of this is the perception within the local community that the government is the enemy of the people, while the oil companies are more open to accommodating community interests. In interviews, residents of Quitupo and Maganja in Palma expressed concerns about government corruption and insisted that they would prefer to receive their compensation from the companies rather than the state.[33] Similarly, in August 2015, during the third community consultation, representatives of the local population declared that they did not trust the government to manage the funds that had been allocated for resettlement and compensation.

Nevertheless, civil society organizations and the 'mobilized' local communities have managed to effect changes in both local and central government behaviour. In 2015, the new central administration acknowledged that CSOs had an important role to play in negotiations over compensation and resettlement. In this regard, it distanced itself from the problems of previous years – ranging from a lack of community consultation on land acquisition to an absence of transparency in the consultation process on resettlement and tension between the state and CSOs.[34]

Despite far from universal acceptance of the CSOs within the local community, they have managed to alter the state's perception of the local community's demands and indeed the role of civil society itself. Moreover, they have increased the local community's leverage during negotiations with investors by educating the local population on their rights to land and natural resources, actively defending the villagers' interests and fighting for more social and economic benefits from the LNG project.

Conclusion

This chapter has analysed the relationship between multinational oil companies (the investors) and local communities during negotiations over compensation for land lost due to LNG investments. This issue has been examined by highlighting the role played by local government in the negotiation process vis-à-vis its ability to protect the interests of the local population. My principal conclusion is that the negotiations over compensation relating to land and economic losses are intertwined with the contested nature of local government politics. In general, local government has been sidelined during these negotiations, which have been dominated by the central ruling elite and the investors. This has eroded local government authority and its ability to protect the local community's interests. Therefore, the type of state that has emerged in the wake of investment in LNG has been strongly influenced by ruling elite politics, which has both undermined and delegitimized local government. In turn, this has had a detrimental impact on the relationship between investors and local communities, which has been distorted due to lack of information and poor rights awareness, and because the ruling elite has become too influential in determining the path of negotiations over compensation.

Notes

1 Padil Salimo (padil.salimo@gmail.com; padil@ruc.dk) is Ph.D. Fellow at Roskilde University in Denmark and the University of Dar-es-Salaam in Tanzania. He is affiliated as a research associate at the Institute for Poverty, Land and Agrarian Studies – PLAAS – of the University of Western Cape, Cape Town. This research is part of his Ph.D. programme, which is funded by the Danish Ministry of Foreign Affairs under the Hierarchies of Rights Programme. The valuable comments of associate members of the Hierarchy of Rights Programme in Denmark, Mozambique and Tanzania are gratefully acknowledged.

2 The Natural Gas Master Plan (NGMP) suggests that the Rovuma Basin may contain more than 200 tcf of recoverable natural gas (Cabinet Council 2014).

3 The company's local branch is called Anadarko Mozambique Area 1 (or AMA1).

4 http://clubofmozambique.com/news/mozambique-waives-financial-benefits-for-eni-and-partners-to-initiate-us8-billion-in-natural-gas/. Accessed 15 June 2017.

5 http://clubofmozambique.com/news/anadarko-may-take-fid-mozambique-lng-next-year-come-production-around-2022-2023/. Accessed 22 July 2017. Additional information from interviews at INP indicates that investment may reach US$50 billion.

6 In this chapter the phrase 'local communities' is interchangeable with 'local populations'.

7 Fieldwork started in 2015 with several meetings held in Maputo; Cabo Delgado Province (in Pemba, Mocimboa da Praia and Palma districts). The gathering of information also involved focus group meetings with members of the local communities in Palma Sede, Quitupo, Maganja and Senga. Preliminary results of this research have been presented in a seminar and conferences at the Institute for Advanced Studies (STIAS) of the University of Stellenbosch; the Institute for Poverty, Land and Agrarian Studies (PLAAS) of the University of Western Cape; the Institute of Resource Assessment (IRA) of the University of Dar Es Salaam; and at the 5th IESE Conference in Maputo.

8 For an elaboration of the analytical framework, see Buur *et al.* (2017). The two other relations are not explored here. The first is the relation between ruling elites and investors, which is founded on the principle of 'compatible interests'. The

ruling elites have the power to decide whether the investment project goes ahead, but they also need investors to secure a source for extraction of rents that the ruling elites need to hold on to their power. Investors need support from the ruling elites for their investment project to be implemented, and to be profitable, as well as to avoid being undermined. The second is the relation between ruling elites and local communities, founded on the principle of 'productive social relations'. Local communities conceive of the state as provider of property security and guardian of individual and communal rights. Therefore, local populations should be able to expect that decisions and actions taken by ruling elites will protect their rights and interests.

9 The IFC's Performance Standard 5, on land acquisition and involuntary resettlement, is applied in cases where people are forced to move to a new location after suffering a loss of land and other resources (Jayawardena 2011; Perera 2014). The Free Prior and Informed Consent (FPIC) approach was established under the UN Declaration of Rights of Indigenous Peoples and the ILO's Convention 169 on Indigenous and Tribal Peoples, which suggest inclusion of the local population as it enshrines the idea of consent, as well as the community's right to veto the commencement of a project (Buur *et al.* 2017; Cotula 2011). The Committee on World Food Security (CFS) endorsed the Voluntary Guidelines on the Responsible Governance of Tenure of Land, Fisheries and Forests, which offers guidance on sustainable development and security of tenure for vulnerable and marginalized people. There are other models, too, such as corporate social responsibility (CSR) and social licence to operate (SLO), both of which are driven by companies. The CSR approach is generally considered to be less appropriate for the desired relationship as it is based on what companies want to offer rather than a process of clear engagement with the local population. The SLO approach introduces the idea of strengthening dialogue with the local population, but some studies argue that there is little difference between SLO and CSR (e.g. Buur *et al.* 2017).

10 In 2015, for example, the then district director of planning and infrastructure had been under investigation in a case involving the illegal allocation of lands (interview with the district administrator of Palma, July 2015).

11 See the Exploration and Production Concession Contract for Area 1 'Offshore' of the Rovuma Basin, 20 December 2006, agreed between the government, AMA 1 and ENH; and the Exploration and Production Concession Contract for Area 4 'Offshore' of the Rovuma Basin, 2006, agreed between the government, EEA and ENH. Both available at www.inp.gov.mz.

12 The sites were identified between Pemba and the Tanzanian border, with the seven then narrowed down to three: namely, the Afungi Peninsula in Palma District, the Londo Peninsula in Metuge District and the Cabo Delgado Peninsula.

13 Personal interview with key officials at INP and ENH, and confirmed with narratives in Chapter 5, 'Consideration of Alternatives', in the AMA1 socio-economic, marine and terrestrial ecology study, conducted by ERM and Impacto.

14 This is aligned to policy for industrialization through natural gas investments, as established in the Natural Gas Master Plan, approved by the government in 2014.

15 Governo da Província de Cabo Delgado, Ofício No. 33/GG/CD/2012, 27 February 2012. The same document was sent to the offices of the Head of State, Prime Minister, Minister of Agriculture and Minister of State Administration.

16 Personal interviews with senior officials at the district government in Palma, April 2017.

17 A PowerPoint presentation prepared by the district government of Palma, 20 September 2016. Complementary information obtained from personal interviews with technicians from district services for planning and infrastructure.

18 Based on personal interviews with officials in the key sectors of the government, who argued that this kind of operation was adopted, even bypassing the law, to

ensure that land was not directly allocated and controlled by multinational oil companies and therefore to guarantee that state sovereignty was not threatened. The government's intention has been to keep land for the development of natural gas infrastructure projects under the control of the National Oil Company – ENH – and thus to give this company a central role in all negotiations with multinationals.

19 The figure is confirmed by details on the map of localization annexed to the provisional DUAT allocated to Rovuma Basin LNG Land (RBLL), issued in Maputo on 12 December 2012, authorized by the Minister of Agriculture and issued by the National Directorate of Land and Forest. The document also says that the 7,000 hectares of land allocated to RBLL is unoccupied, which later became the main source of contestation by local communities and civil society organizations against the government and the multinational oil companies.

20 In interviews, members of the district government in Palma consistently mentioned that the 18,000 hectares of land have been earmarked for ENH's future projects of urban development.

21 The presentation took place on 20 September 2016.

22 That is, 13 December 2012.

23 The Environmental Impact Assessment approved by the government in 2014 and the Resettlement Plan approved in 2016 both refer to specific use of PS-5 and the government of Mozambique's Decree 31/2012.

24 See Anadarko (2015).

25 See Anadarko (2015); MITADER (2016).

26 Decree 87/2013 assigned a concession for maritime terminals and logistics in Pemba and Palma to Portos de Cabo Delgado (PCD), but Decree 4/2016 amended those rights and transferred them to concessionaries in Areas 1 and 4. This regulates how the concessionaires of the Rovuma Basin project meet the requirements of international LNG standards applicable to the Rovuma Basin project infrastructure, in both land and maritime areas, with regard to ownership rights, operation and management, including safety and maritime traffic control. The concessionaires of the Rovuma Basin project are granted exclusive rights of access and operation over maritime and land areas where the facilities are constructed, and effective control over all Rovuma Basin project infrastructure, including the LNG marine terminal and the materials offloading facility.

27 Focus group with local communities in three villages – Quitupo, Maganja and Palma – April 2017.

28 The centre was commissioned to conduct an independent study evaluating the company's proposed scheme for compensation for crops under the LNG project in order to verify whether the proposal was aligned with the 'total cost of replacement' established in PS-5. See Chiulele (2014).

29 Anadarko (2012).

30 Interviews with key actors in Quitupo and Maganja, June 2016 and April 2017.

31 'Rovuma Basin LNG Land', *Bulletin of the Republic*, Series III, No. 68, 22 August 2014.

32 In a letter of 22 April 2013 to the former Minister of Mineral Resources (Ref. No. 145/ENI/13), Eni expresses interest in obtaining DUAT for a site in Quionga and discusses the regulatory and contractual framework.

33 Interviews in Quitupo and Maganja, April 2016 and April 2017.

34 The new government took the decision to postpone the public community consultation that was scheduled to take place a few months after the government's inauguration. This decision gave the new administration time to understand the project, but more importantly it signalled a positive change in its attitude towards CSOs, which had previously been viewed as enemies of development, as the government invited them to participate as relevant stakeholders. An independent evaluation on land allocation to concessionaries in Palma, Afungi, commissioned

by CTV (see Trindade *et al.* 2015), has since been used by the government as a key document to inform the next stage of interventions in Palma. Relations with CSOs have improved, a network for consultations between government, CSOs, companies and other stakeholders has been created, and a network involving those actors has been established and consolidated to deal with land issues.

References

Alden-Wily, L. 2010. Whose land are you giving away, Mr President? Paper presented at the Annual Bank Conference on Land Policy and Administration, Washington, DC, 26–27 April.

Anadarko. 2012. *Social Investment: Community Investment Plan 2013–2014*. Mozambique: Anadarko.

Anadarko. 2015. *Resettlement Plan: Draft for Public Disclosure. Part C: Resettlement Action Plan*. Mozambique: Anadarko.

Barros, J. 2013. Mozambique. In E. Pereira and K. Talus, eds, *Upstream Law and Regulation: A Global Guide*. United Kingdom: Globe Business Publishing.

Borras, S.M.Jr., R. Hall, I. Scoones, B. White and W. Wolford, eds. 2011. Towards a better understanding of global land grabbing. *Journal of Peasant Studies*, 38(2), 209–216.

BTI. 2014. *Mozambique Country Report*. Gütersloh: Bertelsmann Stiftung.

Buur, L., M.L. Nystrand and R.H. Pedersen. 2017. The political economy of land and natural resource investments in Africa: An analytical framework. DIIS Working Paper 2017/2. Copenhagen: DIIS.

Buur, L. and H. Kyed. 2006. Contested sources of authority: Re-claiming state sovereignty by formalising traditional authority in Mozambique. *Development and Change*, 37(4), 847–869.

Cabinet Council. 2014. *Natural Gas Master Plan (NGMP)*. Adopted at the sixteenth ordinary session of the Council of Ministers, 24 June. Maputo: Government of Mozambique.

Cabral, L. and S. Norfolk. 2016. Inclusive land governance in Mozambique: Good law, bad politics? IDS Working Paper 478. Brighton: Institute of Development Studies and Swiss Agency for Development and Cooperation. https://opendocs.ids.ac.uk/opendocs/bitstream/handle/123456789/12187/Wp478.pdf;jsessionid=5E756739CC5A3F2FDD8C39AB2A25B998?sequence=1.

Chamberlin, J., T.S. Jayne and D. Headey. 2014. Scarcity amid abundance? Reassessing the potential for cropland expansion in Africa. *Food Policy*, 48, 51–65. http://dx.doi.org/10.1016/j.foodpol.2014.05.002.

Chiulele, R. 2014. *Avaliação do relatório da compensação das culturas independentes para o Project de Desenvolvimento de Gás em Moçambique (PDGM)*. Maputo: Centro de Estudos de Agricultura e Recursos Naturais, UEM.

CIP. 2016. Newsletter 38/2016. Maputo: CIP.

Cotula, L. 2011. *Land Deals in Africa: What is in the Contracts? Land, Investments and Rights*. London: IIED. http://pubs.iied.org/12568IIED.html.

CotulaL., S. Vermeulen, R. Leonard and J. Keeley. 2009. *Land Grab or Development Opportunity? Agricultural Investment and International Land Deals in Africa*. London andRome: IIED/FAO/IFAD.

Deininger, K. 2011. Challenges posed by the new wave of farmland investment. *Journal of Peasant Studies*, 38(2), 217–247. www.shus.unimi.it/wp-content/uploads/2012/01/jpeasantst_032011.pdf.

Deininger, K., F. Xia, A. Mate and E. Payongayong. 2015. Quantifying spillover effects from large farm establishments: The case of Mozambique. Policy Research Working Paper 7466. Washington, DC: World Bank Group. https://papers.ssrn.com/sol3/papers.cfm?abstract_id=2683691.

Fairbairn, M. 2013. Indirect dispossession: Domestic power imbalances and foreign access to land in Mozambique. In W. Wolford, S. Borras, R. Hall, I. Scoones and B. White, eds, *Governing Global Land Deals: The Rule of the State in the Rush for Land*. Malden, MA and Oxford: John Wiley & Sons.

Filipe, E. and S. Norfolk. 2017. *Changing Landscapes in Mozambique: Why Pro-poor Land Policy Matters*. London: IIED. http://pubs.iied.org/pdfs/17356IIED.pdf.

Gqada, I. 2013. A boom for whom? Mozambique's natural gas and the new development opportunity. South Africa: SAIIA. www.saiia.org.za/occasional-papers/349-a-boom-for-whom-mozambique-s-natural-gas-and-the-new-development-opportunity/file.

Human Rights Watch (HRW). 2013. *What is a House without Food? Mozambique's Coal Mining Boom and Resettlements*. New York: HRW.

International Gas Union (IGU). 2016. *World LNG Report: LNG 18 Conference & Exhibition Edition*. Oslo: International Gas Union.

Jayawardena, S. 2011. *Right of Way: A Journey of Resettlement*. Colombo: Centre for Poverty Analysis.

Jayne, T.S., J. Chamberlin and D.D. Headey. 2014. Land pressures, the evolution of farming system and development in Africa: A synthesis. *Food Policy*, 48, 1–17.

Khan, M.H. 2010. Political settlements and the governance of growth-enhancing institutions. Unpublished paper, SOAS, University of London. https://eprints.soas.ac.uk/9968/1/Political_Settlements_internet.pdf.

Kjœr, A.M. 2017. Land governance as grey zone: The political incentives of land reform implementation in Africa. *Commonwealth and Comparative Politics*, 55(4), 426–443. www.tandfonline.com/doi/full/10.1080/14662043.2017.1272876.

Lambert, A., M. Cabelo, P. Salimo and H. Sueia. 2013. *Midterm Review of the Malonda Program*. Stockholm: SIDA. www.sida.se/contentassets/93db82896d964bf48655d208ffc0c142/mid-term-review-of-the-malonda-program-july-2010-june-2013_3735.pdf.

Lund, C. and C. Boone. 2013. Introduction: Land politics in Africa – constituting authority over territory, property and persons. *Africa*, 83(1), 1–13.

Maugeri, L. 2014. Falling short: A reality check for global LNG exports. Discussion Paper 2014–2011. Boston: Belfer Center for Science and International Affairs, Harvard Kennedy School.

Melina, G. and Yi Xiong. 2013. Natural gas, public investment and debt sustainability in Mozambique. Working paper. Washington, DC: IMF.

MITADER. 2016. *Constatações e recomendações da Comissão Técnica de acompanhamento e supervisão do reassentamento sobre a proposta do Plano de Reassentamento da população afectada na Península de Afungi, Distrito de Palma, Província de Cabo Delgado*. Maputo: MITADER.

Mosca, J. and T. Selemane. 2011. *El Dorado Tete: os mega projectos de mineração*. Maputo: Centro de Integridade Pública.

Nhantumbo, I. and A. Salomão. 2010. *Biofuel, Land Access and Rural Livelihoods in Mozambique*. London: IIED. http://pubs.iied.org/pdfs/12563IIED.pdf.

Nolte, K., W. Chamberlain and M. Giger. 2016. *International Land Deals for Agriculture: Fresh Insights from the Land Matrix: Analytical Report II*. Bern, Montpellier,

Hamburg andPretoria: Centre for Development and Environment, University of Bern; Centre de cooperation internationale en recherche agronomique pour le développement; German Institute of Global and Area Studies; University of Pretoria.

Norfolk, S. and J. Hanlon. 2012. *Confrontos entre produtores, camponeses e investidores na Zambézia, Norte de Moçambique, no contexto de pressões relativas ao lucro em investidores europeus.* Washington, DC: World Bank.

Pedersen, R.H. and O. Kweka. 2017. The political economy of petroleum investments and land acquisition standards in Africa: The case of Tanzania. *Resource Policy*, 52, 217–225.

Perera, J., ed. 2014. *Lose to Gain: Is Involuntary Resettlement a Development Opportunity?* Mandaluyong City: Asian Development Bank.

Salimo, P. Forthcoming. The political economy of land policy implementation in Mozambique. Working paper. Cape Town: UWC.

Schoneveld, G.C. 2014. The geographic and sectoral pattern of large-scale farmland investments in sub-Saharan Africa. *Food Policy*, 48, 34–50. https://doi.org/10.1016/j.foodpol.2014.03.007.

Schreiber, L. 2017. Putting rural communities on the map: Land registration in Mozambique, 2007–2016. Working paper. Princeton, NJ: Innovations for Successful Societies, Princeton University. https://successfulsocieties.princeton.edu/sites/successfulsocieties/files/LS_Land_Mozambique.pdf.

Shearman and Sterling LLP. 2014. Mozambique's new petroleum legislation: Are investors ready to hit the gas?London: Shearman and Sterling LLP. www.shearman.com/~/media/Files/NewsInsights/Publications/2014/09/Mozambiques-New-Petroleum-Legislation-Are-Investors-Ready-to-Hit-the-Gas-PDF-091914.pdf.

Stein, H. and S. Cunningham. 2015. Land grabbing and formalization in Africa: A critical inquiry. Working Paper 124/2015. Leiden: ASC.

Toulmin, C. 2005. *Securing Land and Property Rights in sub-Saharan Africa: The Role of Local Institutions*. London: IIED.

Trindade, J.C., L. Cruz and A.C. José. 2015. *Avaliação jurídica independente aos processos de licenciamento dos projectos minerais e hidrocarbonetos*. Maputo: Centro Terra Viva. www.oam.org.mz/wp-content/uploads/Avaliacao-Juridica-Independente-aos-Processos-de-Licenciamento-dos-Projectos-Mineiros-e-Hidroca rbonetos-.pdf.

UNAC and GRAIN. 2015. *The Land Grabbers of the Nacala Corridor: A New Era of Struggle against Colonial Plantation in Northern Mozambique*. Barcelona: GRAIN. www.grain.org/article/entries/5137-the-land-grabbers-of-the-nacala-corridor.

UPC. 2016. *Consultas Públicas, Manipulação e Falta de Respeito aos Direitos das Comunidades*. Working report. Cabo Delgado: UPC.

USAID (2007). *Land Use Rights for Commercial Activities in Mozambique*. Washington, DC: United States Agency for International Development.

Weimer, B. and J. Carrilho. 2017. *Political Economy of Decentralization in Mozambique: Dynamics, Outcomes, Challenges*. Maputo: IESE.

Whitfield, L. and L. Buur. 2014. The politics of industrial policy: Ruling elites and their alliances. *Third World Quarterly*, 35(1), 126–144.

Wittmeyer, H. 2012. Mozambique's 'land grab': Exploring approaches to elite policymaking and neoliberal reform. Unpublished paper, College of Saint Benedict and Saint John's University. http://digitalcommons.csbsju.edu/polsci_students/3.

World Bank. 2011. *Rising Global Interest in Farmland: Can It Yield Sustainable and Equitable Benefits?*Washington, DC: World Bank. https://siteresources.worldbank.org/DEC/Resources/Rising-Global-Interest-in-Farmland.pdf.

Zoomers, A. 2013. A critical review of the policy debate on large-scale land acquisitions: Fighting the symptoms or killing the heart? In S. Evers, C. Seagle and K. Froukje, eds, *Africa for Sale? Positioning the State, Land, and Society in the Foreign Large-scale Land Acquisition in Africa*. Leiden and Boston, MA: Brill.

6 A radical mineral policy with retribalisation?

Mining and politics of difference in rural South Africa

Sonwabile Mnwana

Introduction

State formation is a contested process, particularly at the nexus of resource extraction and wealth distribution. National and local institutional arrangements that regulate social relations over property are central to the understanding of contemporary dynamics of state power and distributional struggles in Africa. This contribution illustrates this argument with the case of South Africa's post-apartheid mineral policy reform. It demonstrates how this reform, particularly its redress mission, has been significantly compromised by the local institutions that shape the structure of power at the local level. Although the 'new' mineral policy has nationalised all minerals rights and placed them under state custodianship, rural land in the former 'homelands' remains largely under the control of traditional authorities. The rural expansion of the platinum industry has coincided with post-apartheid legislators' attempts to redefine residents in these communal areas as 'traditional communities' ('tribes'), under local chiefs. The post-apartheid state, through several pieces of legislation, has crystallised power over land and landed resources into the institution of traditional authority. Subsequently, chiefs, as assumed custodians of communal resources, have become the mediators of mineral-led development, and mining deals. This has triggered significant conflict over the mineral-rich land and mining revenues. New forms of ethnic and other political identities are also emerging.

What form do redress and development take when pursued through state-owned mineral resources on land controlled by chiefs? Recent studies have shown that ordinary rural residents remain poor despite enormous mining revenues generated from their land. I argue that the gaps in the state's minerals policy, particularly its failure to grasp and address the local power structures and distributional challenges, renders the idea of the national state as a driver of mining-led socio-economic transformation less convincing. To illustrate this argument, I draw on detailed archival and ethnographic research, including in-depth interviews, conducted in the Bakgatla-ba-Kgafela traditional authority area – a platinum-rich community in North West Province – since April 2008. Broadly, the chapter examines the multiple impacts of platinum mining on rural communities that live on the vast platinum-rich land (the platinum belt) in South Africa's North West and Limpopo provinces.

The state and politics of difference

South Africa's rural political landscape is no less complex than the dynamics of state formation and contestation over resources. As such, by following the connections in local struggles over land, authority and resources, one is likely to gain an understanding of how processes of state formation are organised and contested at the local level.

The link between land, authority and contestation over the meanings of statehood, nationhood and sovereignty is nothing new. The post-colonial political experience of citizenship and nationhood in many parts of Africa has been fraught with sharp contradictions and tensions.

Like many post-colonial African states, the post-apartheid state in South Africa has battled to steer a clear course when it comes to aligning the civil rights order (democratic citizenship) prescribed in the country's constitution and the customary rights order that is still prevalent in the countryside. The difficulty in defining citizenship in rural South Africa emanates not only from the ambiguity of governance there, but also from the ever-increasing powers of traditional authorities (chiefs) over people, land and natural resources in the countryside. Chiefs have claimed not only political recognition and custodianship of African culture and tradition but territory – asserting political and administrative control in communal areas that were termed 'homelands' during apartheid. These claims over territory mark the contestations at the heart of state formation, particularly during moments of rapid social and economic change. The post-colonial states have, on several occasions, allowed and enabled traditional (tribal) authorities (chiefs) to reassert their control and power over rural land. Increasingly, chiefs seem determined to contest with national states over political governance and are asserting strong claims over territory in the countryside (Comaroff and Comaroff 2003; Fanthorpe 2005).

The question of difference has dominated recent debates on processes of state formation and paradoxes in the post-colony. For Mamdani, institutionalisation of difference was fundamental to the functioning and accomplishment of the colonial states' system of indirect rule. Armed with experience of the significant failure of direct rule in British and other Western colonies, the colonial state in Africa 'institutionalised difference in both policy and society' (Mamdani 2012, 2). In Africa the colonial powers aimed never to extend national citizenship beyond the minority European settler communities. Through this dual system of rule and rights, the colonial state mastered the evolution of an administratively laborious system which defined and packaged access to citizenship rights and even privilege in two forms: 'racial and tribal' (ibid.). By exclusively defining Africans as 'tribes', the colonial state claimed that it was observing pre-colonial custom.

The institutionalisation of difference, however, was designed not only to deny Africans civil rights and national citizenship, but to divide and identify them as members of different tribes, each of which was defined as a unique, homogeneous political unit under a local despot – a chief – who was a local administrative and political functionary of the central state (Mamdani 1996). But the notion of a crystallised, unchanged custom that the state used to justify its denial of Africans' civil rights was significantly flawed. The content of custom was significantly distorted by the colonial state in Africa (Mnwana 2016). The colonial authorities made significant attempts to 'formalise' or crystallise African custom into a set of rigid rules that could be imposed to deal with disputes in areas where Africans lived. But there was no pre-colonial precedent for this rigid, ubiquitous version of custom which conceptualised and interpreted African custom as Western law – 'legally enforceable rules' that governed all aspects of African life (Mnwana 2016). Mamdani (1996, 110) observes that customary law became both 'all embracing' and divisive. It 'embraced' under the authority of chiefs 'previously autonomous social domains [such as] the household, age sets, and gender'. Yet, the purpose of customary law, Mamdani argues, 'was not about guaranteeing rights, it was about enforcing custom. It was not about limiting the power [of chiefs], but about enabling it' (ibid.).

The resilience of difference in post-colonial Africa has captured the attention of many scholars. The anthropologists Jean and John Comaroff, for instance, have raised and attempted to grapple with some theoretical questions at the core of difference in modern African states. Observing the unrelenting ethnic difference in post-apartheid South Africa, these authors raise two critical questions:

> i How do nation-states in the twenty-first century, nation-states increasingly forced to come to terms with the ethnic heterogeneity of their citizens, deal with the problem of cultural difference?
>
> ii How, in particular, does the Constitution of post-apartheid South Africa – widely believed to be the most enlightened in the contemporary world, the most tolerant of diversity – strike a balance between the 'One Law' of 'The Nation' and the plurality of customary beliefs sustained, as a matter of right, by the various peoples who make up this postcolony?
>
> (Comaroff and Comaroff 2003, 445)

Such questions are central to our understanding of the persistent 'conflict between liberal governance and the call of custom' (ibid., 465). Hence, these authors use these questions in a bid to explain 'why, despite strenuous and thoughtful efforts to resolve … [the conflict between liberal governance and the call of custom], the antinomy persists, why it resists even the best-intentioned, most capacious politics of tolerance' (ibid.). They conclude that this 'ever more problematic relation between the liberal modernist state and the policultural nation' is rooted in the dynamics within the less explored history of difference in Africa, and especially South Africa. They insist that, to understand struggles over identity, culture and democratic citizenship rights in modern South Africa, one needs to trace the dynamics of the 'concrete, ongoing history of difference' (ibid.).

For Mamdani, difference has always been pervasive in both colonial and modern states. However, the modern democratic state 'ensures equal citizenship in political society while acknowledging difference in civil society', while the colonial state 'institutionalised difference in both the polity and society' (Mamdani 2012, 2). Yet, South Africa's modern democratic state seems to have done more than merely 'acknowledg[e] difference in civil society'. The ongoing rural struggles over land and identity demonstrate this, especially in areas where large-scale mining operations encroach onto rural land. We unpack this argument below.

Land and chiefs and 'radical' policy reform

The expansion of platinum mining has resulted in significant shifts in South Africa's social landscape. The primary shift has been largely connected to the mining operations' geographical location. In contrast to gold mining, platinum mining largely occurs on densely populated communal land in South Africa's former 'homeland' areas. These areas fall under the political jurisdiction of several traditional – 'tribal' – authorities, particularly in the North West and Limpopo provinces. The legacies of apartheid, including extreme poverty, high unemployment, poor education and a lack of basic services, all persist in these areas (Mnwana and Capps 2015).

Studies have revealed that platinum mining has not benefited ordinary rural residents in the locales where it is practised. The platinum boom – which continued for almost a decade from the late 1990s to the late 2000s – attracted scores of migrant workers and job-seekers from all over the southern African region. This resulted in unprecedented demand for social services and complex social problems associated with migrant influx in an already land-scarce area. The local social services were overwhelmed and ethnic tension, as well as crime and other social ills, increased (Mnwana 2015b, 2015c; Mnwana *et al.* 2016). On the other hand, the post-apartheid South African state has introduced some radical mineral legislation that has exerted pressure on the mining companies to address the industry's historical injustices, particularly its widespread exploitation of Africans as cheap labour and their exclusion from the ownership structure. In the discussion below, I expand on this post-1994 radical policy shift and its local antinomies.

The expansion of platinum mining on rural land coincided with two processes that help to explain the paradox of the socially ambivalent contribution of the industry in South Africa, despite the strong post-1994 policy framework. The first of these processes may be termed the 'retribalisation' of rural residents. Since the early 2000s, the African National Congress (ANC)-led post-apartheid state has introduced several pieces of legislation that have significantly empowered local chiefs. The Traditional Leadership and Governance Framework Act of 2003 (TLGFA; Act 41 of 2003; RSA 2003) is the main piece of legislation in this regard. It not only empowers traditional (tribal) authorities to preside over precisely the same geographic areas as were defined by the apartheid government but also enables chiefs and their traditional councils to manage communal land and natural resources, economic development, health and welfare, and administer justice.

The second – perhaps more important – process is the state's attempt to reform the mining sector. This chapter presents an analysis which goes beyond the widely reported history of geo-territorial positioning, legal battles and political struggles that ostensibly 'authenticate' traditional communities' claims over the platinum windfall. It is crucial to note that South Africa's history of racial exclusion in the country's major economic sectors, particularly mining, has its structural roots in the erstwhile apartheid state's political economy. Since the death of 'formal' apartheid in 1994, the new neoliberal democratic state under the leadership of the ANC has faced major socio-economic challenges – particularly poverty and sharp inequalities – that comprise unpleasant legacies of the previous regime. The apartheid mining sector, which was dominated by gold mining, enjoyed unparalleled growth and capital accumulation through massive exploitation, proletarianisation and total exclusion of Black[1] people from any form of corporate ownership in South Africa (Bozzoli 1981; Fine and Rustomjee 1996). It is no surprise, therefore, that the post-apartheid government has made radical policy shifts towards the racial inclusion of Africans in all of South Africa's key economic sectors, especially mining.

South Africa's democratic constitution (RSA 1996) served as a harbinger of the predominance of rights, justice and redress in the post-apartheid mineral legislation. For instance, Section 25, sub-section 4(a) of the Bill of Rights states: '[T]he public interest includes the nation's commitment to land reform, and to reforms to bring about equitable access to all South Africa's natural resources' (RSA 1996). Furthermore, the ANC's determination to transform the country's minerals policy and move towards equitable control of natural resource wealth is premised upon a crucial clause in the Freedom Charter of 1955: 'The people shall share in the country's wealth … and … The mineral wealth beneath the soil … shall be transferred to the people as a whole' (ANC 1955).

In an attempt to address some of the apartheid injustices, particularly the racially exclusive ownership structure of the mining industry, the post-apartheid state began to introduce some radical mineral legislation after the 1994 democratic transition. The most prominent piece of legislation was the Mineral and Petroleum Resources Development Act (MPRDA) 28 of 2002 (RSA 2002), which placed all mineral and petroleum resources in South Africa under the custodianship of the state. The state's main mechanism for transforming the racial structure and thickening the social footprint of the mining industry is 'broad-based black economic empowerment' (BBBEE;

RSA 2002, Section 1a). Through this legislation, the state has promoted a range of measures, including black economic empowerment (BEE), mine–community partnerships, continued royalty payments and social labour plans (SLPs) as requirements for mining companies (Mnwana 2015c). The state has also encouraged communities that previously received royalty payments for mineral rights on their land to convert those royalties into equity shares (Mnwana 2014b). In consequence, several communities on the platinum belt have entered into complex arrangements with mining companies – including royalty conversions and BEE partnerships.

The Bafokeng and Bakgatla of North West Province are leading traditional communities in South Africa in terms of investments in mining (through BEE equity stakes) and control over vast mineral revenues. Their diversified investment portfolios (albeit dominated by mining) amount to billions of rand (Mnwana 2014b; Khanyile 2012). Rural communities have entered into other complex deals with mining companies who operate on their land through local chiefs. The latter, as assumed custodians of communal resources, have become mediators of mineral-led development and mining deals. As such, they control mining revenues and champion mining-led community development. This has hampered the state's attempts to redistribute the country's mineral wealth to local communities and historically disadvantaged social categories.

The model of mediation and control of mining revenues by local elites – mainly chiefs – has generated significant tension and conflict in the villages that host vast mining operations in North West and Limpopo provinces. Several groups of ordinary villagers have made strong claims over some of the mineral-rich farms where some of the largest mining operations are situated. They assert that these farms were bought by their forefathers as private properties and so never should have been designated 'tribal' land. As such, they dispute and resist the role of local chiefs as signatories of the mining deals and assumed custodians of mining revenues on behalf of local communities (Mnwana and Capps 2015; Mnwana 2016). The mounting resistance to local chiefs is also rooted in the lack of transparency in their corporate dealings and serious allegations of corruption that are levelled against them by ordinary community members (Mnwana 2014a). The lack of tangible benefits epitomises this challenge. Moreover, mining, especially in rural areas, tends to exacerbate conflict and power struggles.

Mining is strongly connected to power struggles among local elites. This is epitomised by the relentless chieftaincy disputes in several communities on the platinum belt, for instance in the Bakgatla-ba-Kgafela, Bafokeng, Bapo-Ba-Mogale, Langa-Mapela and Kekana (Valtyn) traditional authority areas. Since claims and rights over tribal property are politically mediated, disputes over political power cannot be separated from contestations over resources. So far, the transformations initiated by post-apartheid legislation have not resulted in economic benefits for ordinary residents, since most of the benefits that accrue from community BEE equity deals tend to be captured by those members of the local elite who occupy high positions in the traditional authority structures (Mnwana 2015c; Mnwana *et al.* 2016).

The mediation of mining deals (community-owned BEE equity stakes) and control of (or custodianship over) mining revenues by traditional authorities on behalf of impoverished rural residents tends to establish a form of enclave mining development. The assumption that local chiefs are developmentally orientated, and that rural development should be driven by traditional authorities, facilitates the establishment and sustenance of an enclave local environment for mining capital. Such a local enclave situation is epitomised by two main elements. The first is the establishment of easy access for mining capital to communal land and the minerals beneath it. Vast tracts of agriculturally productive land in the rural areas of Limpopo and North West provinces has been fenced off for mining operations. The mining companies deal directly with local chiefs, which undermines the power, rights and claims of thousands of customary rights holders over their land. Consequently, the livelihoods of many families have been negatively affected. I expand on some of these issues below, but for now it is crucial to highlight that the traditional elite mediation model serves to establish a situation whereby mining capital can gain easy access to rural land and displace thousands of rural residents (Mnwana 2016, 222).

The second element that epitomises a local enclave is the gradual crystallisation or devolution of power to local chiefs, which enables the latter to position themselves as de facto brokers between mining capital and local communities. A situation gradually evolved whereby local chiefs were empowered not only to broker mining deals but also to exercise some repressive functions. Powerful chiefs who control significant mining revenues, as in the cases of the Bafokeng and the Bakgatla-ba-Kgafela in North West Province, have wielded more power since the platinum boom began. This has allowed them to suppress the protests of ordinary villagers who have attempted to hold them to account. They have done this by imposing court orders that prohibit villagers from holding meetings, hiring private security companies and powerful lawyers to silence village activists, and facilitating the fencing off of land that villagers had previously cultivated or used for animal grazing (Mnwana 2014b, 2015c). The chiefs are also playing an increasingly significant role in the procurement of local business services and recruitment processes, which has exacerbated ethnic tension on the platinum belt. In North West Province, some villagers and even local chiefs tend to advocate for the exclusion of non-Setswana-speakers from job opportunities and mining-led local development (Manson 2013; Mnwana and Capps 2015).

The emergence of an enclave in the form of elite capture is one of the prevailing antinomies of South Africa's radical mineral policy reform. The latter, rather than enhancing the social footprint of the platinum industry through BEE and other mechanisms, has served to marginalise the rural poor and has created a situation whereby the benefits of mining are being captured by local elites. The struggles over meanings of statehood and sovereignty in the context of rapid expansion of mining epitomises this paradox. The following case-study of Motlhabe village illustrates this finding.

Motlhabe: a portrait

Motlhabe is one of thirty-two impoverished villages in the 'platinum-rich' Bakgatla-ba-Kgafela traditional authority under Chief Pilane in North West Province. Situated on rocky, dry land dotted with thorn bushes, it lies about 10 kilometres north-west of the Pilanesberg Mountains and about 75 kilometres north of Rustenburg. The narrow tarred road which runs past Moruleng (the main village) ends abruptly about 15 kilometres from Motlhabe, as if to suggest that it falls outside of Bakgatla jurisdiction. Thereafter, a rough gravel road runs past the vast open-cast operations of the Pilaneberg Platinum Mine (PPM). The thick dust that is churned up by the mine's heavy vehicles makes the road dark and dangerous at times. Herds of village cattle that once grazed on land now fenced off for PPM's operations make any journey even more treacherous. The cattle wander in the thick dust, foraging for dry grass and shrubs as they drift along.

Figure 6.1 Village cattle on the gravel road that runs past the Pilaneberg Platinum Mine
Source: S. Mnwana

After crossing a narrow sandy river and heading up a path lined by thorn bushes, one finally reaches a hodgepodge of scattered structures constructed mainly out of corrugated-iron sheets and mud bricks. This is Motlhabe – a village formed by a history of difference and shaped by resistance.

Motlhabe has experienced occasional uprisings ever since mining activities began next to the village in 2008. The residents' resistance was mainly targeted at PPM and the tribal authority. Sometimes they turned violent. In May 2012, for instance, Motlhabe residents barricaded the gravel road next to the mine and burnt a PPM truck. They also demolished a block of single-roomed flats rented out by a local resident to migrant mine workers. The mine had to suspend its operations as a result.

Residents of Motlhabe once used the land now occupied by PPM for crop cultivation and grazing. The villagers felt that the chief, as the recipient of revenues from the mine, was sidelining them. Their main grievance was over the lack of public infrastructure in the village. Except for a small post office and a few schools that the villagers themselves raised funds to build, public services are either poor or non-existent. With intermittent water supply from the Moses Kotane Local Municipality, many villagers have no option but to buy water from the few residents with bore holes in their yards. The latter charge between R5 and R10 for a 20-litre bucket.

For more than two decades, many residents of the village have tried to resist their political designation as members the Bakgatla-ba-Kgafela chieftaincy. This group's resistance to that designation is connected to a protracted land dispute on the platinum belt. The advent of mining in this impoverished area and the lack of benefits accruing to ordinary people seem to have intensified this struggle.

Motlhabe is located on the Welgewaagd 515 (133 JQ) farm, about 3 kilometres south-west of PPM's operations. Many of the residents trace their origins to a group of Bakgatla led by Kautlwale Pilane, the first-born son of the great *Kgosi* Pilane (the founder of the morden Bakgatla chiefdom) from the eleventh house. In the 1910s, this group lived, apparently as labouring tenants, on the Witkleifontein 20 (136 JP) farm, which was owned by a European (White) family at the time. Many of those tenants' descendants argue that Kautlwale's group was politically independent from the Bakgatla-ba-Kgafela. However, as was the case with other sons of the great *Kgosi* Pilane, even if Kautlwale's followers regarded him as their chief, the colonial state never regognised him as such.[2] Hence, there is disagreement about whether Kautlwale was a chief or a sub-chief/headman. Nevertheless, it is generally accepted that he assumed a leadership role over the group of Bakgatla who resided at Witkleifontein. To this day, the elders in Motlhabe still call Witkleifontein Motlhabe-Mogologolo – 'Old Motlhabe'. Some of them were born there. In 1932, Witkleifontein's White owner expelled Kautlwale's people from the farm. At first they tried to resist, but ultimately they gradually relocated in small family groups to Welgewaagd farm, where they settled and established the village now known as Motlhabe.

The Welgewaagd 515 (133JQ) and Witkleifontein 20 (136 JP) farms

There is ongoing conflict over the Welgewaagd and Witkleifontein farms. Welgewaagd 515 (133JQ), which measures 2,370 morgen, 503 square roods, is registered as tribal land, with the title deed held in trust for the Bakgatla community by the Minister of Rural Development and Land Affairs. It was purchased on 6 March 1926 from Francois Hercules Du Toit and ten other White owners at a cost of £3,550,[3] with *Kgosi* Ofentse Pilane[4] of the Bakgatla signing the deed of sale. On approval of the sale, *Kgosi* Ofentse – apparently on behalf of the tribe – was required to pay no less than £2,000 upfront, with the remainder to be paid within the next five years. However, by 1 June 1926, less than three months after the first payment, *Kgosi* Ofentse had already collected and paid a total of £3,000. The outstanding £550 was then paid by the end of August that year. Hence, compared with other farms that Africans purchased through the Bakgatla chiefs, this one was bought in record time. It was registered in September 1926 with the 'Minister of Native Affairs in Trust for Bakgatla Tribe under Chief Ofentse Pilane'.[5]

The original, White-owned Welgewaagd farm was divided into four discrete portions at the time of this ostensibly 'tribal' purchase, with the portion discussed above comprising the largest of the four.[6] The other three portions were owned by two European speculating companies[7] and *Kgosi* Ofentse himself.[8] It was and remains quite common for the Bakgatla chiefs and other members of the ruling elite to hold private titles to some farms in the Bakgatla area. Over the years, these chiefs have sold some of their privately owned farms to the tribe or to individual Africans. For instance, *Kgosi* Ofentse sold Portion B of Welgewaagd to Mr Shadrack Makubire, an individual African buyer, in the early 1940s.[9]

Notwithstanding official documentation of the sale and registration of the land in 1926, oral tradition in Motlhabe disputes the tribal ownership of Portion D of Welgewaagd. A number of residents of the village insist that the land was privately acquired by a small group of families for their own use, not by and for the entire tribe. According to them, these were the families who were residing on Witkleifontein farm under Kautlwale at the time. Since the early 1980s, Kautlwale's descendants, who claim political authority over Motlhabe, have also led the group that claims exclusive ownership of Welgewaagd. As we shall see below, this dispute eventually escalated into a secessionist move that culminated in a lengthy court battle.

The members of the group who claim to be descendants of the families that purchased Welgewaagd have also claimed ownership of the mineral-rich Witkleifontein farm. Identifying themselves as 'Bakgatla-ba-Kautlwale', they submitted a restitution claim[10] for the latter farm in 1998. However, for some reason, this claim was registered under the name of the Bakgatla-ba-Kgafela tribe. Hence, *Kgosi* Nyalala opposed the ba-Kautlwale and pursued the claim on behalf of his Bakgatla tribe. The claim is based on the historical loss of land-use rights on this farm. The ba-Kautlwale contend that their ancestors were the sole occupants of the farm until their expulsion in 1932. In 2010, Mr Mmothi Pilane, one of the leaders of the ba-Kautlwale, explained:

> Nyalala (the chief) is now claiming that the land, which only we as the [b] a-Kautlwale ever occupied[,] belongs rightfully to him. He hired a lawyer to follow up the claim and paid him R20,000 a month[,] collected from the community.[11]

The South African Development Trust (SADT), the state agency for the implementation of the country's land laws, purchased Witkleifontein in 1937. Thereafter, it formed part of the Bakgatla 'native location'. Since this farm had good grazing land, over subsequent decades the people of Motlhabe continued to graze their livestock at a place called Phatswane. Some of this land has now been fenced off to allow PPM to undertake its mining operations.

Ba-Kautlwale? The secession attempt and the Constitutional Court's judgement

There is a strong connection between the contemporary dispute and the history of land purchase and political power in Motlhabe. Power contestation is nothing new in the village. Historically, claims to political power have always been connected to disputes over property. In 1982, Mainole Pilane, a descendent of Kautlwale Pilane, started to claim headmanship of the village. He argued that Kautlwale was headman at Witkleifontein, and that both of his sons – Pilane Pilane and Kobedi Pilane (Mainole's father) – were subsequently headman of Motlhabe. However, Mainole's opponents argued that his claim to headmanship was weak because the apartheid state recognised only one chief of the Bakgatla in South Africa. As such, in the 1950s, all previously autonomous Bakgatla polities in Pilanesberg were integrated into the newly established Bakgatla-ba-Kgafela Tribal Authority, and their leaders became *dikgosana* (headmen).

The dispute over the leadership of Motlhabe intensified in May 1984 when *Kgosi* Tidimane Pilane attempted to appoint Ramotwana Kgotsamaswe Moses Pilane acting *kgosana* in the village. Mainole lodged an urgent objection to this appointment with a local magistrate in which he maintained that *Kgosi* Tidimane's appointment of Ramotwana contravened local custom. He and his supporters also argued that Welgewaagd had been purchased privately by a group of Bakgatla who were under Kautlwale's leadership and resided on Witkleifontein in the 1920s. *Kgosi* Tidimane countered that the headmanship belonged to Mantirisi's descendants, who – according to his interpretation of local custom – were senior to Kautlwale's descendants. He also maintained that Mantirisi's descendants had first settled Welgewaagd and that Portion D of the farm had been purchased by the entire tribe, not by the small group of families who paid allegiance to Kautlwale.

In light of these conflicting claims, the president of the Bophuthatswana Bantustan at the time, Lucas Mangope, appointed a commission under the chairmanship of Mr H.A. Viviers to investigate the dispute. The commission repeatedly dismissed Mainole's claims to both land and headmanship, but he continued to argue his case, which delayed implementation of Viviers' recommendations. In June 1986, Mangope finally accepted the commission's finding that the 'rightful heir is Tlhabane Pilane from Mantirisi's lineage'.[12] However, since the latter was employed as a school headmaster, Ramotwana Kgotsamaswe Moses Pilane was officially appointed acting *kgosana*, just as *Kgosi* Tidimane had wanted two years earlier. Still Mainole did not give up. He filed yet another claim, but lost again in 1991.

The official files pertaining to this dispute reveal that the Bophuthatswana government was unwilling to entertain any challenge to *Kgosi* Tidimane's power, so his interpretation of custom and history was always likely to prevail. For instance, in November 1982, the magistrate in Mankwe District[13] remarked:

> [Al]hough [Mainole's claims and allegations against *Kgosi* Tidimane] may ... appear to be true, they are not so easy to resolve as the chief's councilors are always ready to protect him at all costs. The tribal councilors regard Mr Mainole as a troublemaker in the village. Some even suggested his complete expulsion from the tribal area.[14]

Similarly, four years later, in April 1986, Viviers' commission asserted: 'Mainole ... is in great disfavor with the chief and his uncles. Recognition of Mainole will just create friction.'[15] And in August 1991, Mr Magodiri, the administrator in Mankwe District, informed Mangope: 'Mainole Pilane has vowed publicly that if he can be appointed as headman of Motlhabe ... he will secede from the rule of the Bakgatla-ba-Kgafela.'[16] On receiving this report, Mangope, ostensibly alarmed by the prospect of divisions within the Bakgatla 'tribe', summoned Mainole to his office in September 1991. There is no record of what the two men discussed, but Mainole lost his final claim to headmanship a few months later. Nevertheless, the threat of secession from the Bakgatla chiefdom outlived both Mainole himself and Mangope's regime. Indeed, it continues to pose a serious challenge to the authority of the current Bakgatla chief, *Kgosi* Nyalala Pilane.

The move to secede began in earnest in July 2009, when leaders of the Bakgatla-ba-Kautlwale group delivered a notice to the traditional council of Bakgatla. The notice declared that Motlhabe was no longer under the jurisdiction and administrative control of the Bakgatla chieftaincy. In February 2010, news reached *Kgosi* Nyalala that the secessionists had invited 'the residents of Motlhabe village' to discuss the issue at a public meeting. He filed an urgent High Court application to interdict the leaders. This prohibited them from convening any village meeting without first obtaining the tribal council's permission. Thus began a protracted legal battle between the chief and the Bakgatla-ba-Kautlwale group that would eventually reach the Constitutional Court.

On 30 June 2011, in the North West High Court, Judge Landman upheld *Kgosi* Nyalala's interdicts against two ba-Kautlwale leaders and village activists, Mmuti Pilane and Reuben Dintwe. When delivering his judgement, he declared: 'Any action by a parallel but unsanctioned structure that is neither recognised by law or custom seeking to perform or assume functions that are clearly the exclusive preserve of recognised authorities ought to incur the wrath of law.'[17] The same court and the Supreme Court of Appeal both denied Pilane and Dintwe leave to appeal against the judgement, but their lawyers – from the Legal Resources Centre – subsequently presented the matter to the Constitutional Court. On 28 February 2013, it concluded that the interdicts 'adversely impact on the applicants' rights to freedom of expression, association and assembly' and lifted them with immediate effect.[18] It also affirmed the villagers' right to meet without having to seek prior permission from the chief. This was a landmark ruling not only for the ba-Kautlwale in their ongoing struggle against the Bakgatla chieftaincy but for all traditional rural communities.

A few weeks later, the ba-Kautlwale leaders filed an application to be recognised as an independent traditional authority under the terms of the Traditional Leadership Governance and Framework Act of 2003 (RSA 2003). No decision had yet been reached on this application at the time of writing, and several similar court cases relating to disputes in the Bakgatla area are also pending (see Mnwana 2014a, 2016).

Discussion and conclusion

This chapter has drawn on detailed ethnographic and archival research conducted at Motlhabe village in North West Province in an attempt to demonstrate how the post-apartheid state's radical policy reforms have significantly entrenched the power of traditional authorities in the former homeland areas where platinum mining occurs. Like its colonial predecessor, the post-apartheid state seems to favour granting local chiefs and mining companies control over rural land at the expense of African families and other productive units. Of course, this perpetuates inequality and generates conflict at the village level.

The issues raised by the case of Motlhabe illustrate how notions of statehood and sovereignty are contested at the micro level in the context of radical socio-economic shifts generated by the platinum mining boom in rural North West Province. For instance, why does difference take the form of ethnic and exclusive sub-ethnic group identities in contemporary struggles over land and mining revenues? How do we understand the persistence of ethnic difference and even claims to particular histories, different origins and traditions in the context of rural struggles on the platinum belt?

Evidently, tradition, modernity and development are inseparable in this discussion. From the empirical discussion in this chapter, it seems clear that the South African state needs the involvement of traditional institutions and the revival of ethnic identities to pursue mining development in rural areas with large platinum deposits. This contradicts the view that tradition and modernity occupy opposite poles of the development spectrum and that tradition delays the development of poorer countries (and their impoverished citizens); thus, 'history – the passage of developmental time – would in the nature of things raise the poor countries up to the level of the rich ones' (Ferguson 2006, 177f.). The significant involvement of chiefs in mining deals and emerging ethnic identities in rural South Africa point not only towards a resurgence of the politics of tradition, but towards tradition and evolving histories of difference as essential tools that are used by claimants to legitimise their claims over land, territory and mining revenues. Yet ambivalence and contradictions in relation to the role of chiefs in local economic development abound. For instance, some commentators present them as custodians of 'the traditional cultural fabric' which enhances social capital and cohesion – essential ingredients for congenial local relations and rural development in Africa (Grischow 2008). Meanwhile, others perceive traditional authorities as backward, intransigent and a hindrance to development and accuse them of limiting poor people's land tenure rights security through privatisation and therefore preventing increases in land values and markets (World Bank 1989). Then again, the question of political legitimacy – with the national state and chiefs competing for power and legitimacy in the countryside (Krämer 2016) – remains central in contemporary rural struggles.

Moreover, recent studies on mining and rural struggles in South Africa have increasingly focused on the resurgence of tradition and politics of difference. Elsewhere (Mnwana 2015a, 158–177), I have argued that local struggles in communities that host large-scale platinum mining operations reveal some complex social relationships whereby struggles around the politics of belonging and claims over mining benefits are producing new modalities of local conflict. Comaroff and Comaroff (2009, 7) observe that chiefly power has become increasingly connected to the commoditisation of the politics of ethnic identity, culture and tradition. They describe this process as 'incorporation of identity, the rendering of ethicised populations into corporations of one kind or another' (Comaroff and Comaroff 2009, 21). The Bakgatla, Bafokeng and other traditional communities who are involved in the mining industry on the platinum belt all fit this description. Manson and Mbenga (2012, 109) have argued that struggles in South Africa's former homeland areas, especially on the rural platinum belt, epitomise a revival of previously suppressed ethnic identities, 'leading to forms of a better defined ethnic sense'. All of these processes are strongly rooted in the ability of chiefs, through collusion with the state (and capital, at times), to position themselves as custodians and trustees of communal land (Mnwana 2016). But the resilience of traditional leadership and local modalities remain less understood at micro levels, particularly during moments of radical socio-economic transformation.

Finally, it is obvious that mining capital gains easy access to rural land when authority over communal property is concentrated in the hands of local chiefs. Hence, resistance to mining also tends to target chiefs on the platinum belt. I feel that post-apartheid South Africa's radical mining policy reform did not take into consideration the complex nature of customary rights and power over land and landed resources. As shown this chapter, the emergence exclusive land claims and politics of difference at village level epitomise this paradox.

Notes

1 The term 'Black' is used interchangeably with 'African' in this chapter. It should be noted that the former is a highly ambivalent term which also embodies a somewhat pejorative meaning. Unless explained otherwise, I generally use 'Black' when referring to Africans in South Africa. At times, it is also applied to Indians and Coloureds (as described by the MPRDA's BEE Mining Charter).
2 Although the colonial state never granted Kautlwale official recognition, the people he led still regarded him as *kgosi*.
3 Pretoria National Archives, NTS, Vol. 3514, Ref. 323/308.
4 Chief Lenchwe I's third son, who was the chief (some say regent) of the Bakgatla in South Africa during that period. He was appointed by *Kgosikolo* Isang Pilane (in Botswana) to rule over the Bakgatla.
5 Pretoria National Archives, NTS, Vol. 3514, Ref. 323/308.
6 Portion D, which is now occupied by the villages of Motlhabe and Ntsoana le Metsieng.
7 The South African Townships, Mining and Finance Company owned Portion A, measuring 1,007 morgen, 246 square roods. Karodia Limited owned Portion C, measuring 147 morgen, 404 square roods.
8 Portion B, measuring 503 morgen, 421 square roods.
9 Pretoria National Archives, NTS, Vol. 3514, Ref. 323/308.
10 Under the terms of the Restitution of Land Rights Act 22 of 1994 (RSA 1994).
11 Submission by Mrs Mary Mokgaetsi Pilane and Mr Mmothi Pilane of Bakgatla-ba-Kautlwale to the Rural Development Portfolio Committee on the repeal of the Black Authorities Act Bill, 21 July 2010.
12 North West Provincial Archives (NWPA), File 191, 6/4/2.
13 The Bakgatla area fell under Mankwe District during the Bophuthatswana regime.
14 Letter to the Department of the President of Bophuthatswana, 23 November 1982, NWPA, File 191, 6/4/2.
15 Department of the President, Bophuthatswana, 22 April 1986, NWPA, File 191, 6/4/2.
16 NWPA, File 191, 6/4/2.
17 Pilane and Another v. Pilane and Another (263/2010), 30 June 2011, para. 21.
18 Pilane and Another v. Pilane and Another (CCT 46/12), 28 February 2013, para. 70.

References

ANC. 1955. The Freedom Charter. (www.historicalpapers.wits.ac.za/inventories/inv_pdfo/AD1137/AD1137-Ea6-1-001-jpeg.pdf). Accessed: 28 December 2017.

Boone, C. 2017. Legal empowerment of the poor through property rights reform: Tensions and trade-offs of land registration and titling in sub-Saharan Africa. WIDER Working Paper 2017/37. Helsinki: UNU-WIDER.

Bozzoli, B. 1981. *The Political Nature of a Ruling Class: Capital and Ideology in South Africa, 1890–1933*. London: Routledge.

Comaroff, J.L. and J. Comaroff. 2003. Reflections on liberalism, policulturalism, and ID-ology: Citizenship and difference in South Africa. *Social Identities* 9(4), 445–473.

Comaroff, J.L. and J. Comaroff. 2009. *Ethnicity, Inc.: The Zulu Kingdom Awaits You*. Chicago: University of Chicago Press.

Fanthorpe, R. 2005. On the limits of liberal peace: Chiefs and democratic decentralization in post-war Sierra Leone. *African Affairs* 105(418), 27–49.

Ferguson, J. 2006. *Global Shadows: Africa in the Neoliberal World Order*. Durham, NC: Duke University Press.

Fine, B. and Z. Rustomjee. 1996. *South Africa's Political Economy: From Minerals-Energy Complex to Industrialisation*. Johannesburg: Wits University Press.

Grischow, J.D. 2008. Rural 'community', chiefs and social capital: The case of southern Ghana. *Journal of Agrarian Change* 8(1), 64–93.

Khanyile, G. 2012. Bakgatla tribe men facing corruption probe. iol, 14 October. (www.iol.co.za/news/southafrica/north-west/bakgatla-tribe-men-facing-corruptionp robe-1.1402519#.VCA4PPmSy8A). Accessed 12 July 2013.

Krämer, M. 2016. Neither despotic nor civil: The legitimacy of chieftaincy in its relationship with the ANC and the state in KwaZulu-Natal (South Africa). *Journal of Modern African Studies* 54(1), 117–143.

Mamdani, M. 1996. *Citizen and Subject: Contemporary Africa and the Legacy of Late Colonialism*. Princeton, NJ: Princeton University Press.

Mamdani, M. 2012. *Define and Rule: Native as Political Identity*. Cambridge, MA: Harvard University Press.

Manson, A. 2013. Mining and 'traditional communities' in South Africa's 'platinum belt': Contestations over land, leadership and assets in North-West Province c. 1996–2012. *Journal of Southern African Studies* 39(2), 409–423.

Manson, A. and B. Mbenga. 2012. Bophuthatswana and the North-West Province: From pan-Tswanaism to mineral-based ethnic assertiveness. *South African Historical Journal* 64(1), 96–116.

Mnwana, S. 2014a. Chief's justice? Mining, accountability and the law in the Bakgatla-ba- Kgafela Traditional Authority Area, North West Province. *South African Crime Quarterly* 49, 21–29.

Mnwana, S. 2014b. Mineral wealth – 'in the name of morafe'? Community control in South Africa's 'Platinum Valley'. *Development Southern Africa* 31(6), 826–884.

Mnwana, S. 2015a. Between 'locals' and 'foreigners': Mining and rural politics of belonging in North West Province, South Africa. *TRAVAIL, capital et société* 48(1–2), 157–181.

Mnwana, S. 2015b. Democracy, development and chieftaincy along South Africa's 'Platinum Highway': Some emerging issues. *Journal of Contemporary African Studies* 33(4), 510–529.

Mnwana, S. 2015c. Mining and 'community' struggles on the platinum belt: A case of Sefikile village in the North West Province, South Africa. *Extractive Industries and Society* 2, 500–508.

Mnwana, S. 2016. 'Custom' and fractured 'community': Mining, property disputes and law on the platinum belt, South Africa. *Third World Thematics* 1(2), 218–234.

Mnwana, S. and G. Capps. 2015. 'No chief ever bought a piece of land!' Struggles over property, community and mining in the Bakgatla-ba-Kgafela Traditional

Authority Area, North West Province. South Africa Working Paper 3. Johannesburg: Society Work and Development Institute, University of the Witwatersrand.
Mnwana, S., F. Mtero and M. Hay. 2016. Dispossessing the dispossessed? Mining and rural struggles in Mokopane, Limpopo. Working Paper 7. Johannesburg: Society Work and Development Institute, University of the Witwatersrand.
RSA. 1994. Restitution of Land Rights Act 22. Cape Town: Government Printer.
RSA. 1996. Constitution Act 108 of 1996. Cape Town: Government Printer.
RSA. 1998. Green Paper on Minerals and Mining Policy for South Africa. Cape Town: Government Printer.
RSA. 2000. Draft Minerals and Petroleum Resources Development Bill. Cape Town: Government Printer.
RSA. 2002. Mineral and Petroleum Resources Development Act 28. Cape Town: Government Printer.
RSA. 2003. Traditional Leadership and Governance Framework Act 41. Cape Town: Government Printer.
RSA. 2009. Traditional Leadership and Governance Framework Amendment Act 23. Cape Town: Government Printer.
World Bank. 1989. *Sub-Saharan Africa: From Crisis to Sustainable Growth*. Washington, DC: World Bank.

7 The local state in a new mining area in Zambia's Northwestern Province

Rita Kesselring

Introduction

Zambia is heavily dependent on revenue from copper extraction and export. The councils (district, municipal and city) hosting large-scale mining operations in Zambia receive only approximately 1 per cent (Zambia EITI 2017, 21) of the total revenues from the companies; the largest proportion of the revenue from the extractive industry goes to the national treasury. Councils nevertheless play an important governance role for both investors and residents in the districts or municipalities. They also bear the brunt of regulating the uneven impact of a large-scale mining investment on the lives of the residents. This despite the fact that mining companies employ relatively few workers, measured against a context of high expectations and higher unemployment rates than before privatization and mechanization. In this chapter, I explore the relationship between investors and local authorities at an extractive frontier, and how this engagement shapes stateness – that is, the ideas and practices of the state as negotiated and acted out in the relationship between the state authorities and their constituencies.

In the first years of the twentieth century, Solwezi was established as a tiny administrative centre overseeing mining activities in what was then known as Kaonde-Lunda Province. Only gradually did the administration develop a presence in the region, first the British South Africa Company and later the British Colonial Office. Between 1936 and 1947, the regional office was moved back to Kasempa, where it had previously been situated (Hellen 1968, 229). Between 1946 and 1954, Solwezi District was part of Western Province (today Copperbelt Province), and in the latter year, ten years before independence, Northwestern Province assumed its current form and Solwezi became its capital.

During the twentieth century, Kansanshi mine, situated 10 kilometres north of Solwezi town centre, was only intermittently operative (in the 1920s, 1930s, 1950s and 1970s). In the early 2000s, against the backdrop of the global resource boom, the mine was reopened and quickly grew into the largest copper mine (by output) in Africa. It currently employs a small operations workforce of 2,705 and a further 4,874 contract workers (First

Quantum Minerals Ltd. 2017). However, the reopening of the mine by Canada-based First Quantum Minerals Ltd. (FQML) attracted tens of thousands of migrant workers looking for opportunities in Solwezi, in a country which has suffered since the 1970s first from low global prices for copper, then from the IMF-imposed structural adjustment reforms and the loss of a great number of jobs. People are further attracted to Solwezi District because two additional copper mines west of Solwezi town opened shortly after the reopening of Kansanshi mine: Lumwana mine, owned by Barrick Gold (acquired from Equinox in 2011), in 2008 and Sentinel mine, wholly owned by FQML, in 2015. The number of residents in Solwezi town alone multiplied fivefold between 2005 and 2015 to an estimated 260,000 inhabitants (Preuss and Schmidt-Eisenlohr 2016).

Most of the research on the newest wave of extractivism in Africa focuses on the new and easily identifiable actor, the mine, and on communities' resistance to it (Golub 2014; Kirsch 2014). If local authorities feature at all, they are presented as rather insignificant: powerless against the mines, and largely unable to represent their constituencies. While this might be an accurate overall picture, it glosses over many important issues. In Solwezi, for instance, the municipal council has been *the* steady actor in a rapidly changing environment as it has remained in charge of regulating the effects of the mining boom. How does it deal with the new extractive actor in town, and how does stateness change as a result of this engagement? What can we learn about stateness in Zambia by looking at a moment of rapid spatial-material and socio-economic change? These questions lie at the heart of this chapter.

I will show that the arrival of the mine has had a considerable impact on life in the town and the work of the municipal council, yet the council has made few changes to its governing practices. This has resulted in a situation where the council is attempting to maintain its long-learned practices of governance and bureaucracy under dramatically altered conditions. In some regards, the council's work is easier now due to more and easily collected revenue from the mine, which makes officers more comfortable, lazy and less accountable in the view of both residents and the mining company (see Case-study 1). In other regards, though, the mine interferes with the council's tasks, such as planning processes, which has left the council with diminished authority and extra planning challenges (see Case-study 2). Finally, the council's constituencies have become much more diverse due to considerable in-migration triggered by the mine's employment policies and other factors. As a result, voting patterns and representation have been gradually changing (see Case-study 3).

The council, as I will show, has not addressed the challenge of governing differently in response to these unfolding changes. This fact not only increases the mine's impact and diminishes the council's relative authority; it also weakens the council's accountability towards the residents. Hence, the council's significance in people's lives has declined in both relative and absolute terms.

In the main part of the chapter, I focus on three levels of crystallization (economic, spatial and political) in which the impact of extractive industries on imagined and practised stateness is most tangible. I argue that the mine's power to alter citizens' and residents' relationships to the state rests, on the one hand and to a large extent, on the continuity of the council's practices. The council tends to proceed with its habitual, bureaucratic activities as it did before the mine reopened. On the other hand, however, the mine's presence has had considerable influence on some specific fronts – a process I examine through the example of revenue and revenue collection.

My focus on the ways in which extractive investments influence the legitimacy, capacity and authority of the *local* state entails looking closely at local histories and local dynamics of stateness as well as changes in the relations between local and central government. My approach is ethnographic and my interest anthropological. Between 2013 and 2017, I lived in Solwezi town for a total of sixteen months and conducted research in the municipality (for a time as an intern in the Planning Department) with male and female residents from across the age spectrum in a variety of social milieus and suburbs, as well as workers in the mining complex.

Background: a municipal council in a mining town

Zambia has a total of 109 districts, which are governed by 4 city councils (Lusaka, Livingstone, Kitwe and Ndola), 13 municipal councils and 92 district councils. Solwezi has municipality status and has been preparing for city status since 2015. Solwezi Municipal Council (SMC) consists of the 3 Members of Parliament for the district, 2 representatives of the local chiefs and 22 elected councillors (as prescribed by Section 3 of the Local Government Act). The councillors work part-time and are accountable to the electorates of their respective wards. SMC holds ordinary meetings at least every three months; subject to provisions, these are open to the public.

Before the amendment of the constitution in 2016, the mayor was elected from the councillors. However, under the terms of the new constitution, he or she is elected directly by the electorate and the position is full-time. The full council meets under his or her chairmanship, with administration staff in attendance. Reports contain minutes of the preceding meeting and reports from standing committees. Councillors chair the standing committees, whose meetings are not open to the public. SMC has four standing committees: Finance, Human Resources and General Purposes; Plans, Works, Development and Real Estate; Audit; and Health, Environment and Social Services. The committees' decisions serve as recommendations to the full council.

On the administrative side, the town clerk is the council's chief executive officer. He or she is assisted by the departmental heads for Administration, Finance, Engineering Services, Planning and Housing, and Social Services. In contrast to the elected councillors, the administrative staff are full-time, salaried officers who are in charge of the day-to-day implementation of the council's services.

The Ministry of Local Government and Housing (MLGH) is responsible for overseeing all local government in Zambia. With the enactment of the Local Government Amendment Act No. 6 of 2010, the Local Government Service Commission was established with oversight from MLGH. The commission is mandated to hire, fire, promote, demote and discipline officials. Any official appointed by the Local Government Service Commission is subjected to a system of rotation, intended to prevent corruption. Hence, state officers are often unfamiliar with the culture of their workplace and may even struggle to understand the language spoken by their 'clients'.

Under the terms of the Local Government Act, a council may levy taxes, borrow money, manage and/or own housing projects and control a wide range of public services, such as roads, water, power and health facilities. Moreover, it receives a number of national grants, including the Constituency Development Fund, through the MLGH. In November 2013, the government approved the Revised National Decentralization Policy. The strategy, enacted from 2015 onwards, is 'decentralization through devolution' of power and certain functions, including fiscal decentralization, to the councils. It is meant to give citizens more authority and power in decision-making with respect to local matters. In reality, SMC has been rather

Figure 7.1 District planning officer Adraida Daka and former director of planning Naomi Simwanza at Solwezi Municipal Council
Photo: Rita Kesselring

overwhelmed by this new policy, mostly because of a lack of financial and human resources to undertake its extra functions.

SMC oversees all local government matters for Solwezi District, which, up to recently, covered three constituencies – Solwezi East, West and Central. Solwezi town is situated in the Solwezi Central constituency. Solwezi East is largely rural, while Solwezi West hosts the Lumwana and Sentinel/Kalumbila mines, which have triggered the growth of two new clusters of urban character. During my research, the boundaries of Solwezi District changed per Statutory Instrument No. 39 of 2016. The district was subdivided into three new districts, namely Kalumbila District (formerly Solwezi West), Solwezi District (formerly Solwezi Central) and Mushindamo District (formerly Solwezi East). The current Solwezi District thus primarily covers the urban settlements. Whereas Solwezi District previously contained three large-scale mines – Kansanshi, Lumwana and Sentinel – it now hosts only Kansanshi. This means that not only its area but also its revenue base shrank considerably.

First Quantum Minerals Ltd. and Kansanshi Mining Plc.

Since the early 2000s, Zambia has experienced a revival of the mining sector and hence a foreign investment and construction boom. Today, First Quantum Minerals Ltd. (FQML) is the largest taxpayer in the country, contributing 36.54 per cent to total government revenues in 2015 (Zambia EITI 2017, 18). Its output amounts to 74 per cent of the total copper production and 100 per cent of the total gold production (4,241 kilograms in 2015) in Zambia. It owns 80 per cent of Kansanshi Mining Plc. (KMP) and all of the Sentinel mine (now in Kalumbila District). KMP, which is the focus of this chapter, contributed 23.6 per cent to total government revenues in 2015. The FQML mine complex is registered in Canada but operates from Perth (Australia), London (UK) and Zug (Switzerland).

In Solwezi, KMP, partly as 'goodwill' gestures and partly in lieu of tax payments, rolls out sporadic and highly selective programmes administered through its Corporate Social Responsibility (CSR) Department. These are often poorly integrated into the national development plan; and, aside from placing moral pressure on the mines, neither communities nor the state can control the delivery of such services.

The 2015 slump in global commodity prices

In 2015, the Zambian economy felt the consequences of China's declining demand for natural resources. The kwacha (Zambia's national currency; abbreviated as ZMW) depreciated to half of its value within a few months and the national electricity crisis deepened. The downturn in global copper prices triggered the closure of a mine (Luanshya) and the decision to put others on maintenance (Mopani Copper Mines), but the three mines in Northwestern Province remained open. Unlike other mine operators in

Zambia, FQML has not ceased all investment. KPM continued with the construction of a smelter on site and started to process copper concentrate in 2015.

Case-study 1: the council as selective rent-seeker

During the SMC's full council meeting of 13 July 2015, which I attended, the minutes of the last Finance, Human Resources and General Purposes (FHRGP) Committee meeting were discussed. In that meeting, the FHRGP Committee members also debated the 2015 budget estimates.[1] For the fiscal year of 2015, the approved revenue estimates were ZMW78,608,825 (approximately US$7,860,000), out of which approximately ZMW30 million were scheduled to come from local taxes (the largest portion of which are property rates).[2] The 2015 budgeted expenditure estimates were ZMW89,020,569, leaving the committee with a projected budget deficit of ZMW10,411,743 (approximately US$1,040,000). The full council deliberated on the matter brought forward by the committee and eventually resolved that the item should be noted but also, as written in the minutes, that the 'management should consider the possibility of covering up the budget deficit by surcharging Kansanshi Mine a penalty fee and a service charge for the illegal development of the Smelter and for the construction of the Smelter Road'.

In what way was the development 'illegal'? In 2015, KMP had applied to the council to transform an area of roughly 2,500 hectares from customary tenure to freehold title. As required, the application contained a Form II stating the chief's approval of the alienation. The council was then supposed to fill in a Form III to confirm that the land was under the jurisdiction of the chief and that no other legitimate claims on the land existed, and pass on its recommendation to the Commissioner of Lands. The problem with this particular application was that the application for conversion (and approval of structures) came after the fact. When it submitted the application, the mine had already – without securing the necessary authorization – constructed a copper smelter and the access road leading to the smelter on this land.

What followed was a discussion between elected councillors and appointed officials that is not recorded in the minutes but which I witnessed:

COUNCILLOR 1: Council lawyers should help us and slap them [Kansanshi mine] so that they stop doing illegal things!

COUNCILLOR 2: The avenues they are using are not right. Give them the land they already occupy but charge them ZMW8,000 per plot. And charge them a penalty so that they feel it. They should repay every plot. Let's propose a penalty.

COUNCILLOR 3: The chief can only hand out 250 hectares, can't he? Let's go physically on the ground.

TOWN CLERK: We do an inspection, get the drawings (which we don't have) and then decide on the penalty.

COUNCILLOR 4: They are so corrupt. They don't consult the local authority, instead they consult others [that is, the President]. Let's enter into a lease with these 2,500 hectares.

In this instance, officials and elected councillors were in agreement, but this is not always the case. A typical and recurrent point of disagreement between the two groups is how the revenues from the mining companies ought to be spent and planned in the annual budget.

The mining sector pays roughly 98 per cent of its rates and taxes to the Zambia Revenue Authority (ZRA), but property rates and some negligible annual business fees are paid to the local authorities twice a year. For the fiscal year of 2015, SMC received ZMW25,985,900 (approximately US$2,500,000) for property rates – ZMW14,936,900 from KMP and ZMW11,049,000 from Lumwana Barrick (Zambia EITI 2017). To put this in context, this sum is a little less than half of the total revenue the council collected in the 2014 fiscal year.[3] Also, SMC's property rates for the two mines in 2015 were five times higher than, for instance, those of Kitwe City Council, which hosts seven mining operations, among them Mopani Copper Mines and NFC Africa Mining (copper), Kagem and Grizzly Mining (gemstones). It represents 29 per cent of the total revenue from the mining sector going to all host councils in Zambia (Zambia EITI 2017).

The windfall money

Because it constitutes such a fundamental and substantial part of the annual budget, the revenue collected from the mines is discussed as a separate item and budgeted separately. When the Finance Committee tabled its half-yearly 'Utilisation Report on Funds Received from Extractive Companies in Solwezi District from January to June 2015' to the full council on 13 July 2015, it sparked a lengthy and heated debate. This time, there was a clear division between the elected councillors and the officials, led by the town clerk.

Basically, the report outlined that, out of the ZMW13,028,450, the council spent ZMW2.6 million on salaries, ZMW2 million on the repayment of a loan, ZMW1.8 million on the construction of a civic centre, ZMW1.3 million on vehicles (including a mayoral vehicle) and insurance and ZMW800,000 on councillors' allowances.[4] It was the issue of salaries that triggered the heated debate:

COUNCILLOR 1: I would like to see a new item like 'Funds from the mines should not be used to pay salaries'.

TOWN CLERK (VENTURE KAFULA): When we are budgeting as a council, taxes, fines etc., we put everything in one basket. The first we then pay is manpower. Let's not adopt this item, it is not helpful. Let's leave it at the point that we will control better the funds flowing into manpower.

COUNCILLOR 2: Let the departments do their work and collect taxes and levy. Let's adopt [my fellow councillor's suggestion] as an item.

COUNCILLOR 3: Only when the mine pays, the cheques are moving. The TC [town clerk] should budget how much we collect ourselves. People in Zambezi [another rural district in Northwestern Province], they are paying their workers, there are no mines.

TOWN CLERK: There is no fear that we can't manage this place without the mines. But don't make this into a policy, this does not make sense. Let us maximise on the collections of the revenue from the bus station for instance. We are building a new station now and people will happily pay the fees.

In the end, the full council did not adopt a new policy outlining how the revenue from the mines should be used. However, the debate showed a clear divide between the elected councillors, who were unhappy about what they saw as overreliance on that revenue, and the appointed officers, who denied such dependency. The political wing of the council suspected that the municipality would be unable to manage without the mines' rates. They argued that structural costs, such as salaries, were dependent on the mines' payments (although they said nothing about the mayor's vehicle or their own allowances). They accused the officials of laxity with respect to general revenue collection while they waited for the half-yearly windfall money. The elected councillors thus argued against fiscal indiscipline and inefficient use of rent revenue.

In many ways, the councillors were correct. In what follows, I will show that the council was lax in the collection of revenue, even when it had the chance to broaden its revenue base dramatically with a new valuation roll.

The landlords

All landowners are required by law to pay rates to the council for their properties. The amounts payable are determined as follows: the value of the land and the value of any improvements to that land are added together to generate a 'total rateable value', which is multiplied by the rate defined by the responsible council. Only owners whose properties are captured in the valuation roll are required to pay the rates.[5] According to the Rating Act (Chapter 192 of the Laws of Zambia), the valuation roll is supposed to be revised every five years by a government valuation surveyor, appointed by the Minister of Local Government and Housing. In the Solwezi District, the old valuation roll dated back to 2010, and the valuation surveyor prepared the 2016 valuation roll in 2015.

In the full council meeting of 12 December 2016, the Director of Finance presented his report on the new valuation roll. According to the new valuation roll, including some adjustments due to the division of Solwezi District and the consequent loss of Kalumbila town and Sentinel and Lumwana mines, the new Solwezi District (formerly Solwezi Central constituency) would receive land rates from 4,415 entries, adding up to a total rateable value of ZMW3,306,961,591[6] (approximately US$330,700,000).[7] The old valuation roll had just 2,416 entries.

The modest increase in the number of (primarily residential) entries does not correlate with the reality on the ground. The Solwezi Urban Baseline Study (SUBS), conducted in 2015 with the help of the German development agency GIZ (Gesellschaft für Internationale Zusammenarbeit), gives a more realistic picture of the number of plots. According to this survey's findings, there are 29,750 plots (many of them the result of the subdivision of existing properties) within the proposed new township boundary (Preuss and Schmidt-Eisenlohr 2016, 20).[8] The council therefore loses out on revenue on multiple levels, and neither the council nor the MLGH has made the most of the opportunity to address old failures, such as ignoring houses without house numbers, on the new valuation roll.

At the same full council meeting, members approved new rates to be levied for the different categories of properties. The only rate increase was imposed on mining property (from 0.025 to 0.04 as a multiplier). Based on the valuation roll and the new rates, the council's revenue rose from ZMW33,610,480 under the old valuation roll to an estimated ZMW38,594,765, out of which the Kansanshi mine would have to contribute 65 per cent.[9]

Apart from failing to capture all titled and occupied land in the valuation roll, inefficiency in revenue collection has been a concern of the council's management for many years. In 2014, for instance, the collected revenue represented only 52 per cent of the total revenue estimate. In December 2016, the council was owed ZMW15.7 million for rates and ZMW32 million for other revenue sources. In the full council meeting, the Director of Finance took an unprecedented step by requesting the councillors' help in the collection of revenue:

> As a measure, management appealed that the honourable councilors assist in the sensitization of the residents in wards to pay their bills so that the budgeted activities could be achieved in the year 2017 and years to come … [A]ll the landlords had an obligation to pay the rates twice a year … However a number of landlords had not been fair in the sense that when they rent out their houses they receive reasonable rentals but do not, out of the rentals, pay anything to the Council.[10]

Collecting revenue from ordinary landowners is certainly challenging when there is a lack of financial and human resources, sprawling settlement, an insecure tenure situation, multiple claims of ownership and often a physical absence of landlords. The mining company, in contrast, can be relied upon to conform to the law and pay its local rates (albeit while simultaneously, and successfully, opposing any increase in the national taxation and royalty regime).

This insight into proceedings in the council chamber shows that Solwezi town continues to grow, largely informally, but most of the income comes from just one taxpayer – the mine – which, to a considerable extent, helped generate the influx of people. Officially, in 2017, with the new district boundaries, KMP's contribution to the total property rates paid to the municipality rose to 65 per cent. However, in reality, the percentage was even higher if we factor in non-payments by many other commercial, industrial and residential actors. Ordinary residents and small businesses are either not on the valuation roll, and thus not required to pay rates, or manage to avoid payment by ignoring bills and dodging revenue collectors.

However, paying rates, fees and taxes is crucial to the making of stateness. As a result of the council's lax revenue collection, residents who find it easy to evade taxation have little leverage to claim better service provision. Similarly, elected councillors have little incentive to heed the town clerk's appeal and ask their constituents to pay their rates. When a council relies on just one or two large players for the vast majority of its income, its responsibility towards ordinary resident shifts. This not only affects accountability towards those citizens, but increases the council's dependence on the mines. Solwezi is thus turning into a rent-seeking local polity, mirroring developments at the national – central – government level.

Case-study 2: the mine outpaces the council

The Kansanshi mine paid roughly two-thirds of the council's total revenue in 2017 for two principal reasons: first, many smaller landlords – commercial, residential or otherwise – managed to avoid paying their rates; and, second, the mine covered a large proportion of the district's total area. Due to the nature of open-cast mining, a large tract of the district's land has been transformed from customary to state land, and regional and national forest areas have been decommissioned. But the mining complex also contributes to massive spatial changes *outside* its licence area. In what follows, I elaborate on one infrastructural project spearheaded by KMP which not only changed the environment by its mere presence but also triggered socio-spatial change beyond its concrete surface. I will argue that the mine complex's selective interference in the town's set-up has resulted in a situation where the local authorities have handed over traditional state tasks to a corporate actor. Such infrastructural projects have a negative impact on the council's accountability vis-à-vis its constituents.

The most recent development plan for Solwezi District dates back to 1964. Two later attempts to approve a new development plan – in 1978 and 1990 – both failed. Hence, to this day, the council still works with the utterly outdated 1964 document and an integrated development plan, drafted in 2009 but not actioned because the chief has never signed it. (The current chief has been embroiled in a succession battle over the Kapijimpanga chieftaincy since his predecessor's death in 2008 and he is not allowed to sign any official documents until it is resolved.)

Due to the recent influx of people into the Solwezi area, old and new town residents settle and build on customary land after negotiating a variable or standardized price with the area's headman, without any expectation that municipal services will reach their plot. Sometimes, they pursue the matter and present the chief's written consent to the council; usually, they do not bother to apply for conversion or for permission to develop. Businesses and investors acquiring land under customary tenure are more cautious about converting it to state land and usually present the chief's letter of consent to the council. (However, this is not always done before development commences, as we saw earlier with respect to the mine's construction of a smelter and access road.) After a lengthy, costly and often murky process, they receive the title to the land through the Commissioner of Land although rarely any services, such as water or electricity. As a result, parcels of land under leasehold tenure outside the municipal boundaries now dot the landscape. No one undertakes or imposes coherent planning, access roads are lacking, and a church may easily stand next to a bar.

Solwezi town has one primary road – the T5 – which cuts across dense settlements and the centre of town. The T5 is the main west–east highway in northwestern Zambia. It connects Mwinilunga and Angola in the west to Copperbelt Province in the east. Hence, the trucks that carry Barrick Gold's copper, mined at the Lumwana mine, and FQML's copper, mined at Sentinel mine, drive right through Solwezi town. They not only block other traffic and endanger pedestrians and marketeers selling their produce along the road but regularly get stuck in traffic jams themselves.

With the prospect of processing both Sentinel's and Kansanshi's copper concentrate, and given the paucity of smelter capacity within Zambia, FQML built a new copper smelter on the Kansanshi licence area. At the same time, it built the smelter road to reroute trucks from Sentinel straight to the smelter so they did not have to enter Solwezi town centre (see Figure 7.2). Since the smelter's construction in March 2015, it has processed most of Sentinel's copper concentrate into cathodes and anodes (with small portions processed at Mopani Copper Mines). Some trucks from Barrick Gold's Lumwana mine still cut through the centre of town, but the smelter road has dramatically reduced traffic, noise and pollution in Solwezi.

FQML's Road Division built the smelter road between 2014 and 2015. To conform to Zambian regulations, there is a 100-metre road corridor to avoid accidents when truck drivers lose control of their vehicles. The road will eventually be handed over to the Zambian Roads Development Agency for public use. At the time of writing (February 2018), between fifty and a hundred trucks thunder along it each day, although that number is expected to double in the near future.

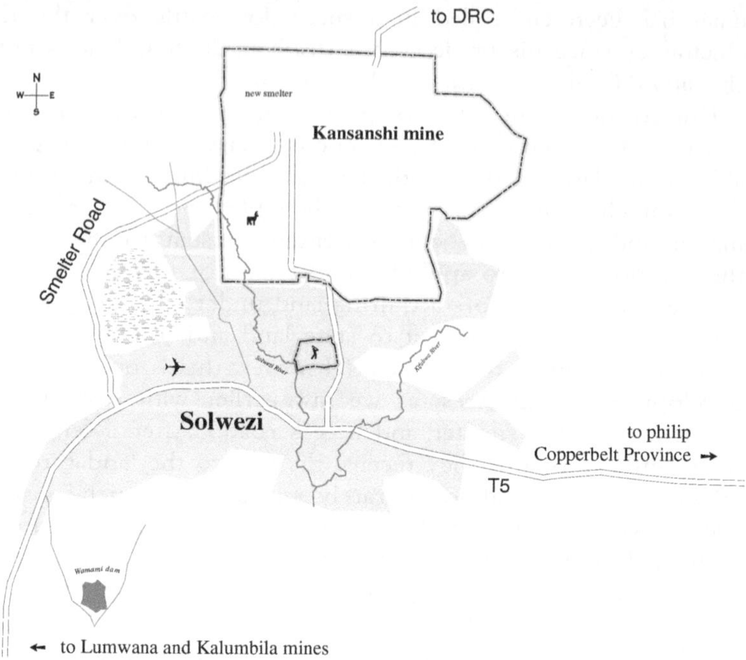

Figure 7.2 Map of Solwezi town, Northwestern Province, Zambia
Note: Grey area depicts actual settlement.
Source: Rita Kesselring

More than eighty households had to be resettled for construction of the road to proceed. Farmers' losses included agricultural land, cultivation potential, annual and perennial crops, fruit-bearing trees, two homesteads and many non-residential structures such as sheds, wells, temporary farm shelters and so on (URS Scott Wilson Zambia 2013, 77). Most of the farmers' homesteads or houses are in adjacent villages, but many live temporarily on their farms when harvesting.

Due to the lack of a national resettlement policy at the time, the mine, through its CSR Department, abided by international standards of resettlement and commissioned consultants to carry out an Environmental Impact Assessment, part of which was a Resettlement Action Plan. Both of these were approved by the Zambia Environment Management Agency and the resettlement process was rolled out in parallel to the construction of the road.

A new road always changes the environment. It influences how people perceive the surrounding areas and it is invariably adopted in various – often unforeseen – ways (Dalakoglou and Harvey 2012; Harvey and Knox 2015; Beck *et al.* 2017). The smelter road was no exception. For a small number of farmers, the road turned out to be a blessing because it facilitated easier access to their fields. Others made the most of the dramatic rise in real estate values in the area by selling their plots of land. However, most of the farmers living or farming adjacent to the road had mixed feelings, at best, or saw their livelihoods destroyed, at worst. They complained of thieves who stole their harvests during the night. Population density in the area rose immediately and continues to do so. And, for many, the CSR Department's resettlement packages – which included some training and limited assistance for the first year after resettlement – introduced a regime which pitted them against those residents who did not enjoy these benefits, contributing to fights with old and new neighbours alike. Moreover, the assistance was insufficient to compensate for the loss of time and labour they had put into the land. Finally, parents feared for their children's safety, as they now had to cross the busy new road to get to school.

For the mine, the smelter road was simply a transport corridor. It was not interested in the additional changes that its construction precipitated, and it gave them little thought during the planning process. The planners merely looked for a route through a relatively thinly populated area so they would not have to resettle too many residents and farmers. However, while the road's course was chosen simply with a view to increasing profits and bypassing the busy town centre, once it was built, the local people started to be affected by it in multiple – often negative – ways.

By pursuing its own logic of infrastructural development in an urban setting, the mine powerfully, if unwittingly, engaged in town planning – a task that should be fulfilled by the municipal council. Second, it laid waste to the council's own spatial planning. The council had initially planned a new residential settlement – the Humphrey Mulemba Villa Park – at the junction of the smelter road and the T5, but it was unable to proceed with this amid rapid informal settlement and a dramatic rise in land disputes. Third, the mine helped to delegitimize the council's authority. Its CSR Department focused on the farmers who lived along the road (with a narrow understanding of the effects of a new piece of infrastructure – a technocratic approach that was approved and supported by the central state organs) and thus singled them out for special treatment. The road, which was built purely to increase a corporate actor's profits, and the accompanying resettlement programme shifted the residents' attention from the council to the mine, and it remains fixed there to this day. If the directly affected farmers need more assistance, they ask the mine for help; if they have a boundary dispute in the resettled areas, they turn to the mine and its state-of-the-art GPS database.

In other words, stateness has been reconfigured by a piece of infrastructure that was designed to aid disengagement with the population and speed up extraction and processing.

Case-study 3: the shifting political geography of an opposition town

Extractivism in a specific locale also changes stateness by way of voting patterns. Due to in-migration, the ruling Patriotic Front (PF) has gained leverage in what has traditionally been an opposition region.

Figure 7.3 Totalling station for Solwezi Central, August 2016 general elections
Photo: Rita Kesselring

For the 2016 general elections (presidential, mayoral and parliamentary), I was accredited as an election observer and thus gained access to Solwezi's polling and totalling stations. These were Zambia's fifth elections in ten years, partly as a result of the deaths of presidents in office and consequent by-elections. Earlier in 2016, the President had signed a constitutional amendment which stipulated that the President should be elected by a majority of the national vote. In August 2016, Zambians went to the polls to elect a new president and parliament and to vote in a referendum on the amended Bill of Rights. The incumbent PF party urged its supporters to vote 'yes' in the referendum, which would be passed as long as it received the support of more than 50 per cent of all eligible voters (a number which is difficult to discern in Zambia).

Against this background, staff and officials overseeing the voting process experienced considerable pressure amid allegations of fraud and vote rigging. The elections had a significant effect on the country and, at the time of writing, the main opposition party – the UPND – was still refusing to accept the results.

Kansanshi polling station

Although the constituency of Solwezi Central clearly voted for the opposition, the results at a couple of the thirty-six polling stations (and one in particular) indicate that voting patterns are gradually changing. Kansanshi polling station in the Kamalamba ward was housed in a tent outside the mine's licence area and was designed to allow Kansanshi employees to vote either before or after their shift, but local residents could use it, too. It had 1,100 registered voters and the turnout was 64 per cent. At all other stations in the constituency, the numbers for male and female voters were quite balanced. However, 84.6 per cent of the registered voters at Kansanshi were men, which supports the assumption that mainly mineworkers voted there.

In the parliamentary elections, 289 votes were cast for the ruling PF party and 396 for the UPND, with just 3 ballot papers rejected. Similarly, the UPND candidate received 372 votes in the mayoral election and the PF candidate 298. Finally, 319 voters gave their presidential votes to the PF and 383 to the UPND, with 3 ballot papers rejected.

The referendum did not come close to reaching the necessary threshold across Zambia, but in Solwezi Central 9,972 people voted 'yes' while 7,393 voted 'no'; thus, a majority followed the ruling party's advice to vote for the constitutional amendments. However, support for the PF's position was much more pronounced at Kansanshi, where 403 people voted for and only 170 against the proposals. This was the clearest expression of a pattern that was visible throughout the town: those areas with large numbers of mine employees and newly arrived job-seekers showed a strong tendency to support the ruling party. Solwezi, in other words, moved closer to the voting pattern on the fiercely contested Copperbelt, where the PF and the UPND were about equal, even though many internal migrants left Solwezi on election day in order to vote in their hometowns.

After a long day of voting and an even longer night of counting, a young, female official at Kansanshi polling station revealed that she had come under intense pressure from PF agents when counting the ballot papers: 'I don't know about those in remote areas – the women – how they handle them [the PF agents]. They really pushed!' Hinting at the general neglect of the province by central government, she said she hoped the UPND would win, because, 'if the PF wins again, Northwestern will be a bush'. Ultimately, the incumbent PF candidate, Edgar Lungu, won the presidential election, but otherwise Solwezi District returned UPND candidates across the board, with every Member of Parliament, every councillor and the mayor all voted in by opposition supporters.

Most of the district's mine employees and those working for contractors arrive with work experience gained in the Copperbelt mines. Their standard of education is above average, as the highly mechanized mines have little need for low-skilled workers. Many in-migrants who are not employed by the mine but come to open businesses in Solwezi are also better educated than the local population, which gives them a competitive advantage. Moreover, most of those who migrate from the Copperbelt speak Bemba and are thus often perceived as 'foreigners' who are likely to vote for the PF, which serves to exacerbate the conflicts between them and the locals.

Figure 7.4 A PF rally at Chavuma Secondary School, Solwezi, Northwestern Province, 8 August 2017
Photo: Rita Kesselring

Despite the rapid growth of its urban population, Northwestern Province still had the second lowest number of registered voters among the country's ten provinces during the 2016 elections. However, Solwezi Central accounted for a fifth of all of Northwestern's registered voters (81,344) – a significant number from a national perspective. Hence, Solwezi is no longer a minor, peripheral town. It is an important urban centre that the political parties cannot ignore. The arrival of considerable foreign investment has not only attracted the attention of the central state and the ruling party but has also changed the agency of the local council and its relationship to its constituencies. Those constituencies have become more diverse and governance more challenging for the local authorities. In contrast to these rapid changes in population, by and large the municipal council continues to represent the original residents, while the administrative staff, as elsewhere in the country, tend to arrive from across the country. In the final section, I will explore what this entails for the relationship between stateness and the extractive industries.

Conclusion: local authorities, stateness and extractivism

In this chapter, I have examined what happens to the local state–residents relationship when a new, economically powerful actor enters a town where the residents have traditionally voted against the ruling party in a context of post-structural adjustment reforms and a receding global commodity boom.

First, at the economic level, we looked at the effects of the collection of revenue from the mining industry on the local authorities. SMC practises a mini-rent-seeking economy that relies on revenue from the mining companies. As a result, residents can avoid paying their rates and thus feel less connected and less obligated to the local authorities, and vice-versa. This, however, does not remain unchallenged. We have seen that there is a chasm between elected councillors and appointed officials with respect to their views on the use of income from the mine for municipal service provision, and that the councillors at least try to represent their constituencies.

Second, at the spatial level, we have seen that the mining company alters the spatial set-up of the town by investing in specific infrastructural projects that serve its needs. It assumes planning tasks that are usually reserved for the state and shapes a particular and competing notion of statehood. The pace and power of the mine's technocratic planning leave the town council with little option but to react and mitigate the consequences. The mine's infrastructural projects thus undermine the council's legitimacy while simultaneously adding to its tasks.

Finally, at the political level, the presence of extractive investors has affected voting patterns in a region that has traditionally supported the opposition. The demographic changes triggered by the mine's recruitment policies and the influx of job-seekers have given the ruling party an entry point into what has long been an opposition stronghold, as was demonstrated in the 2016 elections.

I do not interpret these processes as expressions of the resource curse – that is, the corruption of the state by the extractive industry – as many scholars might. Like the editors of this volume, I feel there is little to be learnt from judging the activities of transnational investors in terms of 'hollowing out' or 'weakening' the state (see Introduction, this volume). Rather, I see a lack of synchronicity in town development and the expansion of the mine, coupled with the investors' capacity to produce relative order to ensure smooth extraction. The result of this uncoordinated situation is profound: governmental regulation declines in relation to that of the mine and probably in absolute terms, too. In other words, the local authorities' significance and range are eroded due to the extractive industry, but not for the reasons that are typically articulated by the resource curse literature. On the contrary, the mine would prefer to work with a *strong* council.

In her introduction to the book *Councils in Action*, Audrey Richards examines various types of council, mainly in Africa but also in Europe. She writes: 'Councils … are governed by conventions and persist in time' (Richards 1971, 1). Although she proposes this definition as an analytical limitation for the diverse councils examined in the book, we can also understand it in empirical terms. In this chapter, we have seen that the municipal council displays extraordinary resistance to change. It reacts to the mine as if not much has happened and fails to adapt its practices to the new circumstances. Indeed, when reading council minutes from the 1980s to today, I was struck by the continuity of the topics that were discussed in the meetings. Generally, there is a striking lack of interest in mining matters. For instance, the Solwezi

District Development Plan for 2006–2010, a forty-seven-page document, addresses mining-related changes with just one word in the preface. Given that the largest copper mine in Africa was establishing itself in the district during those years, the council's indifference seems remarkable.

Whether a town manages to gain its fair share from the extractive industry is up to its residents, civil society and other regional, national and international actors. I have attempted to show that the council chamber has a particularly important role to play. As Spencer (1971, 174) wrote in relation to 'Aberton', an industrial town in the north of England in the 1960s:

> [T]he committee meeting emerges as a focal point in the decision-making process: the success of the system will hinge on the rapport built up between the council members and the officers. While there is an explicit 'master–servant' relationship maintained between them and any issue is finally decided solely by the council members, the latter depend on the officers for technical advice and guidance and the pressures towards certain decisions are by no means one-sided.

Many facets of the political economy of a mining town are negotiated between elected councillors and appointed officials, who listen selectively to their constituencies, NGOs and central government or to powerful economic actors. The council chamber is the space where what stateness means is negotiated and where, without downplaying international and corporate forces, we might see a counterforce to resource extractivism.

Notes

1 'Update on 2015 Budget Estimates', FHRGP/15/06/15.
2 Minutes of the FHRGP Committee Meeting, 17 August 2015; Report of the Director of Finance to the FHRGP Committee, FHRGP/02/08/15. The estimated total revenue for 2015 (in kwacha) included local taxes (30 million), fees and charges (10 million), licences (600,000), levies (3.8 million), permits (1 million), service charges (19 million), other income (500,000), national support (8.8 million) and constituency development funds (4.2 million).
3 Report of the Director of Finance to the FHRGP Committee meeting, 12 March 2015, FHRGP/09/03/15. The collected revenue represented only 52 per cent of the budget estimate.
4 'Utilisation Report on Funds Received from Extractive Companies in Solwezi District for January to June 2015' in minutes of the FHRGP Committee meeting, 17 August 2015.
5 Although, in 2015, the Kalumbila/Sentinel mine was already producing, it was not yet on the district's valuation roll.
6 This is my calculation. The minutes state ZMW3,457,522.05, which is impossible.
7 Report of the Director of Finance in the minutes of the FHRGP Committee meeting held on Monday, 12 December 2016, FHRGP/13/12/16.
8 On average, each plot contains 2.3 households, amounting to a total of 69,500 households and 266,000 people living in Solwezi town (Preuss and Schmidt-Eisenlohr 2016, 61).

9 Report of the Director of Finance in the minutes of the FHRGP Committee meeting held on Monday, 12 December 2016, FHRGP/13/12/16. The council's revenue from Kansanshi mine increased from ZWM16,714,804 per annum to ZMW25,324,000 per annum, added to which SMC will receive ZMW6,518,000 from Lumwana mine as part of the three councils' agreement to share Lumwana's revenue.

10 As reported in the Director of Finance's report to the FHRGP Committee, 12 December 2016, FHRGP/15/12/16.

References

Beck, K., G. Klaeger and M. Stasik, eds. 2017. *The Making of the African Road*. Leiden: Brill.

Dalakoglou, D. and P. Harvey. 2012. 'Roads and Anthropology: Ethnographic Perspectives on Space, Time and (Im)mobility', *Mobilities*, 7(4), 459–465.

First Quantum Minerals Ltd. 2017. *Annual Information Form 2016*. Vancouver: FQML.

Golub, A. 2014. *Leviathans at the Gold Mine: Creating Indigenous and Corporate Actors in Papua New Guinea*. Durham, NC: Duke University Press.

Kirsch, S. 2014. *Mining Capitalism: The Relationship between Corporations and Their Critics*. Berkeley: University of California Press.

Harvey, P. and H. Knox. 2015. *Roads: An Anthropology of Infrastructure and Expertise*. Ithaca, NY: Cornell University Press.

Hellen, J.A. 1968. *Rural Economic Development in Zambia, 1890–1964*. München: Weltforum Verlag.

Preuss, L. and D. Schmidt-Eisenlohr. 2016. *Final Report: Solwezi Urban Baseline Study*. Lusaka: GIZ.

Richards, A. 1971. 'Introduction: The Nature of the Problem', in A. Richards and A. Kuper, eds, *Councils in Action*. Cambridge: Cambridge University Press, pp. 1–12.

Spencer, P. 1971. 'Party Politics and the Processes of Local Democracy in an English Town Council', in A. Richards and A. Kuper, eds, *Councils in Action*. Cambridge: Cambridge University Press, pp. 171–201.

URS Scott Wilson Zambia. 2013. *Access Road to Kansanshi Copper Smelter: Final Environmental Impact Statement*. Kitwe: URS Scott Wilson Zambia.

Zambia EITI. 2017. *Extractive Industries Transparency Initiative (EITI) Eighth Report for the Fiscal Year Ended 31 December 2015*. Lusaka: EITI.

8 Political legacies in Ghana's petroleum industry

Monica Skaten

> Oil is the lifeblood of industry. It is as important for industry as water for human existence. The politics of it is even more complicated.
>
> (President Kwame Nkrumah, 1963)

This quote is an excerpt from Kwame Nkrumah's speech at the opening of Ghana's first (and so far only) crude oil refinery in 1963. In its entirety, the speech reflects not just how important fuel is for various industries, but how Nkrumah envisioned the refining of petroleum to be key for Ghanaian state-building. Ghana's first president emphasised nationalist and pan-Africanist state-building with visions of breaking with imperialism and escaping the international oil companies' energy grip. Domestic petroleum industries could unlock African nations' potential for development and freedom (Nkrumah 1963).

In this chapter, I examine Ghana's oil refinery, its legacy and its place in the contemporary petroleum industry. Ghana's new extractive industry has revitalised the debate regarding the refinery's role in the country's economic development path. The refinery and the workers have political weight that prevents governments in Ghana from making drastic changes regarding the state of the refinery. While crude oil refining is becoming centralised around large-scale refineries in Asia, Europe and the United States, the Ghanaian refinery draws on an important political legacy that has been revamped in the face of recent oil and gas discoveries. Political parties in Ghana have to consider this when devising policies and making financial contributions to the industry, particularly ahead of elections.

While navigating established petroleum politics is crucial to political parties in Ghana, creating new legacies by asserting one's reputation through new projects has become just as crucial for political rhetoric and legitimacy in political campaigning. The introduction and development of new infrastructure, state enterprises and petroleum projects has become key in creating imaginaries of how political parties will provide development and employment to the masses in the twenty-first century. However, demonstrating one's success in the energy sector goes only so far. Investigating and prosecuting political opponents when there is a change in government contributes to painting a picture of one's competitors as corrupt and lacking consideration for the dire consequences that follow from the mismanagement of extractive industries. As such, the early political battles in Ghana's petroleum industry reflect an intense competition for state power and political triumph in future elections.

The two largest political parties in Ghana – the National Democratic Congress (NDC) and the New Patriotic Party (NPP) – have been political rivals since the inception of Ghana's Fourth Republic in 1992.[1] Prior to this transition, Jerry Rawlings led Ghana as a military leader under the Provisional National Defence Council (PNDC) from 1981 to 1992. Rawlings then established the NDC and won the first and second democratic elections in 1992 and 1996. The NPP won the 2000 election under the leadership of its presidential candidate, John Kufuor. The NDC returned to power in 2008 with President John Atta-Mills. Ghana saw its third handover of power in the Fourth Republic with the presidential election of 2016, which was won by the NPP and its candidate Nana Akufo-Addo.

The voting patterns in Ghana confirm the unpredictability of support for the country's political elite. While some regions are seen as strongholds for a particular party, most may be classified as swing states (particularly in the south). The NDC is known to embody an ideology of social inclusion, and it is populist and left wing, while the NPP has a more liberal-democratic, right-wing affiliation, and it is seen as elitist and ethnically exclusive. While the NDC's traditional strongholds are in the three northern regions, and among the Ewes in the Volta Region (Rawlings is Ewe), the NPP has traditionally dominated in Ashanti and the Eastern Region (Jockers *et al.* 2010, 95). However, these strongholds are being challenged, and an increasing number of regions in Ghana are shifting allegiance, increasing the competition and cost of political campaigning (Whitfield 2009, 628–632).

It might seem somewhat early to discuss political legacies in Ghana's new petroleum industry. After all, commercial discoveries were made as recently as 2007 and the country produces less than 200,000 barrels of oil per day. However, the petroleum industry is growing and has become important to Ghanaian economic development. The sale of crude oil is providing much-needed foreign exchange and the production of natural gas is contributing to alleviating a long-standing electricity shortage. The new industry also provides employment and it has stimulated the development of a Ghanaian service sector. The successful management of the petroleum industry is utilised at election times by both major political parties to make promises regarding future discoveries and their benefits for the people and the economy.

Ghana's petroleum industry

There are four Ghanaian petroleum basins, three of which are located offshore. The Western Basin is currently the most active, with production in the Jubilee Field, TEN Fields and the Sankofa Fields. The Central Basin is home to Ghana's oldest oil-producing field, the Saltpond Field. The Eastern Basin includes the Accra and Keta blocks, where exploration has been carried out without much commercial reward to date. Finally, the Voltaian Basin covers approximately 40 per cent of Ghana's landmass and represents country's bid for onshore petroleum extraction (Petroleum Commission 2017).

The history of Ghanaian petroleum activity can be traced back to the turn of the twentieth century: the offshore Tano and Keta basins started small-scale production in the early 1900s. The Saltpond Field has been operating since the 1970s (Appiah-Adu 2013, 17). A Soviet–Romanian team of geoscientists exploring the onshore Voltaian Basin in the early 1960s came across traces of oil and gas. Reports of those findings attracted the attention of the oil giant Shell, which acquired seismic data that led to the drilling of the first exploratory well in the basin. However, the well was abandoned due to the poor quality of the reservoir (Apesegah 2008). It was the discovery of the offshore Jubilee Field in 2007 that put Ghana on the map as a commercial oil and gas producer. As part of the new offshore industry, gas infrastructure has been constructed in the Western Region. The Atuabo Gas Processing Plant and the corresponding transportation infrastructure were finalised in 2015, and a processing facility in Sanzule was scheduled for completion in 2018. While natural gas supplies from the new industry have been processed in Ghana, the crude oil extracted thus far has been shipped to Europe.

Despite the low price of crude oil since 2014/2015, Ghana's petroleum industry has developed rapidly. A development plan for the Greater Jubilee Fields received government approval in October 2017 and is expected to increase production levels in the Western Basin. Ghana has experienced external and domestic macro-economic shocks since 2012, which have impacted economic growth. The unreliable supply and low volume of gas imported through the West African Gas Pipeline forced Ghana to import oil to generate electricity. The dramatically increased fuel bill and electricity shortages have had a substantial negative impact on the economy (World Bank 2015). The growth of the petroleum industry in Ghana has therefore become key to tackling some of the country's economic challenges.

The first decade of commercial petroleum exploitation has not been without its challenges. New petroleum projects have developed rapidly, without consideration for the domestic regulatory framework or whether the hydrocarbon resources actually belong to Ghana. A maritime border dispute, political interventions and corruption investigations have plagued the industry. The rush and the upheaval experienced in the industry to date can be ascribed to the quest to form petroleum legacies in a competitive political environment with urgency from both companies and governments to develop fields for production. In 2011, Côte d'Ivoire claimed that Ghana's petroleum activity in the Western Basin was infringing on Ivorian territory. The maritime border between the two countries had never been demarcated, but both Ghana and the operating oil companies assumed a 'tacit agreement' based on previous oil activity in the area. After several failed attempts at bilateral negotiations, the dispute was submitted to the International Tribunal for the Law of the Sea (ITLOS). An interim ruling in 2015 limited companies operating in Ghana from conducting further drilling in the area. However, three years after the submission of the case, although ITLOS rejected the claim of a tacit agreement, it ruled in favour of Ghana (ITLOS 2017).

While Ghana won the maritime border dispute with Côte d'Ivoire, this maritime conflict reflected the hasty development of the industry. The timeline from discovery to production for Ghana's offshore fields would have been short even if the border had been demarcated. Moreover, the regulatory framework for Ghana's upstream industry dated back to the 1980s, which benefited several companies involved in the Jubilee Field when they sold their shares in 2013 (Larbi 2014). The hasty development can be attributed to a number of factors, such as the high price of crude oil when Ghana first started exploiting its resources. It has also been argued that the increasing cost of political campaigning and the urgent need for cash in the NPP's second term (2004–2008) have been central to the rapid development (Gary 2009, 24; Hickey *et al.* 2015, 9). Hickey *et al.* (2015, 9) further argue that when the NDC returned to power in 2008, it encouraged the further rapid development of the Jubilee Field in the hope that oil revenues would secure another election victory in 2012. Hence, the sense of urgency in the industry was facilitated by the political environment, with both major political parties seeking short- and long-term political gains from the production of crude oil.

In Ghana, there is an ongoing debate over which political party enabled the discovery of the Jubilee Field and the subsequent development of the larger offshore petroleum industry. NDC contends that Rawlings established the legal framework for petroleum exploration in the 1980s and that continuous work and investment by the Ghana National Petroleum Corporation (GNPC) under the PNDC/NDC eventually led to commercial discoveries. Meanwhile, the NPP argues that its restructuring of the GNPC and its investor-friendly policies facilitated the discoveries in 2007 (Hickey *et al.* 2015, 18). While both political parties have sought to develop the industry, this argument over who enabled the discoveries reflects their ongoing rhetorical efforts to create new political legacies.

While the Jubilee Field was discovered during Kufuor's NPP government, 'first oil' was achieved during Atta-Mills' NDC administration. The debate regarding which political party facilitated the discovery of oil and gas might seem innocent, but the continued polarisation between the parties when there is a change of government has had implications for individuals, corporations and the whole industry. The NPP's election victory in the 2000s resulted in major structural changes in the industry, including the restructuring of GNPC and reform of the downstream industry. However, when the NDC returned to power in 2008, it revoked several of these changes and placed a number of key individuals in the Jubilee project under investigation. I examine these processes and the tug of war between Ghana's two main political parties in their bid to establish political legacies in the 'new' petroleum industry. First, however, I examine a long-standing petroleum legacy that demonstrates the significance of infrastructure and political vision in forging state imaginaries tied to the extractive industry. We shall also see how ideas of market efficiency and technical efficiency collide with the vision of national development through an integrated petroleum industry. While Ghana has an oil refinery that is capable of processing domestically produced crude oil, no operating company is willing to supply that refinery. Hence, although domestic political competition influences the outcome of the industry, some processes remain out of the hands of Ghana's political elite.

The Tema Oil Refinery

A grand ceremony attended by a host of national and international dignitaries marked the official opening of the Tema Oil Refinery in 1963 (see TOR 2018). The legacy of Kwame Nkrumah and his vision for the refinery is still present in the contemporary political environment. The discoveries of offshore oil and gas have brought to the fore questions regarding the role of the refinery and its contribution to economic development. With the consequent growth in the extractive sector, successive governments in Ghana have promoted the downstream industry's potential in the belief that it could have transformative capacity in the national economy. Examining the impact of the refinery's legacy in contemporary politics demonstrates the significance of current political competition and its impact on Ghana's petroleum industry. The case of the Tema Oil Refinery highlights that petroleum infrastructure can remain politically important decades after its construction.

The refinery was first mentioned in Ghana's parliament on 4 March 1959. It was part of the Convention People's Party's (CPP's) second five-year development plan, which had the essential aim of increasing living standards for all Ghanaians through industrialisation. The refinery was envisaged as an important component in the creation of an industrial base to drive development, increase agricultural output and eventually alleviate poverty. Two senior ministers from the CPP were sent to Italy to negotiate the construction and operation of the refinery at Tema. The Ghanaian Italian Petroleum Corporation – as the refinery was originally known – was commissioned in 1961 (Biney 2011, 100).

The establishment of the refinery was seen as a major achievement towards Ghana's industrial development. Like other major industrial undertakings, it was developed with external financial and technical assistance – what Nkrumah himself termed 'a common sense and practical approach to industrial development' in a parliamentary debate of 1957 (quoted in Biney 2011, 100). Nation-building through modernisation projects in Nkrumah's newly independent Ghana were often undertaken with expatriate expertise from all over the world (Miescher 2012; Allman 2014,

230). The Italians' experience fed into Nkrumah's vision and goals of nation-building, anti-imperialism and energy independence because Italy itself had progressed from importing petroleum products from multinational oil companies to refining crude oil in domestic refineries in cooperation with Iran, saving itself a great deal of money and creating employment opportunities (Frankel 1966). The Italian administrator Enrico Mattei had been a key player in this development as he had overseen the creation of the National Hydrocarbons Trust (ENI), which had successfully challenged the powerful international oil cartel in the 1950s (Bridge and le Billion 2013, 49). His death in a plane crash just before the opening of the refinery in Ghana fuelled conspiracy claims that plagued the oil industry in the 1950s and 1960s.

Like other major state projects, the refinery was built to impress as a physical structure and tangibly demonstrate its importance in spearheading Ghana's economic, industrial and developmental goals (Killick 1978, 167). It was a supremely modern creation, technologically equipped for industrialisation. Modern infrastructure and equipment signalled the way forward, substantiating the expectations and hopes of the early 1960s. The refinery was set to become part of the backbone of the Ghanaian economy, pumping fuel to industry and agriculture, securing freedom from 'energy imperialists' and materialising the socialist dreams of Nkrumah's independent Ghana.

Brian Larkin (2008) has demonstrated that the arrival of electricity in Kano in colonial Nigeria in 1932 provided an opportunity for a public display of authority. He argues that infrastructural projects can become 'sublime' as we judge them in relation to other objects, distinguishing between what is great and what is worthless. Infrastructural projects, according to Larkin, were necessary gestures for entrenching colonial rule and authority in Nigeria. The will that goes into the construction of such impressive infrastructure does not easily disappear. Larkin (2008, 47) argues that the conceptual horizons of what people expect the technology to do will haunt the infrastructure over time. Like many of Nkrumah's infrastructural projects, the oil refinery did not live up to the expectations that developed for it during its construction. As happened with other projects built with foreign assistance (such as Ghana's aluminium smelter), the Italian operators and multinational oil companies became the refinery's greatest beneficiaries (see Kuruk 1991, 43). This unfortunate development did not, however, diminish the importance of the vision and political will that went into building the refinery. The infrastructure was held up as a symbol of patriotism, political independence and freedom. It was touted as a catalyst for economic growth and development, and, as such, was elevated to a high political status, infused by the vision and early popularity of Nkrumah. This symbolic resonance persists today in political debates, media articles and indeed conversations and claims among engineers at the refinery.

The original agreement between Ghana and the Italians stated that crude oil could be procured freely on the international market. However, if oil and gas were discovered in Ghana, the Italians were obliged to refine the product for the Ghanaian market, provided that the refinery was deemed technologically suitable (Prempeh 2010). While this agreement gave considerable leeway to the Italian corporation, it showed Nkrumah's vision for an integrated petroleum industry at the very inception of the refinery. However, this contract was terminated in 1977 when the government of Ghana became the sole shareholder of the refinery. As it stands today, there are no legal obligations for oil and gas producers in Ghana to utilise the refinery for the processing of domestic crude oil. Indeed, the majority of crude oil refined at the refinery has been procured from Nigeria and Libya, and to a lesser extent from Equatorial Guinea. The refining machinery has proved most effective when processing sweet, light crude oil with low sulphur levels. This type of crude oil has been widely available since Shell and BP made discoveries in Nigeria in the 1950s. These are also the characteristics of the crude oil in the Jubilee Field (Tullow Oil 2017).

The hiatus between Nkrumah's CPP government (1957–1966) and Jerry John Rawlings' period in office (1981–1992) had particularly detrimental effects on the management of the refinery. Military and civilian governments resorted to short-term economic and political survival strategies (Pellow and Chazan 1986, 36), and the Ghanaian economy suffered from decline, high inflation and commodity shortages (Killick 1978; Smilie 1986). A prolific informal economy developed, and the oil refinery became a crucial part of it. Theft of petroleum products by engineers and technicians was common, and more orchestrated large-scale scams happened from time to time. Successive governments used the refinery as their personal filling station, and the debt kept increasing until it threatened the survival of Ghana's banks. These practices at the refinery impacted the way that the public viewed the refinery, as it gradually became a symbol of corruption and inefficiency that benefited the elite who had preferential access to the state.

In 2000, the NDC lost the election to the NPP, and Ghana's president for the next two terms (2000–2008) was John Kufuor. The NPP had promised the electorate an end to fuel shortages and cheaper fuel for Ghanaian consumers. The Tema Oil Refinery experienced a renaissance as petroleum product subsidies were initially high, and the government provided credit to keep the machinery running. While Rawlings had been cautious about delivering crude oil to the refinery, Kufuor provided it with letters of credit and set up a credit scheme for the oil companies in order to encourage the industry to produce a large volume of petroleum products for Ghana's filling stations.

There was another change of government in 2008 when the NDC regained power under President John Atta-Mills. This stirred some conflict in the newly revitalised oil industry (see Gyimah-Boadi and Prempeh 2012; Graham *et al.* 2016). Contracts were scrutinised, some companies were banned from operating in Ghana, and the credit scheme that had kept the refinery running was suspended because, according to the new government, the refinery's debt had spiralled out of control (see Hayford 2009). Some of the oil companies had not paid their bills, but with their high-level political connections they had still been able to operate, creating a problem for the refinery's bank balance. Engineers at the refinery felt that the NPP was supportive of the refinery, while the NDC was supportive of the other state petroleum assets, such as the state-owned Bulk Oil Storage and Transportation Company (BOST).

Working under difficult circumstances, and convinced that the NDC was trying to halt the operation of the refinery altogether, the workers were still utterly shocked by Tullow Oil Ghana's position after production started on the Jubilee Field. The consortium of oil companies operating on the field held a press conference in Tamale, where it was stated that the Tema Oil Refinery was currently unable to refine the Jubilee oil. A journalist asked about the refinery's role in the new upstream petroleum industry and the incorporation of local industries, and a Ghanaian engineer with Tullow Oil Ghana replied that the refinery would need to be retrofitted in order to process the crude oil produced by the Jubilee Field. He claimed that the refinery was able to refine only lower-quality crude oil and then took the opportunity to point out that retrofitting would be very expensive and might even be counterproductive, as further exploration in Ghana might discover other types of crude oil (GhanaWeb 2011).

The NDC was still in power during my fieldwork at the refinery in 2014, and there was widespread resentment over its management of the facility among the workers. They insisted that the refinery was perfectly able to refine the crude oil from the Jubilee Field and that 'someone somewhere' had gone to great lengths to convince ordinary Ghanaians that the refinery was outdated, probably for their own benefit. There was a strong emphasis on the workers' technical prowess at the refinery. A favourite point of reference was US President Barack Obama's visit to Ghana in 2009. His *Air Force One* personnel arrived at the refinery to test its aviation fuel, gave it their seal of approval, and then used it to fuel the plane for the remainder of Obama's Africa tour.

The refinery had received only small supplies of crude oil since the change of government in 2008, allegedly because it was carrying a huge amount of debt. However, my interviewees pointed out that more debt was incurred during the refinery's dormancy. Starting up and shutting down the equipment cost around US$5 million, which increased the refinery's debt at a time when it had almost no income. Everyone knew that the debt was significant. The debate centred on the question of whether it was due to the refinery's own financial mismanagement (as the media and 'experts' often asserted) or to a tendency among government ministries to use it as their personal filling station and help themselves to petroleum products without paying (as the facility's engineers insisted). The engineers viewed the portrayal of their refinery as inefficient – and of the workers themselves as thieves with no technical prowess – as a political manoeuvre. They knew that the refinery embodied an important legacy, and that citing recent developments and presenting it as an outdated piece of infrastructure would justify the NDC's decision to halt the supply of crude oil. However, the workers were fairly confident that the refinery's legacy and importance would be re-established as soon as the NDC saw some benefit in doing so.

As the workers had predicted, in 2016 media outlets reported that the tide had turned for the Tema Oil Refinery. In 2014, President John Dramani Mahama of the NDC had stated in his annual address to the nation that the refinery was in final negotiations with PetroSaudi over a merger (IMANI 2014), yet, two years later, during a visit to the refinery, he declared: 'Government has no intention of selling the Tema Oil Refinery and we will rather assist the refinery to re-establish itself as a vibrant state enterprise in petroleum production' (Benaba 2016). Mahama also stated that the government was planning to build a new crude distillation unit to expand the refinery's capacity and re-establish it as a viable entity and position it as one of the foremost state enterprises in Ghana (TOR 2016).

The refinery had resumed operations in February 2016. The media reported that it had been receiving crude oil from BOST and that the cooperation between the two state-owned enterprises was likely to continue. The refinery had also received financial support from the government, albeit only half of what it had been promised (Ocloo and Mordey 2016). Nevertheless, the workers were happy that the plant had resumed operations. In a demonstration of their appreciation, a group of engineers travelled to Wa in the Upper West Region, where Mahama was holding a political rally. A representative from the union thanked the President for rescuing what he described as a 'crippled national asset' and restoring national dignity and security (Ocloo and Mordey 2016).

The refinery's resumption of operations was also celebrated with a thanksgiving service. The theme was 'Thanking God for Tema Oil Refinery', and the managing director announced, 'The spiritual battle that faced the refinery is over' (Ocloo and Mordey 2016). The revival of the refinery and the thanksgiving service can be viewed as parts of a political ritual. Emphasising the broad significance of the refinery for Ghana's economy and security was in the best interests of the workers, who told me that the atmosphere in the plant had changed since operations had resumed. However, they were suspicious that this had happened in an election year, and wondered if it was just a political move to keep the NDC in power.

Ghana's first president, Kwame Nkrumah, built the refinery in the hope that it would prove to be a major component in an integrated petroleum industry once oil was discovered within Ghanaian territory. For the engineers, the refinery embodied and symbolised Nkrumah's vision and promise; and in the midst of its dormancy, they utilised the symbolic representational history of the refinery to call for patriotism and unity in order to get it running again. Persistent public displays of the government's intention to privatise the refinery, as well as the ongoing unavailability of crude oil for operations, were understood as aspects of the political environment. And while the threats of privatisation were real enough, governments of every stripe recognised the importance of the refinery as a state-owned enterprise that provided a basic public service. The refinery has become synonymous with the provision of petroleum products, and so plays a crucial role in the two main parties' efforts to secure a majority in Ghana's competitive democracy. Neither the NPP nor the NDC wants to be accused of allowing the famous enterprise to fall into terminal decline. However, its commercial viability has long been open to question, and it has relied on government support for decades. As such, successive NDC administrations took the decision to keep it mothballed for most of the 2008–2016 period, authorising its resumption of operations only in the run-up to national elections.

Ghana's competitive democracy, combined with the refinery's political legacy, might hinder the enterprise's privatisation. However, making it profitable and materialising the imagery of national development through an integrated petroleum industry collide with current trends of flow and market efficacy propagated in global commodity trade and the international petroleum industry (Ferguson 2005; Appel 2012). Crude oil from Ghana's offshore fields is shipped to Europe for processing, not because the refinery needs 'retrofitting' but because the Jubilee consortium is more focused on profit than national development. Due to its political legacy and the fierce competition between Ghana's principal parties, the refinery remains dormant for long periods of time and resumes operations only when it is politically expedient to do so. Therefore, its changing fate demonstrates the importance of political legacies in the petroleum industry, currently battled out between Ghana's two main parties, both of which are seeking leverage in order to cement their political legitimacy.

New political legacies in Ghana's petroleum industry

There are two main state-owned petroleum corporations in Ghana's upstream industry: the Ghana National Petroleum Corporation (GNPC), established during Rawlings' military regime in 1983; and the Ghana National Gas Company (GNGC), established by Atta-Mills' government in 2011 in response to the discovery of oil and gas in the Jubilee Field. Governments use these state-owned petroleum companies to forge links between the extractive industry and national development by taking ownership of the industry on behalf of Ghanaian citizens, by establishing control over the domestic gas industry and by providing employment, sponsorships and scholarships. Due to their crucial political and developmental roles, the corporations have become important battlegrounds for political legacies. Ghana has a long-standing political culture in which state-owned companies are valued as key drivers of economic growth and state-building that can be traced back to Nkrumah's economic policies and the continued protection of key state enterprises during the structural adjustment period in the 1980s and 1990s (Adda 1994). Their inherent legitimacy as state entities makes them useful for forging imaginaries of state-building and economic progress for whichever party happens to be in power. Moreover, whenever there is a change of government, the new administration has a golden opportunity to tarnish its predecessor's reputation by scrutinising the contracts it signed and the work it undertook. Any issues that subsequently come to light can be highly damaging to the party concerned due to the importance of the petroleum industry in the national economy. Therefore, accusations of corruption or mismanagement are routinely made during national election campaigns or more generally to harm a party's overall legitimacy.

The upper echelons of GNPC have always been filled by people who are closely affiliated to the sitting president, with the role of chief executive viewed as one of the most prestigious in government. Tsatsu Tsikata, who had a socialist orientation with a national development vision for the petroleum industry, served as head of the corporation from 1988 to 2000. He sought a strong state presence in exploration activities and wanted to utilise domestic resources to develop the industry. However, this was a period of economic hardship for Ghana. Structural adjustment programmes deprived Rawlings' government of ready cash, and there were no commercially viable oil and gas deposits in GNPC's portfolio throughout Tsikata's tenure. As a result, he decided to diversify and invest in cocoa farms, salt production, gold production and the telecommunications industry. These investments were supposed to yield high returns that the corporation could then reinvest in its core oil and gas activities (Hickey *et al.* 2015, 11). However, critics claim that they merely distracted GNPC from its principal task – the search for oil and gas (Hickey *et al.* 2015, 16) – and turned the corporation into a vehicle for the accumulation of personal wealth (Opoku 2010). Similar criticisms have been levelled at the leaders of other Ghanaian state-owned enterprises in the same period (Killick 1978).

When the NPP came to power, Tsikata was accused of causing financial losses to the state and misappropriating public funds and property. His trial began in 2001 and continued for six years before he was finally convicted. He was sentenced to five years in prison, along with several other PNDC/NDC politicians. In light of the close ties between GNPC and Rawlings' government, the new administration embarked on extensive restructuring of the whole corporation (Mohan and Ashante 2015, 8). A downsizing exercise resulted in the dismissal of 90 per cent of GNPC's employees (Hickey *et al.* 2015, 18). Meanwhile, private capital was injected, and the corporation was transformed into a commercial upstream operator in 2002. The NPP also removed the corporation's long-standing regulatory mandate for both upstream and downstream sectors. However, after the NDC returned to power in 2008, the GNPC enjoyed heavy investment in recruitment and capacity-building projects. Technical and political personnel were rehired and the new government re-established the corporation's strong position in the sector, although it did not restore GNPC's regulatory mandate (Hickey *et al*. 2015, 18). A Ghanaian court also overturned Tsikata's conviction and he was freed in January 2009.

Throughout its period in opposition and especially in the campaigning ahead of the 2016 elections, the NPP lobbied for reform of the industry and greater transparency. In accord with its market-led approach, it promised continued exploration through foreign investment and public–private partnerships to build additional processing plants. It also insisted that it would improve the utilisation of gas for electrification and make the Western Region a hub for the oil and gas industry by moving GNPC's headquarters to Sekondi-Takoradi. The latter promise was made in the hope of securing the support of the local chiefs, who had long been demanding 10 per cent of Ghana's petroleum revenue for development of the region, without success.

The NDC also focused on GNPC in its electoral campaign. In particular, it trumpeted its 'community engagement' during an exploration programme called the Voltaian Basin Project. In practical terms, this engagement consisted of semi-rural meetings with various communities to discuss the basin's oil and gas potential and the benefits that would accrue to the residents in the surrounding areas in the form of land compensation and youth employment (GNA 2015). With respect to this project, the NDC government went so far as to award an exploration and production licence to a consortium that included GNPC, a local company headed by an NDC party member and a Swiss–African oil company with no track record in Ghana. However, at the time of writing in 2018, no exploration had been undertaken. Therefore, all of the activity in the Voltaian Basin may be attributed to the area's substantial political significance. It covers four of Ghana's administrative regions and includes a large proportion of the electorate. At an election rally in the Volta Region in 2016, Nana Akufo-Addo promised that the NPP would develop the basin for oil and gas production, foster economic development and create jobs, just as it had in the Western Region.

In February 2011, President Atta-Mills had commissioned a Natural Gas Development Task Force to assess how Ghana could most efficiently develop and utilise its natural gas reserves in the Jubilee Field. GNGC was enacted as a limited liability company in June of that year and given the mandate to build, own and operate the infrastructure required for extracting, processing, transporting and marketing the country's natural gas reserves. Senior NDC politicians were appointed to the GNGC board and management, including Kwesi Botchway (former Minister of Finance) and George Sipa-Adja Yankey (former Minister for Health). Both men were also members of the Natural Gas Development Task Force. The main aim of GNGC was to construct and operate the Western Corridor Gas Infrastructure Development Project (Ministry of Petroleum 2015). As part of the project, the Atuabo Gas Processing Plant was constructed in Nzemaland, Western Region, but was delayed for several months after the main contractor, the Chinese National Petroleum Company (SINOPEC), failed to receive payment from Atta-Mills' government.

In Ghana, both oil companies and the government emphasise the benefits of natural gas for domestic consumption and economic development. They associate the industry with notions of modernity and development, and insist that it will deliver an abundance of cheap electricity and clean fuel for cooking.[2] In an echo of the narrative that has been presented to the citizens of Mozambique (see Symons 2016, 150), the main theme is that gas production is in the national interest. Unlike the crude oil that never reaches the shores of Ghana, the gas is pumped ashore and then processed and consumed by Ghanaians. Unfortunately, though, the national gas company has faced many of the same challenges that have plagued other state-owned corporations in Ghana.

GNGC provides its largest customer, the Volta River Authority (VRA), with gas for the generation of electricity. The VRA is a state-owned company that supplies other state-owned companies with electricity, and as a result GNGC has suffered severe cash-flow problems due to delays in the settling of accounts. One report suggests that the VRA currently owes GNGC US$500 million (Nyavor 2017). Meanwhile, the VRA has stated that it will be unable to pay up until the electricity companies have settled their outstanding bills. For their part, the electricity companies blame their consumers for failing to pay for the power they use. Raising tariffs or forcefully collecting money owed by Ghanaian citizens is not an option as pursuing either policy would directly contradict the gas industry's bold promises and be politically damaging to whichever party dared to broach the subject. Hence, GNGC remains cash-strapped, so further progress on the Atuabo Gas Processing Plant seems a remote possibility. Moreover, the perpetual competition between the two main parties has resulted in frequent changes of personnel in the company's hierarchy, which have hampered its long-term development.

Delays and GNGC's ongoing financial difficulties became a cause for concern for Eni and its development plan for the Sankofa Field. GNGC was forced to provide a financial guarantee for the gas from the field because its limited liability status and poor balance sheets were deemed insufficient. Therefore, it was announced in the 2015 budget plan that GNGC would be consolidated with GNPC, making the former a subsidiary of the latter. This, along with an extensive World Bank guarantee, proved acceptable to Eni and it agreed to press ahead with its plan for the Sankofa Field. Nevertheless, a number of important players were vocal in their opposition to the consolidation of GNGC and GNPC. For instance, Kwesi Botchway, who was still a central figure in both GNGC and the NDC, spoke out against the move (Mordy 2014), even though he must have known that his party did not have much choice if it wanted gas processed at the plant in Atuabo to power future projects. He continued to complain until he was offered a prestigious new role at the National Development Planning Commission.

Predictably, when the NPP returned to power in 2016, it appointed entirely new management teams at both GNGC and GNPC. President

Akufo-Addo seems determined to follow through on his election promise to move at least part of GNPC's headquarters to Sekondi-Takoradi; and at the opening ceremony of the Sankofa Field he announced a campaign to attract investment for further exploration in the Voltaian Basin (Ibrahim 2017). The NPP is also in the process of reviewing and investigating many of the deals that were struck between the preceding NDC government and independent power producers, one of which is known as the 'Ameri Energy deal'. Akufo-Addo's investigating committee concluded that this deal, which included the purchase of ten gas turbines, was 'bloated' due to the payment of an exorbitant US$150 million in commission to Ameri Energy for its construction of the power plant (Lokko 2017). The former Minister of Power, Kwabena Donkor, is currently the subject of a police investigation, and the NPP has effectively abolished his fiefdom by merging it with the Ministry of Energy and Petroleum.

It is still widely believed that oil and gas will play important roles in Ghana's economic development. With a strong emphasis on state-owned corporations in the sector, these companies have become key battlegrounds for political parties to manage their petroleum legacies. Successful management of the petroleum industry will enhance the legitimacy of any political party in Ghana and increase its chances of securing victory in future elections. GNPC control of offshore fields and the domestic gas industry both help to produce national imaginaries of development through the extractive industry.

The EO–Kosmos energy conflict

Since the discovery of the Jubilee Field in 2007, Kosmos Energy (hereafter Kosmos) has had a troubled time in Ghana due to the polarisation of the two main political parties. The change in government from NPP to NDC in 2008 led to questions being asked about Kosmos's entry into the country through its relationship with the EO Group, a Ghanaian petroleum company. Both the new Ghanaian government and the US Department of Justice subsequently launched criminal investigations into the firm. The issue was ultimately resolved and Kosmos still operates in Ghana, but the case reflects the inherent dangers of playing an active role in Ghana's extractive industries, especially when a new government comes to power. In this instance, the new NDC administration sought to expose NPP corruption, tarnish the NPP's reputation and strengthen its own legitimacy by presenting itself as the sensible guardian of the nation's resources. Kosmos simply got caught in the crossfire.

Kosmos is a US exploration company based in Dallas, Texas. It was established in 2003 by the previous management of Trinton Energy, with Jim Musselman in charge. Charles Owusu and Kwame Bawuah-Edusei, two Ghanaian nationals living in the United States, founded the EO Group, contacted Kosmos and proposed exploration in Ghana's offshore waters. Hence, the EO Group facilitated Kosmos's entry into Ghana and directed its attention towards the Western Cape Three Point Block. In return, it received a 3.5 per cent stake in the Jubilee Field. Kosmos also agreed to cover the EO Group's initial costs with respect to the exploration and development.[3]

All of the EO Group's management team had close political connections with the NPP government and mediated the latter's relationship with Kosmos (Gyimah-Boadi and Prempeh 2012, 105). Owusu himself became Kosmos's country representative in Ghana. While Kosmos certainly hoped to establish a good relationship with the ruling party, it failed to do its due diligence with respect to Ghana's party political system. Not long after John Atta-Mills was sworn in as the country's new (NDC) president, a police investigation was launched into the relationship between the EO Group and the previous government's officials amid accusations of misuse of political connections and the forging of signatures on official documents. The police questioned all of the partners in the Jubilee consortium and the government instructed the Bank of Ghana to freeze the accounts of Kosmos and all affiliated individuals (Wikileaks 2009).

In October 2009, Anadarko reported Kosmos to the US Department of Justice in relation to Kosmos's compliance with the Foreign Corrupt Practices Act (FCPA) and possible violations in connection with securing licensing, exploration and production agreements. Up to that point, the two companies had been working together on the Jubilee Field, so theories started circulating about Anadarko's close connections with the new NDC government and its desire to gain a larger share of the Jubilee Field by stabbing its former partner in the back (Bonsu 2010).

In an attempt to restore its reputation and rescue its investments, Kosmos first fired Owusu and then announced its intention to sell its stake in the Jubilee Field – which it estimated at US$4 billion – to ExxonMobil. GNPC had previously expressed an interest in this stake, but with no offer from the Ghanaian corporation forthcoming, Kosmos entered into negotiations with ExxonMobil as planned. However, the NDC administration announced that it would not approve the sale, which increased the strain on its already fraught relationship with Kosmos. The US company responded by declaring that the government was motivated solely by a desire to secure the stake at a knockdown price for GNPC.

Distinguishing between rumours, conspiracy theories and facts is often quite challenging in Ghana (and in the international oil industry), and that is certainly the case here. In an attempt to distance itself further from the accusations of corruption, Kosmos's board of directors removed Jim Musselman. With two of the original front men – Musselman and Owusu – now out of the picture, Kosmos set about repairing its fractured relationship with the Ghanaian government. In December 2010, the two sides signed a truce. Four months later, the US Department of Justice announced that it would be taking no further action with respect to Kosmos and the EO Group.

Foreign extractive companies' use of domestic political elites as silent minority partners for political leverage has been observed elsewhere (Burgis

2015; Soares de Oliveira 2015), but in this case an international regulatory framework was employed to generate opportunities for domestic political gain. The NDC painted the relationship between the EO Group and Kosmos as corrupt not just to secure more shares in the Jubilee Field but to demonstrate that its chief political rival had presided over a crooked administration. The ultimate aim was to convince the electorate that the NPP was selling Ghanaian resources to foreign investors, pocketing vast personal profits for itself and leaving Ghanaians in the dark throughout. The EO Group and Kosmos were used to cast a shadow on NPP's reputation, to the benefit of the NDC and its strategy for developing Ghana's petroleum industry.

Conclusion

The two political parties that have dominated Ghanaian politics for many years – the NDC and the NPP – are in a constant battle over the management of the new petroleum industry, although the imaginary of national development through oil extraction and refining dates back to the time of Kwame Nkrumah. Debates tend to focus on who facilitated the discoveries and which policies generate the greatest benefits for Ghanaians. The importance of securing legacies, short- or long-term, has become key to the political processes in Ghana's petroleum industry, including initiating new infrastructural projects, such as the Atuabo Gas Processing Plant, and prosecuting former state officials to highlight the opposition's contempt for the Ghanaian people. Unfortunately, emphasising one's own positive role in the petroleum industry does not carry as much political clout as painting the opposition as corrupt. So, whenever there is a change in government, the previous administration's energy projects are scrutinised and associated individuals are prone to harassment, prosecution and even imprisonment. While it may be argued that this helps to safeguard Ghana against large-scale corruption, it is also used as a tactic for securing greater political legitimacy vis-à-vis the opposition.

It is important to note that not every political process or project in Ghana's petroleum industry is dictated by domestic political affairs. For instance, the Tema Oil Refinery was deprived of Ghanaian crude oil simply because most of the major corporations prefer to refine their petroleum products at large-scale refineries. And the NDC did not want to make GNGC a subsidiary of GNPC; rather, the World Bank and the operators of the Sankofa Field insisted on the consolidation. Ghana's competitive democracy is central to the development of the country's petroleum industry with respect to both the established petroleum infrastructure, such as the Tema Oil Refinery, and the new processes initiated by the political parties in their quest to forge petroleum legacies. Hence, Nkrumah's quote is worth repeating: 'Oil is the lifeblood of industry. It is as important for industry as water for human existence. The politics of it is even more complicated' (Nkrumah 1963).

Notes

1 Although there are other political parties in Ghana, they do not receive significant support during national elections. For instance, the Progressive People's Party and the Convention People's Party garnered a combined total of less than 2 per cent of the national vote in the 2016 elections.

2 See, for example, Eni 2017.

3 Further details can be found in the documentary of this conflict, directed by Rachel Boynton, *Big Men: Everyone Wants to Be Big* (2013). Available online, http://bigmenthemovie.com. Accessed 8 March 2018.

References

Adda, W.A. 1994. *Public Enterprise Reform: The Ghana Experience*. Available online, http://unpan1.un.org/intradoc/groups/public/documents/aapam/unpan027477.pdf. Accessed 19. 01. 2018.

Allman, J. 2014. Modeling Modernity: The Brief Story of Kwame Nkrumah, a Nazi Pilot Named Hanna, and the Wonders of Motorless Flight. In P. Bloom, T. Manuh and S. Miescher, eds, *Modernization as Spectacle*. Bloomington: Indiana University Press, pp. 229–243.

Apesegah, E. 2008. Hydrocarbon Potential of the Voltaian Basin (Post-Premuase-1 Well). In F. Kalsbeek, ed., *The Voltaian Basin, Ghana Workshop and Excursion*. Copenhagen: Geological Survey of Denmark and Greenland, Ministry of Climate and Environment, pp. 75–79.

Appel, H. 2012. Offshore Work: Oil, Modularity, and the How of Capitalism in Equatorial Guinea. *Journal of the American Ethnological Society*, 34(4), 692–709.

Appiah-Adu, K. 2013. *Governance of the Petroleum Sector in an Emerging Developing Economy*. Surrey: Ashgate and Gower.

Benaba, G.-R. 2016. TOR is Not for Sale – President Mahama. Available online, www.ghananewsagency.org/politics/tor-is-not-for-sale-president-mahama-103659. Accessed 19. 01. 2018.

Biney, A. 2011. *The Political and Social Thought of Kwame Nkrumah*. New York: Palgrave Macmillan.

Bonsu, A. 2010. Anadarko's Romance with Tsikata Exposed. Available online, www.modernghana.com/news/266758/anadarkos-romance-with-tsikata-exposed.html. Accessed 10. 12. 2017.

Bridge, G. and P. le Billion. 2013. *Oil*. Cambridge: Polity Press.

Burgis, T. 2015. *The Looting Machine: Warlords, Tycoons, Smugglers and the Systematic Theft of Africa's Wealth*. London: William Collins.

Eni. 2017. Gas and Renewables for a Sustainable Development of Ghana. Available online, www.eni.com/en_IT/media/2017/11/eni-gas-and-renewables-for-a-sustainable-development-of-ghana. Accessed 25. 01. 2018.

Ferguson, J. 2005. Seeing Like an Oil Company: Space, Security, and Global Capital in Neoliberal Africa. *American Anthropologist*, 107(3), 377–381.

Frankel, P.H. 1966. *Mattei: Oil and Power Politics*. London: Faber and Faber.

Gary, I. 2009. *Ghana's Big Test: Oil's Challenge to Democratic Development*. Accra: Oxfam and Integrated Social Development Centre

GhanaWeb. 2011. Tema Oil Refinery Cannot Refine Jubilee Oil. Available online, www.ghanaweb.com/GhanaHomePage/NewsArchive/Tema-Oil-Refinery-cannot-refine-Jubilee-Oil-208228. Accessed 19. 01. 2018.

GNA. 2015. GNPC Committed to Work with Communities. Available online, www.ghananewsagency.org/economics/gnpc-committed-to-work-with-communities-mould-92718. Accessed 25. 01. 2018.

Graham, E., I. Ackah and R.E. Gyampo. 2016. Politics of Oil and Gas in Ghana. *Insight on Africa*, 8(2), 131–141.

Gyimah-Boadi, E. and H.K. Prempeh. 2012. Oil, Politics and Ghana's Democracy. *Journal of Democracy*, 23(3), 94–108.

Hayford, A. 2009. Tema Oil Refinery Debt: Who is Lying? Available online, www.ghanaweb.com/GhanaHomePage/features/Tema-Oil-Refinery-Debt-who-is-lying-163742. Accessed 25. 01. 18.

Hickey, S., A.-G. Abdulai, A. Izama and G. Mohan. 2015. The Politics of Governing Oil Effectively: A Comparative Study of Two New Oil-rich States in Africa. Effective States and Inclusive Development (ESID) Working Paper Series, No. 54. Manchester: University of Manchester.

Ibrahim, A. 2017. Akufo-Addo Hopes for Fourth FPSO as Search for Volta Basin Oil Goes on. Available online, www.myjoyonline.com/business/2017/july-6th/akufo-addo-hopes-for-fourth-fpso-as-ghana-searches-volta-basin-for-black-gold.php. Accessed 25. 01. 2018.

IMANI. 2014. IMANI Report: Evidence-based Support for Ghana to Ratify the EPA. Available online, www.myjoyonline.com/business/2014/April-14th/imani-report-evidence-based-support-for-ghana-to-ratify-the-epa.php. Accessed 19. 01. 2018.

ITLOS. 2017. Dispute Concerning Delimitation of Maritime Boundary between Ghana and Côte d'Ivoire in the Atlantic Ocean. Available online, www.itlos.org/fileadmin/itlos/documents/cases/case_no.23_merits/C23_Judgment_23.09.2017_corr.pdf. Accessed 22. 01. 2018.

Jockers, H., D. Kohnert and P. Nugent. 2010. The Successful Ghana Election of 2008: A Convenient Myth? *Journal of Modern African Studies*, 48(1), 95–115.

Killick, T. 1978. *Development Economics in Action: A Study of Economic Policies in Ghana*. London: Heinemann.

Kuruk, P. 1991. Renegotiating Transnational Investment Agreements: Lessons for Developing Countries from the Ghana-Valco Experience. *Michigan Journal of International Law*, 13, 43–82.

Larbi, C. 2014. Ghana Loses US$70m. Available online, www.modernghana.com/news/527040/ghana-loses-us70m.html. Accessed 23. 01. 18.

Larkin, B. 2008. *Signal and Noise Media, Infrastructure, and Urban Culture in Nigeria*. Durham, NC: Duke University Press.

Lokko, V. 2017. Ameri Deal to be Abrogated over $150m 'Bloated' Commission – Committee. Available online, http://citifmonline.com/2017/03/27/ameri-deal-to-be-abrogated-over-150m-bloated-commission/. Accessed 25. 01. 2018.

Miescher, S.F. 2012. Building the City of the Future: Visions and Experiences of Modernity in Ghana's Akosombo Township. *Journal of African History*, 53(3), 367–390.

Ministry of Petroleum. 2015. *Gas Master Plan*. Available online, http://pdf.usaid.gov/pdf_docs/PA00M84F.pdf. Accessed 20. 01. 2018.

Mordy, J. 2014. Kwesi Botchway Explodes over Ghana Gas Takeover. Available online, www.myjoyonline.com/news/2014/December-16th/kwesi-botchway-explodes-over-ghana-gas-takeover-we-are-not-minions-to-be-ordered-about.php. Accessed 25. 01. 2018.

Nkrumah, K. 1963. Formal Opening of the Oil Refinery. Available online, http://nkrumahinfobank.org/article.php?id=439&c=51. Accessed 24. 01. 2018.

Nyavor, G. 2017. VRA Debts to Ghana Gas Could Spiral out of Control – PIAC Warns. Available online, www.myjoyonline.com/business/2017/january-17th/piac-warns-against-ballooning-vra-indebtedness-to-ghana-gas.php. Accessed 20. 01. 2018.

Ocloo, R.D. and E. Mordey. 2016. TOR Comes Alive. Available online, www.graphic.com.gh/news/general-news/tor-comes-alive-makes-profit-first-in-seven-years.html. Accessed 10. 12. 17.

Opoku, D.K. 2010. *The Politics of Government–Business Relations in Ghana, 1982–2008*. New York: Palgrave Macmillan.

Pellow, D. and N. Chazan. 1986. *Ghana: Coping with Uncertainty*. London: Westview Press.

Petroleum Commission. 2017. Sedimentary Basins. Available online, www.petrocom.gov.gh/sedimentary-basins.html. Accessed 29. 12. 2017.

Prempeh, P.O. 2010. An Overview of Ghana's Petroleum Downstream Sector. Available online, www.ghanaweb.com/GhanaHomePage/NewsArchive/artikel.php?ID=187641. Accessed 20. 12. 2017.

Smilie, I. 1986. *No Condition Permanent: Pump-priming Ghana's Industrial Revolution*. London: Intermediate Technology.

Soares de Oliveira, R. 2015. *Magnificent and Beggar Land: Angola since the Civil War*. London: Hurst.

Symons, K. 2016. Transnational Spaces, Hybrid Governance and Civil Society Contestation in Mozambique's Gas Boom. *Extractive Industries and Society*, 3(1), 149–159.

TOR. 2016. President Pledges Government's Support to TOR. Available online, www.tor.com.gh/2016/05/10/president-pledges-governments-support-to-tor/. Accessed 25. 01. 2018.

TOR. 2018. The First Inauguration. Available online, www.tor.com.gh/media-gallery/. Accessed 25. 01. 2018.

Tullow Oil. 2017. Jubilee Field. Available online, www.tullowoil.com/operations/west-africa/ghana/jubilee-field. Accessed 25. 01. 2018.

Whitfield, L. 2009. Change for a Better Ghana: Party Competition, Institutionalization and Alternation in Ghana's 2008 Elections. *African Affairs*, 108(433), 621–641.

Wikileaks. 2009. Ghana: Kosmos Energy Update. Available online, https://wikileaks.org/plusd/cables/09ACCRA1339_a.html. Accessed 20. 01. 2018.

World Bank. 2015. Ghana: Sankofa Gas Project. Available online, http://documents.worldbank.org/curated/en/173561467986250592/Ghana-Sankofa-Gas-Project. Accessed 24. 01. 2018.

Conclusion

The political ecology of the state

Elísio Macamo, Jon Schubert and Ulf Engel

Introduction

In this volume, we set out to inquire into how the state as a historically constituted institutional reality changes in the context of an economy increasingly dominated by extractive industries. We assumed, for theoretical purposes, that when extractive industries come into contact with the realities of developing economies they can unleash a crisis of legitimacy for the state. This is due to the potential difficulty of reconciling competing interests that are constitutive of the state. Instead of privileging an approach based on a normative definition of the state, which would lead us, as it has led others,[1] into a description of the shortcomings of the 'African' state, we took an analytical approach, placing the onus on understanding the historically contingent nature of state forms emerging in response to this particular moment. This required from us – a task we gladly passed on to the contributors to this volume – a reversal of the analytical lens away from a concern with how states govern natural resource extraction and towards the political and social processes unleashed by natural resource extraction and their impact on the state.

Africa's fortunes changed radically between 2004 and 2014 with the continent's staggering economic growth rates, induced by a resource boom.[2] This, as is well known, took place against the backdrop of the emergence of non-traditional actors, the so-called BRICS countries, which clearly represent a major shift in both the world economy and international cooperation. These countries gained significant influence over global affairs (see Kragelund 2011; UNECA 2013), especially in Africa, on account of their extensive mining and construction activities, which had a strong impact on the economic growth rates of African countries (Brautigam 2009; Taylor 2016). Especially with regards to concerns over current development thinking, this significant change presented a particularly interesting background against which to look closely into African countries experiencing this boom and what their experience – and their adaptation to the subsequent cyclical downturn – can tell us about the continent's prospects. Understanding how African societies react politically to the waxing and waning presence of foreign investment has also become central to the hope of designing better policy to inform African development. Our focus on extractives is relevant in several respects, chief among which is the controversial nature of their relationship to human rights and to upholding environmental standards. In addition, extractive industries are known to foster deviant political behaviour, such as corruption and neo-patrimonialism, and to generate violent political conflict.

Extractives are, for this reason, an ideal background against which to explore what is happening to the state in Africa – that is, what conceptual challenges the interaction of extractive industries and politics in Africa poses to scholars. As the various contributions to this volume have shown, very significant developments are taking place on the ground, challenging received wisdom concerning how to address the state theoretically and empirically, but also how to calibrate the semantics of the concept itself to the particular circumstances of the African continent. Our major concern in this concluding chapter is to focus on one potentially relevant conceptual implication. It bears on the usefulness of focusing attention on process rather than essence (see Schlichte 2005; Hagmann and Péclard 2010). In other words, the political sociology of the state in Africa, if not elsewhere, requires researchers to approach the state as something that does not stand above the factors that require an entity such as a state to mediate, but rather as something that is continuously constituted by those factors.

The political ecology of the state

There is, in this sense, a particular political ecology to the notion of the state. Central to this ecology is, by definition, the analytical primacy of the interactions among organisms and their environment. As indicated in the Introduction to this volume, the relevant organisms in this particular case are the actors – namely, the extractive industries, local communities, politicians, businessmen, governments and so on. These actors interact in a politically defined environment that coincides with the boundaries of the state, its functions as well as the overall international context within which it is located. While the notion of the state suggests an institutional stability that grants it a ubiquitous status, the state is in fact fluid in nature. This is because, behind the impression of ubiquity, the nature of its functions, the extent to which it is accepted by relevant actors and the respect it commands are subject to constant renegotiation. This is not to deny the real nature of the pain people feel when the repressive arm of the state bears down on them. It is simply to stress process over essence.

The state is not what is, but rather what is becoming. In other words, the political ecology defining the state in Africa calls attention to the need to give analytical primacy to how particular events are constitutive of the state and not how a normative view of the state should preside over the meaning to be given to events. To put it bluntly, in every relevant political moment, the state is up for grabs because the meaning of the interaction of the organisms gives substance to it. With this analytical perspective, we draw a clear line between ourselves and normative approaches to the state. Much effort has gone into defining state 'fragility' (see a good summary offered by Olowu and Chanie 2016, 2–3), thereby placing an explanatory onus on precisely the things that analysis should account for. In other words, by insisting on identifying indicators of failure, one glosses over the fact that what is seen as failure is actually the outcome of the interactions between actors and their environment. What needs to be understood is how this interaction produces the outcomes designated as 'failures'. Only in this way, we submit, can research produce an analytically useful account of the state in Africa and elsewhere.

The analytical perspective suggested here therefore casts a critical look at the focus of the political sociology of the state on its perennial nature and functions. A minimal definition of the state along the lines of the Weberian focus on the monopoly of legitimate means of violence is required to have an empirically stable object. However, any approach that goes beyond this and takes certain properties for granted risks not only deploying the concept in a normative way but also failing to give an adequate account of what is actually taking place on the ground. As pointed out in the Introduction to this volume, taking certain properties for granted leads researchers to place undue emphasis on such normative notions as good governance while failing to acknowledge that they are also parts of the register from which actors draw to give meaning to the state. Moreover, normative approaches prevent researchers from paying sufficient attention to how practices render visible dimensions of the concept that generally fall outside of the field of vision of such normative approaches.

The study of extractives has shown how problematic such normative accounts can be. Much research effort, for example, has gone into drawing attention to how the fragile institutional framework of developing countries, including adverse international conditions, may turn resource wealth into a 'curse' (Basedau and Mehler 2005; see also Saylor 2014). Fears that extractive industries in Africa may be unable to solve the problems of poverty and social injustice drew from lessons from the past. These fears helped shape the philosophy behind the new aid architecture that was so fundamental to the consensus shared by the OECD's Development Assistance Committee (Mosse and Lewis 2005), emphasising policy reform as opposed to aid transfers within the general framework of market liberalism and new institutionalism. While there is much to criticise in this shift (see Ferguson and Gupta 2002), there is also much to commend, especially in terms of the emphasis placed on ownership as opposed to conditionality.

The idea of ownership seems to acknowledge the equality of partners in development. Conditionality, in contrast, requires a firm idea of the state around which policy interventions are structured. In other words, conditionality draws from a normative account of the state yielding recommendations concerning the kind of institutional arrangements required for the policies to work. It is not surprising, therefore, that the new aid architecture assumes, for example, that countries need good institutions based on the principles of good governance. Unfortunately, it is very difficult to translate this assumption into practical action. We know from experience that most economically successful countries tend to have a good institutional framework. Whether such an institutional framework is a precondition for their success or an outcome of that success is a question seldom asked. Here is where a consideration of the political ecology of the state – as may be derived from the implications of the studies presented in this volume – becomes relevant.

The usefulness of the political ecology of the state is particularly visible in the context of studies in contentious politics, as is largely the case when one deals with extractives. Enquiring into the role of resources in promoting or undermining development requires consideration of 'interactions in which actors make claims bearing on shared interests or programs, in which governments are involved as targets, initiators of claims, or third parties' (Tilly and Tarrow 2007, 4). While collective action and contention can – and do – occur in non-political settings (i.e. when discussing small or big individual questions), the inclusion of political (i.e. governmental) actors has been essential to democratisation processes in various countries at various times, as Tilly (1997, 2007) shows by drawing on several examples. Like structural adjustment, good governance or social accountability, 'democratisation' – when considered to be the goal and outcome of large-scale development initiatives – somehow loses its originally meaningful potential and becomes just another attempt to control historical processes.

Critical authors, such as Scott (1998), Abrahamsen (2000) and Sabaratnam (2017), have gone so far as to suggest that the aim of the new reform agenda may be to make developing countries legible and objects of neoliberal disciplinary intervention. Yet, though tainted with a normative utopian development rhetoric, if democratisation is seen as a process that favours 'broad, relatively equal political participation combined with binding consultation of political participants on governmental personnel, resources, and policy plus protection of political participants from arbitrary action by governmental agents' (Tilly and Tarrow 2007, 66), it does, in fact, seem desirable. Interestingly, contentious politics are not viewed as safeguards for democratic conditions: according to contention studies, de-democratisation is as likely an outcome of contentious processes as is democratisation (see Tilly 2006; see also Macamo 2011). By equal measure, drawing from the political ecology of the state, what the literature would take to be 'state failure' may be understood as an acknowledgement of the open nature of historical events. 'Failure' would not be the most appropriate word, though, as it speaks to what the state should be. The political ecology of the state, however, acknowledges outcomes as contingent upon particular interactions among organisms and their environment.

This insight raises an important epistemological issue. Research cannot be premised on normatively predictable outcomes of the kind one often finds in studies of the state. Not all states respond in the same way to the events that constitute them. The belief that there is one universally valid norm for the evaluation of historical change reveals a highly problematic teleological assumption underlying how we deploy concepts to make sense of Africa. This assumption posits the world as rationally ordered and therefore capable of responding to causal stimuli. The problematic effects of such views are particularly evident in the development community's concern with implementing purportedly universally applicable plans and initiatives in order to foster development. Hence, development policy has been designed as if positive development outcomes could be conceptualised as a direct response to a discrete set of the 'right' factors, incentives and attitudes implemented by reasonably acting individuals and institutions (see also Abrahamsen 2000; Macamo 2013).

By doing so, however, the past decades of institutionalised aid have led to problematic thinking about politics in Africa. In addition to being highly normative, this thinking has failed to understand the changes that are currently taking place on the African continent. For, clearly, though representing a comforting vision, the idea of social and political progress taking place in a linear and causal way cannot be upheld as either realistic or practicable. The political ecology of the state allows us to approach local politics in ways that force us to be sensitive to contingency.

Closing remarks

The resource boom was and continues to be an opportunity for Africa, much as the subsequent bust represents a challenge for resource-dependent countries. These changing dynamics provide an opportunity for new research as they create room for questions to be asked that are of central importance not only to our ability to understand what enables development, but also to challenge our ways of accounting for historical change and the constitution of social worlds. While a considerable body of literature has paid attention to the resource boom, most of it has tended to recycle older debates that do not seem to confront the epistemological assumptions underlying development thinking and do little to improve social science's ability to be a valid participant in these debates.

This volume engages development policy and practice as well as social science. It challenges the causal and linear assumptions of the former to the effect that development can be engineered through the 'right' kind of policies. It argues for the primacy of social action embedded in local contexts as the better bet in assessing potential development outcomes. A public and scholarly debate has arisen over whether extractive industries benefit Africa and to what extent the recent resource boom could be made productive for the respective countries' development. Researchers have been concerned with assessing the seemingly positive and negative outcomes of foreign investment, including corporate social responsibility (CSR) programmes, and have often concluded by demonstrating their ambivalent social, economic, political and environmental effects on local communities (Bryceson and MacKinnon 2012; Ngomba-Roth 2007; Owen and Kemp 2014; Rajak 2011; Taylor 2016; Wolff 2013). A fundamental critique has been that multinational corporations were part of a neo-colonial project of economic imperialism that produced unsustainable development, created further dependency and caused more damage than good. While researchers were quick to highlight the weakness of African governments and civil society groups vis-à-vis foreign capital (Beckmann *et al.* 2010; Fraser and Larmer 2010), many have failed to enquire deeper into the relationships that have been evolving between mining communities and political representatives. Thus, rather than lamenting the growing irrelevance of the state, the crumbling of sovereignty or the effacement of political logics against economic logics under the onslaught of global corporate forces, in this volume we have attempted to chart the *kind of state* that emerges (Magnon-pujo 2011, 3) from the negotiations around the management of the extractives sector and the diverse political repertoires the various actors in this ecology invoke to advance their respective positions. The political ecology of the state could enable us to appraise the ways in which an original political sphere has been developing in these countries, within which the relationship between state and society is being (re-)negotiated in novel ways, yielding important challenges to scholarship. This approach opens up interesting pathways into the role of deliberation in constituting political spaces. Extractive industries unleash debates showing how actors construct a sense of political obligations, identities and roles.

So far, scant attention has been paid to the potential of local contentious politics in revealing the conditions that favour, or undermine, progressive social change and positive development outcomes in the light of resource abundance. Here, we should note that we do not conceptualise 'local' as the opposite of 'external', 'global' or even 'national'. Rather, by 'local' we mean the historically contextual nature of the interaction between actors and their environment. Extractive industries unleash political processes involving collective claims-making. These, in turn, provoke reactions on the part of the local (and national) institutional political environment. These – at times violent and dangerous – expressions of citizens' discontent attest to an actively engaged population claiming its actual participation in a political cause. And even if no one knows the direction the process will take or the changes it will precipitate, the fact that it involves an actual negotiation of interests between the affected population and stakeholders from politics and economy raises hopes for an open path to state consolidation that is genuinely sustainable because it is locally grounded.

Just like 'the state', 'development' resists definition and assessment in the way the international development apparatus has thought about it. Rather, it is a deeply political and contingent matter. The political ecology of the state can make a case for an understanding of development as a constantly contested and changing process shaped by local politics: that is, how a political community engages decision-makers, contests policies and stands its ground. The nature of local politics does not have to be avowedly democratic, but by privileging how states constitute themselves historically we can determine under what conditions contention yields democratic politics and development. In other words, the chances of developmental success depend to a considerable extent on the nature and quality of everyday political negotiations of interests between citizens and their politicians, rather than on normative large-scale transparency and accountability programmes (see also Jenkins 2001).

Notes

1 One example that illustrates this point is a book by Pita Ogaba Agbese and George Klay Kieh Jr., who, in their very first paragraph, write: 'In both scholarly works and in the popular press, much has been written on the failure of the state in Africa. Incessant political instability, high crime rates, lack of access to education and healthcare, deteriorating public infrastructure, and environmental degradation are a few of the features that have come to characterize the modern African state. Scholars and lay people use these as concrete indicators of the failure of the African state to perform its fundamental duties as a modern state. The catalogue of failure is quite depressing' (Agbese and Kieh 2007, 3).

2 See www.mckinsey.com/insights/economic_studies/whats_driving_africas_growth. Accessed 1 January 2018.

References

Abrahamsen, R. 2000. *Disciplining Democracy: Development Discourse and Good Governance in Africa*. London: Zed Books.

Agbese, P.O. and G.K.KiehJr, eds. 2007. *Reconstituting the State in Africa*. Houndmills: Palgrave Macmillan.

Basedau, M. and A. Mehler. 2005. *Resource Politics in Sub-Saharan Africa*. Hamburg: Institute of African Affairs.

Beckmann, B., S. Buhlung and L. Sachikonye, eds. 2010. *Trade Unions and Party Politics: Labour Movements in Africa*. Pretoria: Human Sciences Research Council.

Brautigam, D. 2009. *The Dragon's Gift: The Real Story of China in Africa*. Oxford: Oxford University Press.

Bryceson, D. and D. MacKinnon. 2012. *Mining and Urbanisation in Africa: Population, Settlement and Welfare*. Abingdon: Routledge.

Ferguson, J. and A. Gupta. 2002. Spatializing States: Toward an Ethnography of Neoliberal Governmentality. *American Ethnologist*, 29(4): 981–1002.

Fraser, A. and M. Larmer. 2010. *Zambia, Mining, and Neoliberalism: Boom and Bust on the Globalized Copperbelt*. New York: Palgrave Macmillan.

Hagmann, T. and D. Péclard. 2010. Negotiating Statehood: Dynamics of Power and Domination in Africa. *Development and Change*, 41(4), 539–562.

Jenkins, R. 2001. Mistaking 'Governance' for 'Politics': Foreign Aid, Democracy and the Construction of Civil Society. In S. Kaviraj and S. Khilnani, eds, *Civil Society: History and Possibilities*. Cambridge: Cambridge University Press.

Kragelund, P. 2011. Back to BASICs? The Rejuvenation of Non-traditional Donors' Development Cooperation with Africa. *Development and Change*, 42(2), 585–607.

Macamo, E. 2011. Social Criticism and Contestation: The Politics of Anger and Outrage in Mozambique and Angola. *Stichproben, Wiener Zeitschrift für kritische Afrikastudien*, 20, 45–68.

Macamo, E. 2013. The Compulsion to Do the Right Thing: Development Knowledge and its Limits. In U. Engel and M.J. Ramos, eds, *African Dynamics in a Multipolar World*. Leiden: Brill.

Magnon-pujo, C. 2011. La Souveraineté est-elle privatisable? *Politix*, 95, 129–153.

Mosse, D. and D. Lewis, eds. 2005. *The Aid Effect: Giving and Governing in International Development*. London and Ann Arbor, MI: Pluto Press.

Ngomba-Roth, R. 2007. *Multinational Companies and Conflicts in Africa: The Case of the Niger Delta – Nigeria*. Hamburg: Lit Verlag.

Olowu, D. and P. Chanie, eds. 2016. *State Fragility and State Building in Africa: Cases from Eastern and Southern Africa*. London: Springer.

Owen, J.R. and D. Kemp. 2014. Mining and Community Relations: Mapping the Internal Dimensions of Practice. *Extractive Industries and Society*, 1(1), 12–19.

Rajak, D. 2011. *In Good Company: An Anatomy of Corporate Social Responsibility*. Stanford, CA: Stanford University Press.

Sabaratnam, M. 2017. *Decolonising Intervention: International Statebuilding in Mozambique*. London and Lanham, MD: Rowman & Littlefield International.

Saylor, R. 2014. *State Building in Boom Times: Commodities and Coalitions in Latin America and Africa*. Oxford: Oxford University Press.

Schlichte, K. 2005. *The Dynamics of States: The Formation and Crises of State Domination*. Aldershot and Burlington, VT: Ashgate.

Scott, J.C. 1998. *Seeing Like a State*. New Haven, CT, and London: Yale University Press.

Taylor, I. 2016. Dependency Redux: Why Africa Is Not Rising. *Review of African Political Economy*, 43(147), 8–25.

Tilly, C. 1997. Parliamentarization of Popular Contention in Great Britain, 1758–1834. *Theory and Society*, 26(2/3), 245–273.

Tilly, C. 2006. Contention and Democracy in Europe: 1650–2000. Cambridge: Cambridge University Press.

Tilly, C. and S. Tarrow. 2007. *Contentious Politics*. Boulder, CO: Paradigm Publishers.

UNECA. 2013. *Africa–BRICS Cooperation: Implications for Growth, Employment and Structural Transformation in Africa*. Addis Ababa: UNECA.

Wolff, S.M. 2013. *In a State of Becoming. Local State Making and Citizen Making in Tanzania's Mineral Margins*. København: Center for Afrikastudier.

Index

Taylor & Francis Group
an informa business

Taylor & Francis eBooks

www.taylorfrancis.com

A single destination for eBooks from Taylor & Francis with increased functionality and an improved user experience to meet the needs of our customers.

90,000+ eBooks of award-winning academic content in Humanities, Social Science, Science, Technology, Engineering, and Medical written by a global network of editors and authors.

TAYLOR & FRANCIS EBOOKS OFFERS:

A streamlined experience for our library customers

A single point of discovery for all of our eBook content

Improved search and discovery of content at both book and chapter level

REQUEST A FREE TRIAL

support@taylorfrancis.com

Routledge
Taylor & Francis Group

CRC Press
Taylor & Francis Group

For Product Safety Concerns and Information please contact our EU representative GPSR@taylorandfrancis.com Taylor & Francis Verlag GmbH, Kaufingerstraße 24, 80331 München, Germany